Published in association with the
International Peace Research Association

NEW AGENDA
FOR PEACE RESEA

New Agendas for Peace Research

Conflict and Security Reexamined

EDITED BY
Elise Boulding

Lynne Rienner Publishers · Boulder & London

Published in the United States of America in 1992 by
Lynne Rienner Publishers, Inc.
1800 30th Street, Boulder, Colorado 80301

and in the United Kingdom by
Lynne Rienner Publishers, Inc.
3 Henrietta Street, Covent Garden, London WC2E 8LU

Library of Congress Cataloging-in-Publication Data
New agendas for peace research : conflict and security reexamined /
    edited by Elise Boulding.
        p.   cm.
    Papers, presented at a gathering of peace researchers in July 1990
on the occasion of 25th anniversary of the end of World War II.
    Includes bibliographical references and index.
    ISBN 1-55587-290-5 (hc)
    1. Peace—Research—Congresses. 2. Security, International—
Research—Congresses. I. Boulding, Elise.
JX1904.5.N49   1991
327.1'72'072—dc20   91–31610
                                                        CIP

British Cataloguing in Publication Data
A Cataloguing in Publication record for this book
is available from the British Library.

Printed and bound in the United States of America

The paper used in this publication meets the requirements
of the American National Standard for Permanence of
Paper for Printed Library Materials Z39.48–1984.

Contents

Acknowledgments

I wish to thank Lois Muller for her careful preediting of the papers included in this book and for her painstaking work with references. I also want to thank DeLinda Wunder for her conscientious work at the computer, getting the manuscript into one consistent format, and Marty Gonzales for coordinating the process from paper collection to manuscript.

—*E. B.*

Introduction:
What Is Possible

ELISE BOULDING

The euphoria over the end of the Cold War that began in the fall of 1989 was still at its height in early July 1990, when the international gathering of peace researchers whose work is reflected in this book took place. As will be seen, peace researchers never shared that euphoria. While others were pronouncing the end of history and a corollary end to the need for research on the causes of war and the conditions of peace, the gathered scholars soberly assessed new challenges: the changing nature of conflicts and increasing sources of insecurity. Looking to the future, they considered where and how new peace-building capacities might be emerging to deal with new threats and insecurities.

While this is a sober book, it is far from a pessimistic one. The very fact that peace researchers have immersed themselves in the years since World War II in the realities of arms races and East-West and North-South conflicts gives them a sense of time and historical process that enables them to see the emergence of new problem-solving capacities even while conflicts themselves seem to increase. Peace researchers have always understood that the boundaries between internal and interstate conflicts have been arbitrary and fluid in the extreme. The current rise of new-old ethnic-based nationalisms in Eastern Europe, their persistent recurrence in large parts of Africa and Asia, and the outbreak of North-South conflicts in a particularly confused manner in the shape of the oil war in the Gulf come as no surprise to peace researchers.

Just as the euphoria of 1989 and 1990 were premature, so is the current despair about the state of the world. A realistic understanding of the nature and structure of human conflicts can lead either to worst-case or best-case scenarios, depending on the choices the analyst makes. Security strategists tend to create worst-case scenarios. Peace researchers explore best-case

1

scenarios, looking for the emergent possibilities for peace building that exist in every human crisis. It is these emergent possibilities that this book offers.

This is how the peace research community celebrated its twenty-fifth anniversary at the University of Groningen, Netherlands, its birthplace a quarter of a century ago: by looking ahead to what needs to be done in the next quarter-century. It is our joy to know that a new generation of scholars is entering into this work with the same zest that an older generation brought to the "invention" of this interdisciplinary field in the decades after World War II. The goal is now, as it was then, to render obsolete the field of security studies based on the military defense of nation-states.

The chapters included here were all presented in an earlier form at special plenary sessions of the Twenty-fifth Anniversary Conference. They have been organized into three sections to reflect the progression of thought at the conference—from an examination of the nature of current conflicts (Part I, New Faces, Old Conflicts) to a rethinking of what is meant by security (Part II, Reconceptualizing Security) to an exciting overview of new inventions in conflict resolution (Part III, New Security Technologies).

Part I, New Faces, Old Conflicts, begins with the startling assertion by Hylke Tromp of the Netherlands that everybody "lost" the Cold War, since we now have a militarized world in which all states have access to weapons of mass destruction, and the two major contenders in the Cold War are each in a seriously deteriorated condition in terms of internal problems. In short, the tasks of peace research are just beginning to unfold. The peace research methodology of multidimensional analysis of states and human societies will continue, but the components of the required analysis have greatly increased in complexity.

The omnipresence of enemy imagery in all aspects of relations among states, and in relations among ethnic, racial, and religious groups within states, which has so strongly resurfaced at the end of the Cold War, is in itself a conflict multiplier; it therefore claims increasing attention from peace researchers. The enemy image phenomenon is a problem of denial of identity to the other, a refusal to recognize the meanings that conflicts have to one's adversaries. This behavior, as Eva Senghaas-Knobloch of Germany points out, is a symptom of the underdeveloped condition of civil societies and a serious obstacle to the new social learnings that must take place if Europe— and other parts of the world—are to achieve multiethnic stability.

The denial of identity to the other is at the heart of the rage, described so vividly by Solomon Nkiwane of Zimbabwe, that Africans feel toward former colonizers. The rage at Western indifference to Africa is hardly lessened by the fact that Africans are all too apt to see themselves through the belittling eyes of those same Westerners. The rediscovery of Africa's own place in history and the recovery of self-respect is a precondition for internal conflict resolution and for Africa's being able to make its own unique contribution to the international community of states.

Birgit Brock-Utne, of Norway and Tanzania, speaks of another kind of denial of identity—the denial of the place and role of women in every society on every continent, with specific examples from Europe and Africa. This denial, which greatly weakens the problem-solving capabilities of any human group, is another aspect of the underdeveloped character of contemporary civil society spoken of earlier by Senghaas-Knobloch. But Brock-Utne is optimistic that a partnership between women and men can emerge as the values of nurturance, nonviolence, and equality show their pragmatic worth in the marketplace.

The problem of denial of identities takes on another dimension as Kumar Rupesinghe, of Sri Lanka and Norway, discusses the disappearance of boundaries between internal and external conflicts, making the conventional paradigm of interstate relations in international relations theory irrelevant. The widespread internal violence that keeps spilling across national boundaries is a storng indicator of the extent to which states have not met the needs of national groupings within their borders. New constitutive orders will be required to meet the needs of multiethnic societies in a world of deteriorating and diminishing resources.

It is clear from the discussions in Part I that new types of conflict are appearing that cannot easily be handled by the military security strategies of nation-states. Part II, Reconceptualizing Security, offers several different perspectives on rethinking security. Taking as her point of departure the traditional concept of security through military defense, US defense analyst Randall Forsberg makes a straightforward statement that now, at the end of the Cold War, when no great power is threatening any other, is a moment of rare opportunity: it is a time to recognize that high-tech military defense reduces overall security, and that cheaper and more effective strategies like nonoffensive defense and international peacekeeping forces can provide a more stable peace. The alternative is an increasingly deadly arms race. What can move international actors away from that trap? The social imagination to see what a new security order could look like and the courage to abandon old habits and try new strategies.

Should we use the term *security* to refer only to security from military threat, or should we add other types of threats such as environmental deterioration and economic oppression? This is the issue addressed by Lothar Brock of Germany and Patricia Mische of the United States, from differing perspectives. Opting to keep the narrower military definition, Brock points out that environmental threats have always been part of the techniques of warfare, but that conflict itself, whether environmental or economic in nature, should not be confused with war. Brock warns that abandoning the specificities of the nature of environmental degradation as contrasted to the nature of war, might itself in fact lead to the use of ecological security as an excuse for military action, thus launching a new series of ecowars. He recommends, instead, treating environmental degradation as a problem in sustainable development. Since the real problem is getting states to cooperate, says Brock, action should be focused on the development of cooperative interstate ecological projects, such as transboundary peace parks.

Mische, on the other hand, points out that the military should not be permitted a monopoly of the term *security,* since security systems existed long before the invention of warfare; peace researchers, as well as peace movements, must reclaim misused words. Mische sees security not as the traditional steady state concept that Brock refers to, but rather as an organizing principle stimulating a dynamic evolutionary process in a total system context, and thus essentially multidimensional in nature. When it comes to practical solutions, Brock and Mische are not so far apart. Both recommend nongovernmental (NGO) and intergovernmental initiatives for cooperation in ecological and economic arenas across national boundaries to reduce threat and increase well-being. Mische's Earth Covenant brings these initiatives directly to the level of individual human behavior in a moving way.

Whether or not the term *security* is used to cover more than military threats to human well-being, it is clear that the nature and variety of threats is multiplying. Ursula Oswald of Mexico focuses on the economic dimensions of those threats, highlighting the suffering of the Third World as a result of having been used as the First World's backyard for plunder and pollution. Oswald calls for a kind of security based on a new type of autonomous, human-centered development, involving recognition of ethnic, social, and economic differences and the principles of ecofeminism. Achieving this kind of society will require a new type of education, a reshaping of culture. Thus, the themes of human learning, recognition of social identity, and the strengthening of civil society, so important in the discussion of the changing faces of conflict in Part I, reappear as dimensions of security at the close of Part II.

The multidimensionality of security becomes very clear in Part III, New Security Technologies. Reports directly from the scene of action by a former guerrilla fighter, a mediator, a UN official, and a peace educator give us glimpses of new approaches to threat reduction and peace building in the midst of conflict situations.

Winifred Byanyima, with all the clarity of a former resistance fighter, describes the strategies used by the Uganda National Resistance Movement to develop a new political culture of peaceful conflict resolution after a long period of brutal dictatorship and civil war. The movement based its strategies on the insight that the enemy was attitudes and perceptions, not soldiers. Revenge and terrorism were explicitly rejected. Education, respect for tribal identities, the restoration of local decisionmaking, and participatory inclusiveness at the national level were the tools for rebuilding Ugandan society. The active participation of women at all levels in this rebuilding and a strong national commission on human rights have been important in keeping the democratization process on track.

Hendrik van der Merwe, a South African pioneer in the development of mediation centers and training in mediation for black and white South Africans, describes the difficulty for a country torn by black/white and black/black struggles, of moving from an all-or-nothing, win-lose mentality to an openness to negotiation and willingness to compromise. Severe power imbalances, and the fact that South African blacks have been victimized by modernization to a more extreme degree than in other countries of the South, complicate the negotiation process. In the face of the enormous challenges of restructuring the society and creating a new constitution, a new educational system, and new economic solutions to the problems of massive black poverty, van der Merwe and his colleagues courageously offer teams of black and white mediators prepared to go anywhere and work on any problem. Their task is to help develop a new culture of conflict resolution at the grassroots level, linked to indigenous values.

To move from efforts in Uganda and South Africa to rebuild peaceable conflict-resolving cultures through education and training in mediation, to the good offices missions of the Secretary-General of the United Nations, is not as big a step as at first it might seem. The four good offices cases described by Juergen Dedring of the Secretary-General's Office of Research Collection and Information are all examples of United Nations efforts to facilitate the rebuilding of conflict-resolution capabilities in conflict-torn situations. The good offices mission concept represents a unique approach to conflict resolution that involves a skilled behind-the-scenes interweaving of interests and factions from the UN Security Council and the UN General Assembly with national and local interests and factions to come up with tension-reducing alternative courses of action in often dangerously intractable confrontations. This type of quiet diplomacy is not like traditional great-power secret diplomacy. The goal is conciliation. Good offices missions, as conducted by the Secretary-General and his aides, are characterized by great versatility and flexibility and facilitate solutions satisfactory to all parties. Internal and external conflicts are tightly intertwined in the four situations given: Afghanistan, Namibia, Central America, and Cambodia. We see again the salience of the point made by Rupesinghe in Part I that state boundaries have lost their traditional meaning. While none of these conflicts have been "solved" at the time of reporting, it is clear that creative potentials for problem solving have been strengthened. Dedring suggests that the gradual increase in the number of good offices missions over time may be taken as an indicator of a major reshuffling of the international system toward expansion of the problem-solving and peacekeeping capabilities of the United Nations system.

How peace education can meet the challenge of replacing the culture of militarism is addressed at the close of this section by Riitta Wahlström of Finland. Wahlström's theme in a sense has already appeared in three other papers: Byanyima, van der Merwe, and Dedring are all talking about the creation of new problem-solving, peace-building cultures. Wahlström gives more space to describing the invasiveness of militarism—the way it permeates the institutions and values of civil society—than in presenting peace education itself. The assumption behind this approach is that peace education cannot begin without full recognition of this permeation, and the "cultural conversion" has to take place bit by bit in every aspect of modern culture, from children's play life to the conduct of corporations. The civil society must reclaim its own autonomy. If partriarchy and the complex of values associated with dominance and power and the obliteration of diversity have set the ground rules of the old society, the partnership relation among women, men, and children and the complex of values associated with nurturance, listening, mutual aid and respect for diversity must set the ground rules for the new society. Peace education will help develop the new ground rules.

At the beginning of this introduction I said that this is not a pessimistic book. What are the grounds for optimism evidenced by the authors?

- An awareness that dependency on military solutions to problems is learned behavior that can be unlearned
- Demonstrations that conflicts can be demystified by increased understanding of the actual threats to human well-being, in all their variety, that characterize the modern world
- A conviction that the civil society can be equipped with problem-solving and conflict-resolution skills that will release it from its dependence on military force
- Most important, the examples we have been given of societies that have been deeply traumatized by violence and brutality, yet have been able to move to new understandings, discard enemy images, and engage in cooperative reshaping of their own social order—as Kenneth Boulding frequently reminds us, "What exists, is possible."

PART I

NEW FACES, OLD CONFLICTS

One thing peace researchers know about conflict is that it is ubiquitous. Since no two human beings are alike, wherever two individuals, groups, or states are gathered, there will be differences in perceptions and preferences. It is how those differences are managed that concerns the peace researcher. Murder and war lie at one extreme of the conflict management continuum and integrative behavior at the other, with a great variety of negotiating behaviors covering the vast middle ground. In short, most conflict is managed by means considerably short of war. But the forms conflict take change over time. In what follows, the great variety of conflicts is examined and their rate of multiplication emphasized. But at the same time, there is a strong note of pragmatism: humans are capable of social learning, and they are also inventive. The civil society will find solutions that force cannot generate.

—E. B.

CHAPTER 1

Peace Research at the End of the Cold War

HYLKE TROMP

Unless it is resurrected by artificial respiration, the Cold War is over. Nobody won. Everybody lost.

The Soviet Union and its former satellites are faced with stagnation, pollution, corruption, crime, unemployment, alcoholism, illiteracy, and an increasing national debt.

The United States and its allies—still—are faced with stagnation, pollution, corruption, crime, unemployment, alcoholism, and other drug abuses, illiteracy, and an increasing national debt.

Both sides in the Cold War have secretly dumped industrial, chemical, and nuclear wastes on their own soil, contaminating the air, polluting the water, and poisoning their territory in order to defend it.

Both sides in the Cold War have overstretched their economies, as well as the social structures of their societies. The Soviet Union is now in a state of poverty usually found only in Third World countries. The United States is now a state with a foreign debt unsurpassed by any other country.

Both sides in the Cold War have cut expenditures for education and social welfare in order to pay for the research, development, production, and deployment of new generations of weapons systems. As a consequence, they are now faced with disintegration, alienation, illiteracy, organized crime, drug abuse, and high levels of unemployment.

Organized crime and corruption are rampant in the United States and have become clearly visible at all levels of society, as is continually demonstrated by the power of crime organizations and by unfolding scandals in government agencies such as the Pentagon. Organized crime and corruption have become institutionalized in East European societies, where Communist Party bosses have been revealed to be mirror images of crime bosses in the United States.

The abuse of alcohol in the Soviet Union has risen to such a level that

9

Gorbachev started his term of office with a declaration of war on alcoholism. The abuse of hard drugs in the United States, steadily rising after the Vietnam War, has reached such a level that the Reagan government had to declare a war on drugs.

At the same time, both "superpowers" were forced by their respective ideologies and the economic systems based on them, to pay enormous amounts of money to millions of people for doing nothing, even if that expense goes under different names: "full employment" in the Soviet Union, "unemployment" in the United States.

Ironically, democracy and totalitarianism have both produced huge bureaucracies unable to deal with the problems they are supposed to manage.

The former superpowers, however, have succeeded in one respect. They have militarized the world. There is no place on earth that cannot be destroyed within minutes by one of their nuclear-tipped missiles. There is not one state that cannot get loans to buy the outdated equipment of the superpowers for defending their "democracy" (virtually nonexistent) or their "independence" (completely nonexistent). Nonstate actors, varying from terrorists to ethnic groups, have virtually unlimited access to weapons of all kinds. The weapons trade has become the world's most profitable business. In an armed United States more than 30,000 citizens are killed annually by fellow citizens using these weapons during what is officially the longest peace in recent history.

Ending the Cold War was a difficult process. It required a revolution from above, because a revolution from the bottom would never have succeeded. It was a revolution because it involved changing foundations instead of appearances (as détente). Foremost, however, it had to be a revolution in thinking, that is, in perceiving and interpreting reality. That is the real revolution because it requires giving up the belief in basic but outdated and unrealistic assumptions about where the threat to peace comes from and how it should be countered. It also requires giving up beliefs about what military power and the use of political violence might achieve and forsaking the persistent notion that nuclear deterrence assures eternal peace. Changing such beliefs came closest to what a conversion is in religion. It required the social change following the transfer of power from one generation to another, from the Byzantine gerontocracy of octogenarians to the cohort of fifty-year-olds, as happened in the Soviet Union.

As a consequence, ideological and doctrinal debates have led to chaos and uncertainty. Politics are now characterized by oscillations and contradictions around old and new basic assumptions and their perceived consequences for the conduct of policy. Social unrest, upheavals, secession movements, and right- and left-wing fringes and sects now dominate the scene. All groups involved in this, however, have easy access to all kinds of weaponry. If they feel the need, they will use their arsenals to demonstrate how just, rightful, or serious they are, following the example set by states in the history of the anarchical state system. Peace has not broken out, even if the direct threat of nuclear war between the superpowers seems to have become a nightmare of the past.

Still, it is no longer rational to pursue political goals by military means. The record of the past century is disastrous. Whoever declared war, started war, or relied on military means to achieve political goals has discovered that the costs always surpassed the benefits—if they survived the decision to go to war, politically or physically. Only in exceptional cases has there been a clear victory, as when the United States defeated Grenada. There was never a clear benefit, not even for the victor. Many actors have been destroyed by the war they started for some limited goal: the German Empire, the Austro-Hungarian Empire, the Ottoman Empire, the Russian Empire. All main actors in the First World War, they no longer existed when that war ended, their chief of state having been overthrown or murdered. War as a political instrument has become a completely unreliable tool. Japan and Germany were defeated in the Second World War. Only a few decades later, they have emerged as real superpowers, if not in a military sense. The results of war have become completely unpredictable. The war over the Falklands/Malvinas between Argentina and England was officially noted as a British victory. However, it gave democracy to Argentina and Mrs. Thatcher to England.

Contrary to still vehemently held beliefs and assumptions underlying the policy-making process, the main instrument of power politics is no longer military power. It is economic power. Only in such exceptional cases, in developing countries, or by regressive politicians is war still seen and applied in, or by the Clausewitzian sense of a continuation of politics.

That does not mean that there is peace—even if war has always been exceptional. Precisely because war is no exception, it gets tremendous coverage in papers and history books. However, the number of annual casualties of war probably does not now exceed the number of traffic casualties on a world scale (more than 500,000 in 1988). Of a world population of more than five billion, the number of people involved in or actually fighting a war is negligible. As a cause of death, war might range last.

But peace is not to be equated with the absence of war. War is only one of the strategies in which political violence is applied. It concerns the specific case where states are using armed, uniformed, and trained men and women to decide an issue by force, sometimes even according to previously agreed-upon rules and laws. The use of violence for political purposes, however, is not limited to states. Nonstate actors and even individuals have always used violence, and now they will increasingly claim the right to do so, if not by proclamation then by action. The militarization of the world through the East-West conflict and its consequences, such as the arms race, have made weapons abundantly available for anyone who has a score to settle. As a consequence, political terrorism, appearing as a major problem since 1968, is gradually replacing war; it threatens, terrifies, and kills innocent people to achieve some political goal, and employs "strategies" such as hijackings, bomb attacks, hostage taking, and direct murder. Officially acknowledged as "low-intensity conflict," its social consequences are still being played down. It is war, but in a different form.

These developments may change the scope of peace research, but not its purpose. Preventing political violence remains the main issue. It is essential to describe and analyze the causes of political violence and to prescribe what should be done to prevent the escalation of violence. This encompasses more than simply counting weapons systems, predicting technological improvements, and assessing consequences for military strategy, which is actually the field of "strategic studies." It requires much more difficult studies and analyses of all aspects of the state of human society: cultural, psychological, sociological, economical.

Peace research is not over because the Cold War has ended. It is just beginning.

CHAPTER 2

Social Learning and Conflict Resolution in a Changing Europe

————————————— EVA SENGHAAS-KNOBLOCH

NEW DIRECTIONS IN CONFLICT RESEARCH

The Sociopsychological Perspective

Political and social processes, structures, and norms can be analyzed from the point of view of observers. However, it should not be overlooked that processes, structures, and norms are produced by people who act by attributing meaning to their actions. This means not that the actual results completely correspond to the subjective meaning of these actions, but that the great changes taking place in Europe can be fully comprehended only if one tries to describe the subjective side of the events and processes.

The meaning of subjectivity in international politics, especially in the context of East-West relations, becomes clearer when we regard ourselves as both the agents of and those affected by the action and, thereby, not only pursuing interests but also striving to satisfy specific psychic needs, particularly security needs. With this emphasis on the subjective dimension it is possible to shed light on sociopsychological dynamics—thus taking up the very concern of the social scientists who were invited by UNESCO in 1948 to define its mission and who urged research related to the causes of war and the conditions of peace.[1]

Overcoming Enemy Images

Sociopsychological dynamics in international politics can perhaps best be illustrated by referring to a widely circulated comment made by Georgi Arbatov, a leading Soviet expert on the West, shortly after Mikhail Gorbachev assumed the office of secretary-general of the Communist Party of the Soviet Union in 1985. Arbatov said at that time that "Gorbachev had

13

done great harm to the West by robbing it of its enemy image." This very mode of speech lends expression to sociopsychological dynamics as a central aspect in the East-West conflict that contributed to an enemy image syndrome with the following characteristics: real conflicts of interest and power became mixed with suspicion of anything originating from the other side, as well as attitudes of hostility and an ongoing arms race under the premises of nuclear deterrence.[2]

This syndrome prevented a collective process of real social learning in the realm of disarmament, although since the Cuban missile crisis, the political class in the United States and in the Soviet Union has been aware of the common vulnerability of the two countries and the obsolescence of nuclear weapons. They failed to arrive at disarmament agreements because of an institutionalized chronic suspicion fed by an aura of hostile secrecy in all security matters and in real political aims. The breakthrough—which Arbatov's comment refers to—was made possible because of the radical confidence-building gestures of the East since 1985. The central elements of Soviet political behavior since that time met exactly those criteria that the different classical psychological schools in the West put forward to overcome the enemy image syndrome in the context of the East-West conflict:[3]

• Openness about one's own political aims, the credibility of which are all the more indisputable the more they are linked to a self-critical reorganization of one's own systems and policies. The break with the Brezhnev Doctrine on the part of the Soviet government provided the US administration and the Western population, tired as they were of the endless arms race, with evidence of the integrity and trustworthiness of the declared new policy.
• Strict observance of treaties, especially when they signify certain disadvantages for one's own side. An example of this is the INF treaty, which required more disarmament by the East than by the West.
• Emphasis on common aims and tasks. Such a reorientation of foreign policy was ushered in by Gorbachev's speeches in 1985, the tone and content of which were a signal of a fundamentally new political stance to both the national and international public. In emphasizing the common problems of civilized societies and tasks of humanity, Gorbachev broke with previous Soviet policy, which always allocated priority to the interests of the Socialist bloc.
• Since the Soviet "policy of new thinking"[4] was also extended to its relations with the other countries in the "brotherhood of socialist nations," this policy enabled advances toward radical change in Poland and Hungary, which then provided the foundation for the democratic revolutions in the other countries of Eastern Europe in the autumn of 1989. The new governments in Poland, Hungary, Czechoslovakia, and the USSR describe

the situation as a return to "the cradle of European civilization."[5]

• A self-critical reflection of one's own collective involvement in the history of violence. The new policy of transparency and openness (glasnost) in Soviet society meant a break with the tradition of glossing over the problems within the borders of the USSR and enabled the motive of self-enlightenment, the aim "to live the truth," as stated by Vaclav Havel, the new president of Czechoslovakia, to be extended to the field of international relations.

All these new policy features combined to produce internal and external change. In particular, the change through openness and the emphasis on matters of joint concern also created a climate in the West in which the personal credibility of Gorbachev was recognized in the political class as well as, or even more so, among the general population in Western countries.

We are thus able to define the elementary sociopsychological insight known as "Deutsch's crude law":[6] A social relation based on suspicion and hostility strengthens a structure in which such behavior is produced and viceversa; behavior characterized by openness and willingness to cooperate contributes to a structure that is supportive of cooperation.

Challenges of the New Situation in Europe

Let us apply this insight to the new situation in Europe. What exactly is the situation there now?

The mechanisms that blocked social political learning and were generated by the enemy image syndrome have been overcome as far as the old East-West conflict is concerned. Since the new Soviet foreign policy has agreed to a unified Germany, there will be disarmament on all levels and a de facto nuclear-free zone in Central Europe. With respect to the old adversaries of the Cold War, ways and means have been found to distinguish between attitudes of hostility, opposing interests, and misunderstandings.[7] But beyond this line of nearly obsolete confrontation, the magnitude of the problems and conflicts that were previously hidden from view or suppressed are now becoming visible: ecological challenges, economic disparities, identity conflicts, and ethnonationalist struggles for autonomy or independence.

It is no wonder then that by mid-1990 the festive mood that characterized the end of 1989 and the beginning of 1990 gave way to a mood of weariness, a loss of orientation, and even a sense of depression, particularly in Eastern Europe. While a citizen of the GDR was cited in November 1989 as having said, "It's like a dream," Vaclav Havel stated in his inaugural speech for the Salzburg Festival in July 1990 that the "velvet revolution" in Czechoslovakia was a beautiful dream from which it was painful to awaken to the burdens of everyday life. He used the metaphor of Sisyphus to spell out the psychological problems; he felt a sense of absurdity, "an experience similar to what Sisyphus would have experienced if his rock had, one day, remained on top of the hill and had not rolled back. This alludes to the experience of a Sisyphus who was not prepared for the possibility that his work might succeed."[8]

The self-observation on the part of Havel as a member of the most conscious part of the democratic political movement in Eastern Europe also applies to the subjective state of matters in the broad spectrum of the population. The successful liberation from political coercive rule is not necessarily sufficient for the development of collective interests in the new shaping of political, economic, and social affairs.

According to the theory of etatist societies, for example, Melanie Tatur's theoretical case study on Poland,[9] the erosion of illegitimate rule in Eastern Europe did not free highly developed and differentiated, though thus far suppressed, interests and forces, but made evident a "societal vacuum." The political project of the critics of the old regime, the project of "civil society," turns out to be a developmental project. The described individual and collective grievances concerning the loss of orientation must be understood as symptomatic of this societal vacuum, which has to be filled by the creation of new, differentiated societal interests and autonomous rules of intrasocietal integration.

In this situation of high societal vulnerability, two different modes of coping with the emerging problems become visible: individual rescue strategies of refugees and collective strategies of self-determination. In the first case, individuals leave their place of residence in order to find a new home, mainly in Western Europe. They have lost confidence in the traditional collectives to which they originally belonged. In the second case, conflicts of legitimacy very often become intertwined with conflicts of collective autonomy, aggravated by economic and social problems.

In the first case, the result is internal conflict mainly in the affluent countries of Western Europe to which the refugees address themselves. These conflicts center on matters of sharing material benefits and to some degree on identity problems within the framework of a multicultural society. They might also become an issue in international diplomacy (visa questions, for example).

In the other case of collective self-determination, the issue is not a struggle over a better share of material goods, though the conflict might manifest itself in such demands. Rather, the issue is the need for identity recognition, which is linked to a sense of security. In other words, identity conflicts grow out of the search to satisfy inalienable human needs and the means employed to achieve that goal. The main examples of this kind of conflict in contemporary Europe are struggles involving national or ethnonationalist autonomy or even sovereignty, as in Yugoslavia or the Soviet Union. In any case, the common feature here is a political authority that assumes general recognition but whose legitimacy is rejected. Subjects of conflict are the territorial borders that circumscribe the sociocultural space in which the desired collective self-determination can take place and a sense of security is provided. Internal problems translate themselves into international problems.

Problems and Prospects of Intersocietal Conflict Resolution

Many of the contemporary movements for separation and independence initially articulated themselves as concerns about ecological disaster, protection of the homeland, and efforts for cultural autonomy. In May 1990, a representative from Estonia formulated the problems of her country as problems of denied sovereignty. She said that the ecological situation was dependent on those "who rule over the land." *Land* here has a double meaning. On the one hand, it is the soil, nature, and natural resources; on the other hand, it is also the territory over which one has or does not have sovereign power.

We find that regional autonomy and independence movements raise ecological issues as quasi-anti-imperialist issues, whether it is in the Baltic countries, in the Ukraine, or on Corsica. Whenever the conflict takes on such articulation, the struggle is no longer focused only on opposing interests that can be negotiated. The struggle is also concerned with recognition of profound needs. Conflicts of interest can be settled by compromise, provided that the opposing interest has received its recognized legitimate articulation. This condition of recognition is the difficulty in the case of conflicts related to needs, particularly security needs and the collective sense of the self.[10] The political means through which these needs of identity should presumably be satisfied may be inadequate, and the needs themselves may be obscure for the people concerned. Yet, whenever these deeper needs are not recognized and met, anxiety arises and the conflict, now exploitable for the Machiavellian creation of the enemy image syndrome, can become protracted and potentially violent.

In Europe we apparently need new structures of communication and cooperation to prevent destructive forms of conflict articulation and—using a term coined by John Burton[11]—to "provent" conflicts from becoming endemic. To "provent" hostility and violent conflicts, we have to create and set up new sociopolitical structures in Europe

- To facilitate legitimate articulation of concerns and needs,
- To respect diverging interests, and
- To urge cooperative action

on the intergovernmental *and* on the nongovernmental or intersocietal level, the level of civil societies. If we really want to develop nonviolent relations between individuals and collectives in the "cradle of European civilization," then we have to create pan-European forums for the multiple concerns of citizens in Europe. We need institutions to appeal to, and we need authorities having the function of ombudspersons.

The task of shaping intergovernmental European institutions will have to be carried out at the conferences convened within the scope of the Conference on Security and Cooperation in Europe (CSCE) process, in which all European countries, the United States, and the Soviet Union are represented. In this context I want to stress the need for an additional process of democratic integration from below, the first step of which was the Helsinki Citizens' Assembly, held in October 1990 in Prague. For every type of political issue on the intergovernmental level there needs to be a corresponding network of concerned citizens in Europe acting on issues related to human rights and the position of minorities; security policy; economic questions; and ecological challenges.

The combination of autonomy conflicts and ecological problems is motivated primarily by an unjust exploitation of natural resources. This type of conflict can be tackled by a policy that would give room for autonomy or even complete independence. But the intrinsic characteristics of ecological problems could also be perceived with respect to common problems that require cooperation beyond all forms of and efforts for political separation.

If one looks at pollution as a result of "normal" industrial production and consumption, cooperation could be based on the perception of commonly shared predicaments caused by the insensitivity to ecological questions stemming from the traditional model of industrial growth. This may provide an understanding of the mutual ecological dependency that has resulted from the international nature of environmental pollution of water, ground, and air, and of the need to jointly conduct an anticipatory, democratic assessment of technological advances in the service of a "sustainable development."[12]

One could say that the environmental problems and the unresolved issue of an anticipatory, democratic assessment of technology together constitute a security dilemma of a new type that takes the place of the traditional dilemma of sovereign states. The old security dilemma was founded on an international political structure in which individual states tried to gain security against each other. The new security dilemma centers on the premise that it is no longer within the sovereign power of states to protect their populace from the harmful effects of the traditional industrial model of growth. This new quality of security issue may be suited to viewing traditional political means of delimitation and separation in relative terms. These traditional means for delimitation or deterrence in the field of security policy are patently unsuited to providing protection against common problems.

However, the necessary international cooperation in the field of environment and technology is greatly encumbered by the asymmetry of initial conditions in the various countries inside and outside Europe. Therefore, there is a need to develop specific procedures that allow for a compromise between the interests involved in a short-term solution of the most urgent problems at the local level and the interests involved in a general, long-term restructuring process toward an ecologically oriented economy. This is where the challenges lie for the structures of intra-European conflict articulation and conflict resolution still to be developed.

The necessary cooperation between government representatives with respect to ecological tasks will not gain momentum unless the driving force comes from issue-oriented, decentralized networks among citizens of Europe. Intersocietal, decentralized forms of cooperation are absolutely essential for the new system of international cooperation within Europe. Modern industrial societies are highly vulnerable, particularly in Europe. Competent as well as loyal members of society are needed if catastrophic accidents and damage are to be avoided. An approach emphasizing centralist control is likely to be counterproductive.

Under the conditions of growing cultural, economic, and ecological interdependency, decisive importance has to be attached to direct and personal communication between the citizens of the European states and collectives. Insight into the substance of environmental problems can promote attitudes of cooperation and solidarity as well as an institutionalized framework in which competence and solidarity can be developed and strengthened.

OUTLOOK

The growing extent to which social and ecological concerns in Europe as a whole are becoming interwoven signifies that modern industrial societies are highly vulnerable and are in need of a new type of cooperative security policy and peaceful resolution of conflicts. This very fact, however, has to be made an issue among the citizens of Europe in order to counteract the revival of traditional security policy. Citizens' forums might help eventually to create a multiple loyalty, a multiple identity as citizens of a specific collective in Europe and of Europe. Distinguishing between conflicts of interest, misunderstandings, and hostility continues to represent the permanent task of the democratic institutions[13] in Europe in their efforts for peaceful resolution and "provention" of conflicts.

NOTES

1. See "Common Statement," in Hadley Cantril, ed., *Tensions That Cause*

War (Urbana: University of Illinois Press, 1950), 17–21. For an outline of respective problems, see Eva Senghaas-Knobloch, "Zur politischen Psychologie internationaler Politik," in "Aus Politik und Zeitgeschichte," *Beilage zum Parlament* 23 (12) (1988):14–23.

2. This description of the "enemy image syndrome" is derived from Kurt R. Spillmann and Kati Spillmann, "Feindbilder: Entstehung, Funktion und Möglichkeiten ihres Abbaus," *Züricher Beiträge zur Sicherheitspolitik und Konfliktforschung,* vol. 12, 1989.

3. This argumentation is spelled out in Eva Senghass-Knobloch, "The Political Psychology of the East-West Conflict and Beyond," in *Towards a Future European Peace Order?* ed. European University for Peace Studies (London: Macmillan, forthcoming). This study takes as a reference point the large wealth of analytical material on the psychology of the Cold War by Milton Rosenberg, "Attitude Change and Foreign Policy in the Cold War Era," in *Domestic Sources of Foreign Policy,* ed. Milton Rosenberg (New York: Collier-Macmillan, 1967), 111–159. See also Anne Ostermann and Hans Nicklas, *Vorurteile und Feindbilder* (Munich: Urban & Schwarzenberg, 1976); Rolf Breitenstein, "'Feindbilder' als Problem der internationalen Beziehungen," *Europa Archiv* 44 (7) (1989):191–198; Günther Wagenlehner, ed., *Feindbild, Geschichte, Dokumentation, Problematik* (Frankfurt: Umschau, 1989); Horst E. Richter, *Zur Psychologie des Friedens* (Reinbek bei Hamburg: Rowohlt, 1982); Birgit Volmerg, Ute Volmerg, and Thomas Leithäuser, *Kriegsängste und Sicherheitsbedürfnis* (Frankfurt: Fischer, 1983).

4. The potential radicalness of these new developments was underestimated for quite some time; cf. Zdenek Mlynar, "Der Ost-West-Konflikt als Strukturmuster in Europa und die Rolle des Sowjetblocks," in *Ost-West-Konflikt: Wissen wir, wovon wir sprechen?* ed. Christiane Rix (Baden-Baden: Nomos, 1987), 201–235. Mlynar pointed out the problems in making such assessments at a 1986 symposium on the theme "East-West Conflict: Do We Know What We Are Talking About?"

5. See, for example, the remarks of Dashichov, the Soviet historian, made during an interview on February 8, 1990 (recorded in the "Frankfurt Rundschau," 6): "The USSR left European civilization about sixty years ago, forty years ago in the case of the East European states, and now we are returning to this European cradle, to European civilization. This must be founded on the basis of pan-European values. These fundamental values are now being worked out and formulated in the fields of politics, economics and morals. Perestroika also signifies the return to these human, I would say, basic European values." The president of Czechoslovakia, Vaclav Havel, presented his ideas in, for example, his speech before the Polish Sejm on January 21, 1990 ("The Future of Central Europe," *New York Review of Books* 37 [5] [1990]:18f).

6. See Morton Deutsch, "Fifty Years of Conflict," in *Retrospective on Social Psychology,* ed. Leon Festinger (Oxford: Oxford University Press, 1983), 65.

7. From the substantial literature on the theme of "misunderstandings," I refer here only to Daniel Frei, *Feindbilder und Abrüstung* (Munich: Beck, 1985).

8. Vaclav Havel, "Von der Angst in Mitteleuropa," in *Angst vor Deutschland,* ed. Ulrich Wickert (Ulm: Hoffman & Campe, 1990), 326f.

9. Melanie Tatur, *Solidarnosc als Modernisierungsbewegung: Sozialstruktur und Konflikt in Polen* (Frankfurt: Campus, 1989); Melanie Tatur, "Zur Dialektik der 'civil society' in Polen," in *Demokratischer Umbruch in Osteuropa,* ed. R. Deppe, H. Dubiel, and U. Rödel (Frankfurt: Edition Juhrkamp,

1991), 234–255.

10. See John Mack, "Nationalism and the Self," *The Psychohistory Review*
2 (2–3) (1983):47–69.

11. John Burton, *Conflict: Resolution and Provention* (London:
Macmillan, 1990).

12. See Volker Hauff, ed., Report of the Brundtland Commission on the
Environment and Development, *Our Common Future* (Greven: Eggenkamp,
1987).

13. See Volker Rittberger, "Frieden und Friedensfähigkeit," in *Perspektiven
der Friedensforschung,* ed. Bernhard Moltmann (Baden-Baden: Nomos, 1988),
65–83.

CHAPTER 3

Africans Read Their Past and Look to the Future

——————————————— SOLOMON NKIWANE

One of the healthy aspects of the contemporary international political system is that Africa is finally being recognized and accepted as an essential part of the world community.

Although this is never admitted publicly, for centuries Africa was considered a place where people, usually Europeans, could find cheap labor, usually slaves, and usually free for the taking.[1] It was a continent where alien cultures and political structures were introduced at the expense of the local systems without much thought about the fate of indigenous cultures and structures. These, and other activities of the outside world in Africa over five centuries, not only contributed to the under-development of Africa, but also created an image of Africa as a continent without any past, present, or future.[2]

It is in this context that Africa as a region and African issues are usually understood—and thus never taken seriously. Africa has been regarded as the outpost of the Europe-centered world, good enough for exploitation and for plundering. For some, this is the only important thing about Africa. (One of my favorite questions to US high school children is this: "What do you think is the most important thing about Africa?" Almost invariably, the answers include animals, hot temperatures, famine, or military coups. It is never the peoples of Africa.)

Fortunately for Africa and the rest of the world, the modern international political system, which began with the Peace Treaty of Westphalia in 1648, at the end of the Thirty Years' War, has undergone dramatic changes. The French Revolution, which culminated in the battle of Waterloo in 1815, saw the sweeping into oblivion of the dynastic and nobility systems of Europe, to be replaced by the new era of international politics in which peace and security was guaranteed through a balance-of-power mechanism.

Further nodal changes in the world system occurred after World War I and

World War II. It was, however, the changes in the international system following World War II that had a telling impact on the African continent. The thirty-year period from 1960 to 1990 will be remembered in history as Africa's liberation decades. Within that relatively short time, forty-two of Africa's present fifty-two independent states gained their political independence.

It is often not appreciated, especially in the developed world, that Africa has its own views of the world, especially of the international political system. One often gets the impression that African views about the rest of the world are either nonexistent or not to be taken seriously.

Yet, relations between Africa as a region and the rest of the world depend, to a large extent, on whether the non-African world recognizes some of these African views. (Of course, that is only one side of the equation. We are all probably more familiar with how Africa is perceived by the rest of the world, which will be assumed in this chapter but not discussed.)

Africa's perceptions of the world have had a lot to do with the manner in which Africans were brought to participate in the modern industrialized world, which is mainly dominated at the present time by West European civilization. Some of the institutions and events that have strongly influenced these perceptions are:

- The African slave trade
- European imperialism and colonialism
- Africa's participation in World War I and World War II
- The decolonization process and liberation
- Postindependence internationalism

Entering the 1990s, however, one is struck by the unfolding revolutions in the Soviet Union, Eastern Europe, and Southern Africa. It is not very difficult to predict that these current developments in the international system will have far-reaching implications for Africa's perceptions of the changed and changing world. In fact, we are probably witnessing the beginning of major changes in the international system itself, which, in Africa at least, will result in national, subregional, and continental self-appraisal, and ultimately greater self-reliance. Perhaps the 1990s will usher in an era in which Africa will be taken seriously by the rest of the world. But this will depend on how African peoples and their governments react to the phenomenal changes that are now taking place all over the world. Africa's reaction to those changes will determine its standing in the world of the twenty-first century.

For Africa, the 1990s represent the first time since the continent was invaded by the Europeans that one can say the continent enjoys substantial freedom from political control by the external world. The decade of the 1990s will be one of reflection on the past centuries and of hard thinking about Africa's future.

PAST AFRICAN IMAGES OF THE WORLD

Until the turn of this century, and in many cases since, Africa was treated by the Western world, especially by the Europeans, as if it were not part of this planet. On the whole, the peoples of Africa were treated as if they did not belong to the human species. Evidence of this is abundant in history. This is despite historical findings indicating that Africa may be the cradle of the human race.[3]

There is little argument now among historians that the peak of Africa's civilizations prevailed between the fifth and fourteenth centuries A.D. This period, sometimes called "Africa's Golden Age," was characterized by thriving empires from the western coast of Africa to the Horn of Africa. The African states of Ghana, Songhai, Sudan, Monomotapa, just to mention a few, were in fact the envy of whatever political entities existed in Western Asia and Europe at the time.[4] Information reaching the outside world about these thriving African empires led to all kinds of speculation, and to adventures and explorations into the interior of the African continent. The result was the discovery of Africa's untapped riches. Unhappily, for Africa, there followed centuries in which the continent was robbed of its human and natural resources.

First by the Arabs, and then in a more systematic and efficient manner by the Europeans, tens of millions of Africa's young people were removed and sold like cattle into slavery. No one really knows exactly how many Africans were captured and transported to the Americas. Estimates range from thirty million to sixty million. What complicates the picture even more, and defies any quantification, is that perhaps as much as 50 percent of this "human cargo" was dumped in the Atlantic Ocean as not being suitable for the American slave market. It is now common knowledge that the unhygienic conditions in the ships sometimes resulted in outbreaks of disease that contaminated the Africans who were being readied for sale. Naturally, no Spaniard or American trader would want to buy contaminated or diseased slaves.[5]

The slave-trading period was followed by the plunder and looting of the raw materials of the African continent for the benefit of the people of Europe. This was the imperialist and colonial period, which was prosecuted in earnest after the Berlin Conference of 1884-1885. From then on until the end of World War II, Africa was militarily and politically brutalized and controlled by force of arms. Centuries of African achievements and civilizations were destroyed under the heavy-handed enforcement of Western values and cultures.[6]

The French colonial policies of "assimilation" and later "association" were nothing less than a cover-up for destroying African culture. The Africans were being "assimilated" into the French culture because African culture was considered inferior. The view from metropolitan France was that the best thing Africans could do for themselves was to abandon their own culture and become "Black Frenchmen" or "Black French women." Belgium's colonial policy of "paternalism" implied that Africans were so childlike that they needed the guidance of metropolitan Belgium forever. What was even more painful about the "paternalism" of the Belgians was that under that system, Africans would be forever children, never to grow up. The *assimilado* policy of the Portuguese was a brutal version of assimilation, by which every educated or Christianized African found in Angola, Mozambique, or Portuguese Guinea would be physically uprooted and shipped to Portugal. This was no gracious act of assimilation, but a deliberate act to keep the indigenous population illiterate and ignorant about the world around them in order to ensure cheap slave labor for the colonies.

The British colonial system of "indirect rule" appeared on the surface to respect the African way of life by having African peoples' own traditional leaders, or those of their kith-and-kin appointed by the British, to rule over them. This was, in fact, a cynical and dehumanizing policy whose essence was to suggest that Africans were just not good enough to participate in the modern world in which the English were supposedly preeminent.

The above portrayal of the world that Africans were being brought into, haphazardly, was a harsh and uncompromising world. Understandably, Africa's perception of that world was negative. To discerning Africans, the foreign intruders, whether they described themselves as adventurers, missionaries, colonizers, merchants, or traders, were all representatives of hostile nations that displayed a total disregard, let alone respect, for those peoples who happened to be different in color and culture to theirs. In fact, if anything, the thrust and agreements hammered out at the Berlin Conference of 1884–1885 by the European powers represents the most eloquent testimony to the Europeans' total nonacceptance of the peoples of Africa as belonging to the same species of humans as the Europeans.

The harsh realities of the past few centuries in Africa have had far-reaching implications for international relations, including international relations today. The fact of the matter is that Africans cannot be expected to forget easily what happened to them in past centuries, even if they wanted to. The colonial systems are still too fresh in the minds of whole generations of living Africans to be treated as if they were remote history. African perceptions of a past characterized by violence against them, their enslavement and dehumanization, cannot be expected to result in the automatic enhancement of a harmonious and peaceful world. Much work needs to be done to change Africans' perceptions of the harsh world from which we have all emerged. No one suggests that it will be easy. Until that is done, however, relations between the North and South or between the European nations and those of Africa, will continue to exhibit only tolerance at best. Suspicion, doubt, and anger continue to exist in the African mind.

The question is: What can be done to change Africans' perceptions of the past? Perhaps little, inasmuch as it is impossible to change history. But, hope does lie in the fact that the world has not remained static. The contemporary international system is different from that in which Africa played only a victim's role. How does the present international system differ from the previous ones? What changes have taken place that may change Africans' perceptions of the world?

S. F. Northedge has characterized the period from 1815 to 1914 in world history as "a hundred years peace."[7] It may have been a hundred years of peace for Europe, but for Africa, it was "a hundred years of hell." That "hundred years of peace" was subsequently shattered by the First World War.

The end of World War I brought about dramatic changes in the international system—changes that had direct implications for Africa. Point Five of Woodrow Wilson's Fourteen Points, at the Versailles Peace Conference in 1919, emphasized the need to recognize the principle of self-determination for peoples throughout the world. Although Woodrow Wilson was probably thinking of self-determination in terms of the peoples of Europe only, it was not hard for alert African nationalists to link the principle of self-determination with the thrust of the pan-Africanist movement, which had been launched in 1900. They argued that if self-determination was good enough for the peoples of Europe, it was equally good and necessary for the peoples of Africa.

However, the fact that the principle of self-determination was not meant for Africa was evidenced by events in the continent during the period 1919-1939, the so-called period of the "universal collective security system." Several European powers took advantage of the lull at this time to consolidate their "territorial acquisitions" in Africa. Others used the period for continuing their "pacification" of their newly acquired possessions in Africa. In fact, Italy even used the period to try to colonize Ethiopia. The only tangible gain for Africa was the granting of political independence and sovereignty to Egypt in 1936. Otherwise, the colonial systems in Africa remained intact, and Africa continued to be treated, at best, as an appendage to Europe.

Changes in the world that could be said to have positively affected Africans' perceptions of the world resulted from World War II and events since then. A large number of Africans participated in World War II, especially under the French and British military. African soldiers' general experiences in that war, and what they saw of their white soldier colleagues, convinced the Africans that, contrary to what they had been led to believe,

Europeans were as human as anyone else. The myths of European or white superiority over the black man evaporated into thin air. This was as much an education for Africans as it was for Europeans.

To get Africans to enlist for the war effort in large numbers, European colonial powers hinted unsubtly that the war effort by Africans would be rewarded by granting political independence to the colonies. Be that as it may, the course of World War II and, in particular, the herculean efforts and resources expended to execute the war to a victorious conclusion, exhausted and weakened the colonial powers so that they lost the will, resources, and military power to maintain the colonies. Notwithstanding the feeble efforts by Portugal to hang on to its African colonial possessions under the guise of such subterfuges as calling the colonies "overseas Portugal," it was only a matter of time before all the colonized peoples would seek, and be granted, political independence. Even the economic recovery of Europe, as a result of the infusion of US financial assistance under the Marshall Plan of 1948, could only slow down—not derail—the pan-Africanist objective of total emancipation of the African continent from alien control.

AFRICA IN THE POST–WORLD WAR ERA

The most significant change in the post–World War II international system was the dramatic increase in the number of sovereign states. Until 1945, Europe and its allies had dominated the international system by sheer weight of numbers, that is, the number of sovereign states. After 1945, however, the picture changed dramatically. As a result of the decolonization process, spearheaded and coordinated by the United Nations, over 100 former colonies sought and were granted political independence within a relatively short space of time.

The newly independent states had several common features, the most important of which were: (1) all the newly independent states had the historical experience of having been colonized by European powers; (2) they all belonged to the nonwhite races with different cultures from those of the Western world; and (3) they were all economically underdeveloped and militarily weak. These were the ingredients for a new voice in the international system. The concerns of the countries of the so-called Third World would be proclaimed by their own representatives; no longer would the former colonial powers be allowed to make a pretense of speaking on behalf of nonwhite peoples in world forums.

With respect to Africa, the changes in the international system were even more startling. When the United Nations was established in 1945, there were only four sovereign states in Africa: Egypt, Ethiopia, Liberia, and the Union of South Africa. But only fifteen years later, in 1960, the number of independent states in Africa had increased to ten, with the addition of Libya,

Sudan, Morocco, Tunisia, Ghana, and Guinea. By the beginning of 1961, Africa had boosted its number of independent states to thirty-one. This trend has continued; Namibia became independent on 21 March 1990, making it the fifty-second member of the Organization of African Unity (OAU).[8]

Suddenly, Africa's voice is being heard loud and clear in the international community. Most of what is being heard from Africa is not very palatable to the older members of the international community, especially to the former colonial powers. The reason for the unpalatability of the African views is that, for the first time, Africans, through their political spokespersons, are ventilating their perceptions of a world that is past, but a world that, nevertheless, remains real to them. This has often led to accusations that African leaders are too preoccupied with the past to the detriment of the present. The developed world, especially Western Europe, would rather forget the unpleasant past and get on with the exigencies of the present world as if the past did not matter.

AFRICA IN THE 1990S

To give maximum attention to the present complex world, African states and the African peoples in general would do well not to dwell too much and too long on the past. After all, what has occurred in history cannot be changed, although much can be learned from the past. What needs to be understood, however, is that Africans marching with the times and changing their perceptions of the world accordingly cannot be divorced from the sweep of history. I believe that Africans' understanding of historical continuity is very sound, especially in their understanding that the present and future cannot be built from nothing. The world also needs to be reminded that until the end of World War II, Africa *had* a view of the world, but that view was muted or denied. It is a healthy prospect for international relations to know what Africa's view of the previous international system was. That may lead to a better understanding and appreciation of Africa's changing perceptions of today's world.

Since the early 1960s, but in particular since 1963, when the OAU was established, Africa has tried to present a united front in the world. Buttressed by the Non-Aligned Movement, with the support of the Soviet Union and the other socialist countries of Eastern Europe and elsewhere, most African states have chosen a socialist orientation in their socioeconomic paths to development. The lips of African leaders have frequently framed the ideology of Marxism-Leninism as the cure for all the ills that Africans suffered, and continue to experience, especially under European imperialism, capitalism, and neocolonialism. This behavior has earned the African states not only condemnation from the Western European states and their allies, but accusations of being "communist." The irony of all these condemnations of

Africa is that out of fifty-two countries, only three or four have at any time claimed to be "Marxist-Leninist."[9]

However, the dramatic changes that have been unfolding in the Soviet Union and Eastern Europe may have great impact on Africa's own self-image. Africa's major weakness has been the tendency to see itself through the eyes of the rest of the world, East or West, rather than through its own eyes—no wonder the Western and Eastern worlds have been tempted to view Africa as either pro-West or pro-East! The implications of glasnost and perestroika have a stunning effect in Africa. While several African countries have declared their intentions to establish multiparty states, several hardliners are determined to hang on to their one-party democracies. The split that the changes in the Soviet Union and Eastern Europe have caused in Africa tells how greatly dependent Africa has been on the outside world, not only for economic assistance, but also for ideas of governance.

These changes are forcing Africans to alter their images of the world. Fortunately or unfortunately, the real world has changed. It is no longer the self-serving monster it once was, closed in on itself, functioning at the expense of Africa. No African leader can, or should be allowed to, find ready shelter in blind adherence to archaic images of the past. The temptations to do so are there, especially given the endemic political and economic mismanagement, and crises, facing most African countries today. Nevertheless, if Africa is to move with the rest of the world into the twenty-first century, it will be necessary for the continent to break out of the trap of its rigid perceptions of the world—perceptions that have only helped those in power to find scapegoats for their failures, without necessarily finding solutions to Africa's pressing problems.

Finally, as the decade of the 1990s progresses, one sees the unfolding events in the world as the opportunity for Africa to discover itself. Africa needs to develop a philosophy of self-reliance to the point where it will no longer judge itself on the basis of images held by others. The one thing Africa needs most entering the twenty-first century is self-respect. That will not come about as long as Africa looks at itself through the eyes of other regions of the world. Only by learning to accept itself, and its problems, can Africa hope to renew its contributions to world civilization in the twenty-first century.

NOTES

1. It will never be known for sure how many young Africans were captured and sold into slavery. The major complicating factor is that many of the captured slaves did not reach the Americas for a variety of reasons, including disease and death.

2. The peak of the introduction of alien cultures in Africa, at the expense of the local cultures and structures, was during the colonial period, i.e., from 1884–

1885 to about 1960. The French replaced African culture by their policy of *assimilation*; the British introduced *indirect rule*; the Belgians had their *paternalism*; and, finally, the Portuguese established *assimilado*.

3. See Phyllis M. Martin and Patrick O'Meara, eds., *Africa*, 2d ed. (Bloomington: Indiana University Press, 1986), especially Part II.

4. Solomon M. Nkiwane, "An Evaluation of the Exhibit of African Emblems of Wealth," presented at Report of the American Numismatic Association, Colorado Springs, Colorado, 1-16 July 1981.

5. UNESCO, *The African Slave Trade from the Fifteenth to the Nineteenth Century* (London: Heinemann; Berkeley: University of California Press, 1980); A. Adu Boahen, ed., *General History of Africa*, vol. 7, *Africa Under Colonial Domination, 1880–1935* (London: Heinemann, 1985).

6. See Leslie Rubin and Brian Weinstein, *Introduction to African Politics* (New York: Holt, Rinehart & Winston, 1977), 28-65.

7. S. F. Northedge, *A Hundred Years of International Relations* (London: Duckworth, 1960).

8. The OAU was created in 1964; its headquarters is in Addis Ababa, Ethiopia.

9. Until about 1989 the following African states were considered Marxist-Leninist: Angola, Congo Republic, Guinea-Bissau, and Mozambique. However, since the dramatic changes that recently overtook the Soviet Union and Eastern Europe, it appears that these countries have abandoned their Marxist-Leninist orientations.

CHAPTER 4

The Feminist Experience and Social Change in Europe and Africa

_____ BIRGIT BROCK-UTNE

The changing face of Europe can be analyzed from many perspectives. Mine will be a feminist one, insisting that the way women think and live matters and that changes must be analyzed according to the effects they have on women and children.[1] My perspective is also transnational, following the philosophy adhered to by Virginia Woolf in her beautiful novel _Three Guineas_. Here she says: "As a woman I have no country. As a woman I want no country. As a woman my country is the whole world."[2] (Right now, the single country closest to my heart is Tanzania, where I have been working and living for three and a half years.)

I shall try to shed some light on the following question: Do the majority of women in Europe and the rural women of Africa have reasons to be happy with the changes going on in Europe? I shall spend the first third of my statement looking at the political changes—changes in the direction of a more open society, a freer press, multiparty systems—the glasnost changes. The next third will be devoted to the economic changes—economic restructuring, trade liberalization—the perestroika changes. The last third will be devoted to a feminist Pragmatopia built on a partnership model of social organization and caring market behavior.

GLASNOST FOR WHOM?

What effects will the recent changes in Eastern Europe in the direction of elections, multiparty systems, and a freer press have on African countries, several of which have modeled themselves after the Soviet Union, having one-party systems and a politically censored press? This question is now being debated all over Africa by African politicians and African intellectuals. In particular, French-speaking countries like Benin, Côte d'Ivoire, Gabon,

Guinea, and Madagascar have been eagerly discussing and are already partly introducing multiparty systems. In Algeria and Tunisia, the framework for a transition to multipartism has been laid.[3] In Zaire, President Mobutu Sese Seko's promise that there would be free elections in April 1991 with three competing political parties, and that a new constitution would be created to ensure the democratic rights of the people remains unfulfilled, as of the fall of 1990. We shall hope that among those drawing up the new constitution, when it finally happens, there shall be included some strong women working for the rights of women.

If not, we may discover that issues concerning women have once again been "forgotten." This happened in Namibia. On 21 March 1990, when Namibia officially became independent, all the racially discriminatory legislation was automatically repealed, especially the powers given the administrative governor under the so-called AG8. Racially discriminatory legislation was done away with, but repealing sexually discriminatory regulations was "forgotten." Independence had been won. We may ask for whom? Not for the married woman. When a black Namibian woman marries today, she legally becomes a minor. She is not allowed to have her own bank account; she cannot own property. The South African government had also imposed an extremely sexist tax regulation on its colony, Namibia, taxing married working women more heavily than men in the same job. Recently both the *Times of Namibia* and *The Namibian,* two leading newspapers in Namibia, displayed pictures of the couple Libertine Amathila and Ben Amathila with their paychecks. Libertine Amathila is the minister for Local Government and Housing while her husband, Ben Amathila, is the minister for Trade and Industry in the newly formed Namibian government. Though they receive the same initial salary, the amount on her paycheck is much lower than on his because she is more heavily taxed. When I wanted to know the rationale behind such a sexist practice, my Namibian friends answered me: "Do you think the South African government ever gave us a rationale for their regulations? This sexist regulation they did not even impose in their own country but in their colony Namibia. The bad thing was that we did not do away with it when we achieved independence. Women's issues were somehow forgotten. Now we shall have to see to it that they will be dealt with." I have given this recent example from Namibia just to emphasize that any researcher who tries to analyze the extent to which a country has achieved independence or democracy and does not include in his or her analysis the rights and position of women will end up with a distorted picture and invalid research. For women, the removal of colonial rule might just mean that they are now ruled by males of their own color.

In a recent workshop on democracy and development in Africa held at the University of Dar es Salaam, the law professor Issa G. Shivji spoke about how the debate on democracy among African scholars was threatening to become an unabashed celebration of *liberalism*. He found that the moderates had faith in liberalism and imperialism and the radicals exhibited faith in the African state. What he saw as common to both groups of intellectuals and to the African politician—militant or otherwise—was "virtually a total lack of faith in the masses of the African people." He reminded the listeners that "after three decades of independence nowhere in Africa do we have either independence or socialism, whether defined in terms of social-democracy or Marxism-Leninism. What we do have though are 'national liberation movements' ruling through the barrel of the gun and 'mass parties' riding on the backs of the masses and presiding over authoritarian legal and political systems."[4] Ben Turok, in the same seminar, talked about the false assumption that the removal of colonial rule would usher in democratic government. Though he did not dispute the power of international capitalism to constrain and control African economies, he was equally concerned about the role of what he called "a domestic power block in and around the state" in safeguarding foreign interests and at the same time serving its own. He describes this domestic power block as "almost entirely male."[5] The block is entrenching its own political power and economic privileges, becoming ever more parasitic and leading to the further polarization of society. African politics, according to Turok, has remained the preserve of this bloc, a tiny sector of society. The majority of the people are still locked into subsistence agriculture (where women are predominant) and are excluded and marginalized from national political life.

Some African men admit that the marginalization of the African woman from national politics cannot be blamed solely on former colonial governments or the many northern male "experts" coming to teach new farming methods to men without realizing that in Africa most of the farming is done by women. Certain traditions in African society also work to the detriment of women's participation in political life. The director of the Forestry Division in Tanzania, E. M. Mnzava, tells about a survey of the attendance of villagers in 257 villages in Tanzania carried out by the Forest Division in Dodoma. The village meetings were very well attended by almost all the males in the village and 89 percent of the women. However, among those villagers participating in discussions only 7 percent were women. Mnzava comments: "One of the reasons for this situation is that according to traditional norms women are not supposed to talk in front of men nor are they supposed to challenge the latter."[6]

Also, in Tanzania a discussion on the opening up of a multiparty system has begun, not only among intellectuals, but also among politicians.[7] In an interview in the newspaper *Mzalendo* (the Patriot) on 25 February 1990, the chairman of Chama cha Mapinduzi (CCM), the only legitimate political party in Tanzania today, Julius Nyerere, said: *"Ukiona mwenzio ananylolewa na wewe tia maji"*—"If you see your comrade being shaven, you should get hold of water"—meaning since like-minded countries are changing, we should also be prepared for changes. Later in the same interview, Nyerere claimed that the fact that Tanzania at the moment had only one party was just a form of social organization that had been important at this time in history. *"Chama kimoja siyo Dini,"* he said—"One party system is no religion."[8] But the splitting of a male political elite into several political parties does not necessarily mean more democracy for the masses, especially not for the women. In the European Economic Community (EEC), which consists of twelve of the richest countries in Europe, nine of which are former colonial powers, one finds formal democracy and multiparty systems; yet, 75 to 92 percent of the unprotected labor power within the European common market is female.[9]

Even in countries that have had so-called free flow of information for many years, that flow is a lot freer for some people than for others.[10] We have a vast number of studies demonstrating the male dominance of the media—how, for instance, the news items on television are selected from a male's world and point of view, how men are interviewed when women could have answered as well or better. Women have trouble getting their writings published, especially if they write from a feminist perspective.[11] In times of economic decline, feminist journals are among the first to fold. Through interviews Robin Morgan has had with some exiled Russian feminists in Vienna, we know how these women were treated in the Soviet Union when they tried to publish a feminist magazine giving information on the actual conditions of women in that country in relation to abortion, contraceptives, single motherhood, wife battering, and so on. They were terrorized by KGB men who attacked and threatened to rape them; they were imprisoned and interrogated, and the four leaders were finally exiled. They tell that even dissident men rejected their writings and called their work frivolous.[12]

PERESTROIKA—TO WHOSE BENEFIT?

The common market countries of Western Europe are very much governed by the type of economic thinking that also serves as a model for Eastern Europe. The result of this thinking has led to a steady increase in the femininization of poverty. In the EC countries, forty-four million people are now living below the poverty line. Most of these people are old women and single mothers. Unemployment for men within the EC is now on the decrease, but this is not the case among the women. Birgit Wiig holds that unemployment can be three to four times as high for women as for men within the EC countries, if you look at the number of women employed in relation to the number of men in waged employment.[13] In this calculation, hidden unemployment, which is especially high among women, is not counted. Waged employment seems important because only those who have some social rights within the EC are employed full-time. Housewives, part-time workers (almost exclusively women), youth, and old people (most of whom are women) are the great losers. The Nordic countries have been proud of their relatively high degree of equality and health care for all—rich and poor—in their welfare states. It should be of interest to those who would like Norway to enter the Common Market to see what has happened to the welfare state in Denmark, the only Nordic country so far to enter the EEC. The restructuring of the economy on which Eastern Europe is embarking, involving an opening up for private enterprise and investments, may be necessary to resurrect life in a stagnating economy. However, the side effects of the liberalization will be many and are likely to hit women the hardest, whether we are talking about women in the Eastern bloc countries, in the European Community, or in the Third World.

Many a politician in the Third World has feared that the new romance between the First World and the Second World will cause the First World to lose interest in the Third World. For instance, much of the economic support Poland has received recently from Western countries has been taken from development budgets, from money that normally would have been used for aid to Third World countries.[14] The EEC, the United States, and Japan have also recently decided to give Poland and Hungary the same preferential trade status as they now give imports from Third World countries.[15] Women in Third World countries, however, may say that it will not affect them very much whether their country gets developmental aid or not. That aid is seldom given to women and often even makes women's lives more difficult. Neither have Third World women profited much from the loans their governments have received, yet they are now repaying the debts to the countries in the North with the lives and the health of their children and themselves.

Women and children are the ones who are hit hardest when repaying the debt burden; preference is given to the cultivation of cash crops instead of food crops and subsistence agriculture. In Tanzania, for instance, women contribute over 80 percent of the total labor force in agricultural activities.[16] Women have special responsibility for subsistence farming for feeding their families. However, when the best land is taken for cash crops and the cash is used by the men for their own priorities or by the government to repay debts to the countries in the North, life for women and children in the South becomes increasingly more difficult. They have to walk longer distances to gather fuelwood and to grow crops on less fertile land.

The IMF conditionalities also hit women and children especially hard, since the softer sectors of society like health and education are the sectors being starved. The worsening social conditions are noted in all recent surveys of poor Third World countries like Tanzania. They are often attributed to the structural adjustment programs.[17] These programs are the special kind of perestroika or economic liberalization imposed by the First World on the

Third World. The negative effects of these programs hit hardest those who are weakest and most vulnerable: women and children. As Hilkka Pietila quite correctly remarks, the word *adjustment* is often used in development discussions without being clarified in relation to those whose lives are at stake. "What is to be adjusted and why, by whom and on whose terms?" she asks.[18] I would also like to add: "Who will bear the burden of the adjustment and who will profit from it?"[19]

PRAGMATOPIA

I have so far sounded rather pessimistic, holding that neither glasnost nor perestroika are feminist concepts or hold much promise for women. Yet, there are possibilities—also from a feminist perspective—to be optimistic when looking at the changes taking place in Europe. The changes have for the most part been proceeding nonviolently, in the spirit of Bertha von Suttner, not of Alfred Nobel. We find a Gorbachev following up the thoughts of Bertha von Suttner, the thoughts she shared with Tolstoy and the csar of that time.[20] However, the changes in the political climate have not come about because of one man, but because of strong popular government and critical movements in the East as well as in the West. In these movements women have been in the majority and have done the basic work, though it has been documented in the peace movements in the West that even in cases where women had collected almost all the signatures in a peace campaign, the handing over of the signatures at a televised ceremony was done by peace movement males.[21]

In the manifesto adopted by the Nordic Women for Peace, and presented to the Secretary-General of the UN at the UN Decade for Women Conference in Copenhagen in June 1980, the Nordic women demanded:

- Disarmament to secure a lasting peace!
- No to War!
- Food instead of arms!

When, ten years later, we look at these demands, the events in Europe have given us some reasons to be optimistic, especially when it comes to seeing realized the first two of these demands. Real disarmament has at long last begun. Wars may become obsolete. Money saved on military budgets in the North could now be used for a redistribution of the resources to also serve the poor in developing countries. However, here we should not rely too much on governments. The United States, for instance, has already made clear that money saved from its military budgets will be used to fulfill the aim of reducing public expenditures within the United States.[22]

As I see it, the great challenge of the 1990s will be to work against the ever-increasing structural violence both within countries and between the North and the South. In an analysis I made earlier of the way women work for peace, I found that their work builds on three principles: the principle of nonviolence, the principle of life as the ultimate value, and the principle of transnationalism.[23]

The principle of nonviolence is a principle calling for inventiveness and creativity and for looking for the power of the allegedly powerless. Women, for instance, see that the fact that women do most of the unpaid household chores around the world, such as buying and preparing food, not only leads to the oppression of women but can also be used to cultivate what I would call a "caring market behavior." By caring market behavior I mean a behavior where business is governed not solely through principles of profit but through an ethical conscience. An example of this is when the Labour government of New Zealand refused to let ships into its harbors without a declaration that they did not carry nuclear arms, the papers in the US news media told of the US government's plan to boycott goods from New Zealand. Women from the United States and Canada then began campaigns to ask for and buy goods from New Zealand. The campaigns, which took place outside the big supermarkets in more than a hundred cities in the United States and Canada, were very successful. The women even coined a new word for these campaigns: "girl-cott." Girl-cott, as well as boy-cott, is ethically conscious, or what I have termed "caring market behavior." Through boy-cotts people are organized to *not* buy goods from certain regimes, such as South Africa with its apartheid policy or companies like Nestlé with its Third World baby milk advertisements. Girl-cotts instead are *positive* actions where people are encouraged to buy goods from certain regimes or producers—for example, from New Zealand, from women's collectives, and from Third World countries.

I hope the use of girl-cotts will be accelerated on the way to our new "Pragmatopia." In her fascinating book *The Chalice and the Blade*, Riane Eisler argues for the necessity of returning to a partnership model of social organization, a model built on equality, nonviolence, and caring. We need to work out what she calls a *Pragmatopia,* which in Greek means a real place and a realizable future, as contrasted to the term *Utopia,* which literally means "no place."[24] Eisler's book takes us back into our history and shows us how the roots of our present global crises reflect the fundamental shift in prehistory from technologies that sustain and enhance life to technologies designed to destroy and dominate. It develops the story of how the original partnership direction of Western culture veered off into a bloody 5,000-year dominator detour of androcratic rule. Our mounting global problems are in large part the logical consequences of a dominator model of social organization at our level of technological development and hence cannot be solved within it. Eisler shows how, through new ways of structuring politics, economics, science, and spirituality, we can move into the new era of a partnership world, a world where people do not dominate each other or Nature.

The Pragmatopia—product of women and men from the East, West, South, and North—should be built on feminist peace development principles. When women work for peace—whether direct or indirect, personal or collective—it is a peace without violence.[25] We are struggling for a society with a high degree of equality, a society where all children, all adults, and the environment matter.[26] We are not working for a society where women dominate men, but for a society run on a partnership model. Partnership model societies tend to be not only more peaceful, but also much less hierarchic and authoritarian.[27] The governing values of the Pragmatopia will be the caring and life-enhancing values, not the values of greed, materialism, and domination. The work that has to be undertaken to construct the Pragmatopia that will best enhance the life of humans and Nature can be considerably facilitated if we would all listen to women—for a change.

NOTES

1. Birgit Brock-Utne, *Feminist Perspectives on Peace and Peace Education* (New York: Pergamon Press, 1989), 15.
2. Virginia Woolf, *Three Guineas* (London: Hogarth Press, 1938).
3. Charles Quist Adade, "Does Africa Need Glasnost?" *Africa Events* 6 (1) (January 1990): 20-21.
4. Issa G. Shivji, "The Pitfalls of the Debate on Democracy," paper for the workshop "Democracy and Development" held as part of the Conference on Alternative Development Strategies for Africa organized by the Institute for African Alternatives at the University of Dar es Salaam, 12-14 December 1989. (To be published in the *Codesria Bulletin*, Dakar.)
5. Ben Turok, "No Democracy, No Development?" paper for the workshop "Democracy and Development" held as part of the Conference on Alternative Development Strategies for Africa organized by the Institute for African Alternatives at the University of Dar es Salaam, 12-14 December 1989.
6. E. M. Mnzava, "Women, Energy and Food: The Development Triangle in Tanzania" (Forest Division, Dar es Salaam, 1988), 8.
7. Birgit Brock-Utne, "Afrikansk Glasnost. Kronikk," *Dagbladet*, 19 April 1990, 4.
8. Saidi Nguba, "Mwalimu Nyerere aelezea mabadiliko ya Ulaya Mashariki" (Mwalimu Nyerere analyzes the changes in Eastern Europe), *Mzalendo*, 25 February 1990, 3.
9. Else Skjønsberg, *Om Kvinner og EF* (About women and the European Common Market) (Oslo: The Women's University, 1990), 27. (To be published by the Information Campaign on Norway and the Common Market.) See also Margret Krannich, "The Impact of the EC Internal Market on the Situation of Women," Women's Bureau of the Green Group in the European Parliament, 1989.
10. Birgit Brock-Utne, "Women and Third World Countries—What Do We

Have in Common?" *Women's Studies International Forum* 12 (5) (1989): 495-503.

11. Dale Spender, *Women of Ideas and What Men Have Done to Them* (London: Routledge & Kegan Paul, 1982).

12. Robin Morgan, "The First Feminist Exiles from the USSR," *Ms. Magazine*, November 1980, 49-56, 80-83, 102-108.

13. Birgit Wiig, "Kvinnens stilling i EF" (The position of the woman within the European Community), in *Fakta og meninger om Norge og EF* (Facts and opinions about Norway and the European Economic Community), ed. Per Lund, Kristen Nygaard, and Birgit Wiig (Oslo: The Information Campaign on Norway and the Common Market, 1989), 77.

14. Tom Vraalsen, "Nye ¥st/Vest-forhold; hva er konsekvensen for Nord/S¢r forholdet og tradisjonell bistand?" (New East/West relationships: What are the consequences for the North/South relationship and traditional aid?), *UD-Informasjon*, no. 7, 22 February 1990 (Oslo, The Foreign Ministry).

15. Knut Vollebæk, "Vil avspenningen mellom ¥st og Vest f¢re til skjerpet konflikt mellom Nord og S¢r i 1990-årene?" (Is the détente between East and West going to lead to a sharpened conflict between North and South in the 1990s?), *UD-Informasjon*, no. 6, 19 February 1990 (Oslo, The Foreign Ministry).

16. E. M. Mnzava, "Women, Energy and Food: The Development Triangle in Tanzania" (Forest Division, Dar es Salaam, 1988).

17. ILO, "Distributional Aspects of Stabilization Programmes in the United Republic of Tanzania, 1979-1984," *Report of an ILO Mission* (Geneva: ILO, 1988).

18. Hilkka Pietila, "The North is the South's Problem," *Peaceletter*, no. 2 (1988): 7-11.

19. Birgit Brock-Utne, "Listen to Women for a Change," presented to a meeting of the Worlds, Joensuu, Finland, 19–23 June 1990. (To be published in *Peaceletter*, no. 1, 1990.)

20. Ibid. See also Birgit Brock-Utne, *Educating for Peace: A Feminist Perspective* (New York: Pergamon Press, reprinted in 1987 and in 1989), 37–45. A Korean edition was published in Seoul in 1986; a Norwegian edition appeared in 1987 (Oslo: Folkereisning mot krig); an Italian edition appeared at the end of 1989, published by Edizione Gruppo Abele; and a Russian translation is under way.

21. Brock-Utne, *Educating for Peace,* 68.

22. With reference to the Gramm/Rudman bill, see Vraalsen, "Nye ¥st/Vest-forhold."

23. Birgit Brock-Utne, "Rauhan Kasvatus. Rauha saa alkunsa naisten mielissa" ("Women and peace. Peace starts in the minds of women"), a Finnish translation of a commissioned paper written in English for a UNESCO conference in New Delhi, 1981 (Helsinki: Naiset Rauhan Puolesta, 1982. Reprinted in 1983), 85; Brock-Utne, *Educating for Peace,* 37–70.

24. Riane Eisler, *The Chalice and the Blade: Our History, Our Future* (San Francisco: Harper & Row, 1987), 239.

25. Brock-Utne, *Feminist Perspectives on Peace and Peace Education,* 39–64.

26. Vandana Shiva, "India—The Abundance Myth of the Green Revolution," in *Women and the Environmental Crisis*, Report of the Proceedings of the Workshops on Women, Environment and Development, Nairobi, 10-20 July 1985 (Nairobi: Environment Liaison Centre, 1985). Irene Dankelman and Joan Davidson, *Women and Environment in the Third World—Alliance for the Future*

(London: Earthscan Publications, in association with the International Union for Conservation of Nature and Natural Resources, 1988).

27. Eisler, *The Chalice and the Blade*.

CHAPTER 5

The Disappearing Boundaries Between Internal and External Conflicts

KUMAR RUPESINGHE

New types of conflict are appearing as we near the year 2000. Boundaries between internal and external conflicts will have to be redefined and more attention focused on internal armed conflicts.[1] In this chapter I will explore the reasons for this phenomenon and emphasize the emergence of identity conflicts as being of special significance. The search for identity appears to the Western liberal as a problem of "fundamentalism." The challenge for the liberal paradigm would be how to engage in a constructive discourse that can accept a multiethnic, plural, global order. In other words, how can the peace research community and policymakers in general communicate to non-likeminded communities and address the issues of internal wars and violence? The demise of the communist utopia does not mean that problems have been shelved. Accumulated historical conflicts will assume a new salience and intensity, and it is likely that these conflicts will become more violent and intransigent.

This is a complex subject, particularly at a moment in history when it is difficult to make clear distinctions between external and internal conflicts. The concept of nonintervention in internal affairs is crumbling as conflicts within and between states get inextricably interlinked. The social conflicts in Central America, the Islamic revivals in Asian and African countries, the destabilization of Southern Africa, the disintegration of the Soviet empire and its subsequent fragmentation, the drug-financed rebellions in South America and Southeast Asia, the resurgence of ethnicity and nationalism, and the complex pattern of refugee movements from South to North are examples that belong to our generation. The globalization that characterizes economic, environmental, and political processes is having an impact on many societies. Powerful tendencies are at work to exacerbate conflicts, and the widespread diffusion of consumerism has accentuated cultural homogenization and modernization, creating a rise in expectations. On the other hand, the process of homogenization is strongly resisted by some cultures and peoples, leading to a localization and internalization of conflicts. These are problems that face the global community, whether it be as a community of citizens or of princes.

In the past there have been periods of relative stability followed by periods of upheaval and rapid change.[2] The present conjuncture is significant if only because the crisis has not been accompanied by a general war. Transitions have usually been nonviolent and have involved large-scale democratic change. The cumulative effects of these changes have undermined existing paradigms of world order. There is a blurring of traditional conflict paradigms. This is most obvious in the changing perceptions of the East-West and North-South conflicts, interstate and internal conflicts, and those generated by environmental degradation. Contemporary forms of insecurity, be they ethnic conflicts, human rights issues, or environmental degradation, are incompatible with conventional paradigms of international relations theory or current utopian thinking. There is a definite need to evaluate and begin to extrapolate present trends for the future.[3]

When we are discussing boundaries and conflicts, we are discussing boundaries as defined by the state system. The number of states has increased over the years so that at present the United Nations has a membership of 170. It is precisely the elaboration and evolution of this state system that will come under increased pressure. Most Soviet republics are claiming independent statehood. Examples elsewhere include Quebec, Eritrea, and Tamil Eelam.

There are simultaneous threats to the state system posing new challenges to peace and order in the future. On the one hand, the process of democratization has opened up new conflicts, such as challenges to the unitary state in many countries. Often, countries that are in the process of acquiring democracy have no tradition of governance, conflict management, or a culture of tolerance; it is in the lack of space for new forms of governance that conflicts so generated have the potential for escalation and violence. Democratization will itself generate new conflicts, and the inability of fragile states to manage this will be a cause for concern.[4] In the absence of an institutional capability to manage conflicts, it is likely that authoritarianism will reassert itself. Claims made upon the state on the basis of the right to self-determination, territorial claims, minority assertions, and popular assertions for democracy are likely to lead to "Lebanonization" and fragmentation of some societies.[5] On the other hand, we are also witnessing the consolidation of larger entities such as the "European Homeland."

What we are seeing today is an extremely volatile and fragile international environment. Global changes are not necessarily reflected in institutional changes in the state system or within the international system. This disjuncture between the global changes, peoples' initiatives, and the international institutions, whether they be the United Nations, the International Monetary Fund, or the World Bank, requires the formation of new global institutions to manage these concerns.

THE END OF HISTORY AND THE END OF WARS

Recent global changes have prompted many hypotheses. Among the more interesting formulations are Francis Fukuyama's "The End of History," heralding a triumph of liberalism, and John Mueller's thesis that major wars between nations are on the decline. While open to criticism, both these ideas represent innovative challenges for debate and discussion. It is significant that these theses have appeared at this particular time.

Fukuyama states that "something fundamental has happened in world history," and that recent events—particularly the rise of reform movements in the Soviet Union and Eastern Europe and the spread of consumer culture throughout much of the world—indicate "the triumph of the West, of the Western idea."[6]

> What we are witnessing is not just the end of the Cold War, or the passing of a particular period of postwar history, but the end of history as such: that is, the end point of mankind's ideological evolution and the universalisation of Western liberal democracy as the final form of human government.[7]

John Mueller holds that "major countries of the developed world had managed to remain at peace with each other for the longest continuous stretch of time since the days of the Roman Empire."[8] Calling this prolonged avoidance of war "history's greatest non-event," he advances an explanation that is, to say the least, controversial. Mueller believes war is going out of style—is it also going out of business?

> The long peace since World War II is less a product of the recent weaponry than the culmination of a substantial historical process. For the last two or three centuries major war—war among developed countries—has moved toward terminal disrepute because of its perceived repulsiveness and futility.[9]

Mueller points to a shift in cultural values so profound in some parts of the world as to banish war from the mind. Fukuyama, on the other hand, celebrates the triumph of the liberal ideal and sees it as the final embodiment of history. Both these contributions touch on several possible areas of agreement—the decline of the Cold War, the reassertion of democracy and liberalism, and the possibility of a lasting peace. Peace, in their view, is the absence of direct violence. I would, however, use their theses as entry points to address the issue of internal wars and violence.

Fukuyama underestimates the manner in which the new international division of labor will further exacerbate conflicts.[10] The new international division of labor will heighten existing inequalities and lead to a greater marginalization of populations. Fukuyama proposes a notion of the uninterrupted evolution of capitalism as a world system. There are likely to be serious internal problems within the transition to capitalism itself. There is no built-in insurance that capitalism will develop into democracy, for it is likely that it could also lead to fascism. The new multipolar configuration is bound to encourage more capitalist competition and trade wars and the search for markets.

The world is moving away from bipolarity, but a multipolar axis may mean more insecurity and turbulence. Fukuyama does not reflect on the crisis of modernization. Consumerism, capitalist development, and modernization are confused and conflated, resulting in the notion that the spread of consumerism equals liberal democracy—as if the Western model could be easily replicated in other parts of the world.[11] Further, it is precisely the confrontation of modernization and consumerism that affects the identity of large populations. Consumerism creates a revolution of expectations that cannot be fulfilled. Totalitarian regimes may be produced as a result of unfulfilled dreams and a profound sense of alienation and deprivation.[12] The struggle for democracy will itself reawaken sleeping conflicts such as those over territory and identity.

In the way the debate has been formulated, there is no reason to assume that the hegemony of the "market economy" is assured. Is the market the issue or is it the need for institutions that sustain capitalism? Another model that has been projected for emulation is the growth performance of newly industrializing countries (NICs) of Southeast Asia.[13] Whether the Soviet Union or Eastern Europe will be able to create a free market remains to be seen. Will the market be the answer to regulated societies that have the institutions necessary to sustain capitalist development? Will the triumph of the market mean the surrender of sovereignty and controls over the national economy? The introduction of a free market requires widespread changes in property relations, including the dominance of private property. Such changes will require major political changes not without serious conflicts. We are witnessing transitional regimes, and it is likely that there will be regression, i.e., many societies going backward toward more militarization and authoritarian rule.

DISAPPEARING BOUNDARIES IN THE GLOBAL ORDER

The East-West Conflict

The relaxation of the Cold War will have profound effects on the world order. With regard to the Soviet Union and Eastern Europe it means the dismantling of parts of the Soviet empire, the decline and collapse of Stalinism as a way of politics, and the demise of socialism from above. But for how long the process will be managed effectively remains to be seen.

The transition from Stalinism and one-party rule to multiparty democracy will be extremely problematic, and a new tradition of governance and institutions governing civil society will have to be built over a long period of time. The transition is likely to be turbulent.

The relaxation of the Cold War heralds new conflicts and the awakening of sleeping conflicts. We are already witnessing the appearance of armed conflicts in the Soviet Union and Eastern Europe, especially Yugoslavia, and increased ethnic tensions.

The reintegration of Eastern Europe into a common European homeland means that Europe inherits a Third World in its own backyard. The periphery of Europe (which has now been incorporated), including the countries of Eastern Europe, will occupy the attention of the European Community. There will be increasing numbers of claims on the welfare budget of European countries from Eastern Europe. The evolution of the European Community and the elimination of boundaries in 1992 means that control policies have to be evolved and unified to keep the South out of fortress Europe.

North-South Conflicts

Changes in the East-West conflict will, however, also have profound effects and mean a blurring of old distinctions between the North and the South. Will the disappearance of serious East-West conflicts lead to increased North-South conflicts? The first casualty may be the concept of the Third World itself. There are already notions of a fourth and fifth world, indicating that the stratification of the Third World is according to income levels and other indicators. Some regions will be marginalized and will most probably revert to subsistence. Over a billion people will not overcome the poverty trap for at least several decades.

The most articulate expression of the North-South problem was the demand for a new international economic order, which was vetoed and pronounced dead by Reagan at the Mexico summit in 1986. Postponing structural issues means that these will emerge with greater salience in the future.

The demographic distribution is worth considering and will provide an idea of the changes of power and distribution within the global community. As the twentieth century draws to a close, the five billion human beings who inhabit the earth are not distributed uniformly over the globe. There will be areas of great concentration in the rich zones, depopulation in others (because of degraded ecological systems), vast migration movements, and an expansion of refugees both internal and external.

Barring drastic changes in the natural conditions of the planet and in the demographic behavior of the population, the population in developed capitalist countries will have decreased to 484 million. Under such conditions, the age structure of the population will suffer far-reaching changes. One consequence is that the percentage of elderly will double and social security systems will be unable to offer the same level of services as are available today. With regard to the population of Eastern Europe and the Soviet Union, it will grow from the current 393 million to 510 million around the year 2065. However, while average rates of birth in these countries would be around 2.3 percent, in the Soviet republics of central Asia, the birth rate would be around 4.5 percent and 6 percent.[14] The distribution of population and power has been dramatically presented by Johan Galtung as follows:

> Essentially ethnic composition will change the nature of the society, with continued decline of the classical WASP as dominant culture in the former Anglo-Saxon territories; decline of the Russians in the Soviet Union; decline of the Scandinavians in the Nordic countries, etc. The imbalance of overpopulated/underpopulated regions is untenable in the longer run in a rapidly interconnecting world.[15]

Changes in the new international system and regional configurations will make economic development more uneven within nations and, in some cases, whole regions will be forced to retreat into primitive economic existence. There will be greater economic polarization, and more countries will be forced to accept very stringent conditionalities from the world financial institutions. Subregions, such as the Sahel in Africa, will continue to reproduce poverty, and it is likely that there will be new forms of recolonization of parts of Africa. Recolonization means that expatriates, aid flows, and controls will exercise a greater influence on large parts of Africa. These economic tensions will accentuate conflicts. The other most important feature is the consequence of environmental degradation of some areas, resulting in large shifts of population due to desertification, armed conflicts due to environmental degradation, and lack of resources.

There will also be a further fragmentation of the so-called Third World. In the short term, resources will be diverted to Europe, and investments and development assistance transfers to developing countries may be the casualties.

Another important factor for several countries in Latin America is the international drug trade, which has had a profound effect on the social structures of Peru, Bolivia, and Colombia. The drug trade permeates politics, the military, and the economic life of significant communities. It also fuels the traffic in arms and provides resources for the guerrilla and the military. To many peasants it provides a source of income. It constitutes also a North-South problem. The drug trade is, in addition, a manifestation of class war. Will the drug bourgeoisie replace the old feudal latifundia? There is also a relationship between external debt and drugs. It is likely that the war on drugs proclaimed by the present US administration may provide the excuse for US hegemonic designs over the Western Hemisphere.[16]

New conflicts created by the drug economy have been expressed by a Peruvian intellectual as follows:

Society is narcotised, making social relations still more violent, imposing mafia rule and disorganising the social elements, which, before the proliferation of drug traffic, had been supporters of the fight for popular alternatives. Politics is cocoalized, squeezing out the democratic space that the workers and people have attained through mobilization, and destroying formal democracy, which the peripheral bourgeoisie imposes.[17]

The links between the drug trade and the debt burden are also interesting. John Kerry, US Democratic senator from Massachusetts, who chaired the Subcommittee on Drugs and Terrorism of the Senate Foreign Affairs Committee, maintained in 1989 that "it is calculated that more than 50,000 million dollars—most from drug sales—are laundered annually through banks of the US and other countries."[18] The links between the drug trade and the external debt is well analyzed by R. T. Taylor:

The cocaine economy forms the biggest component of an international drug complex whose gross annual revenues in the US alone may top 100 billion dollars (though by definition, all such numbers are soft). That drug complex, in turn, is probably the largest single component of a global black economy that makes nonsense of conventional financial statistics. . . . And the complex feeds the growth of "narcocracies" whose financial power overwhelms the economy of small countries, undermines the fiscal integrity of large countries, and subverts the political and judicial process everywhere it reaches.[19]

Connections between drugs, arms sales, the military, and the guerrilla are not restricted to Latin American countries; such connections have been established in the region of Pakistan/Afghanistan and in Southeast Asia.[20]

The connection between drugs and small arms is difficult to establish but there is some evidence for it:

> A powerful arsenal of Israeli arms, found in the possession of drug-traffickers, arrived in Colombia via Antigua and Barbados, at which authorities the Colombian government registered a strong protest.[21]

The role of intelligence agencies in the drug trade has been well documented as has the relationship of drugs to arms. It has occurred mostly in secret, and not so secret, wars, including those in Vietnam, Afghanistan, and Nicaragua.[22]

Internal and International Conflicts

The boundaries between internal and international conflicts are being redefined. Mueller[23] has argued that there is a significant shift in the culture and norms governing war and peace in the advanced democracies. Many have noted the absence of interstate wars in the last few years. Mueller argues that a change in norms and culture in the developed world may help lead to the obsolescence of war in the Third World. He notes that there have been virtually no wars among the forty-four wealthiest countries, and that war has taken place almost exclusively within the Fourth World. He observes that when countries improve their standard of living, they will find the prospect of war to be decreasingly attractive because they will have more to lose. Another interesting proposition is that war outside the developed world has tended to take place among new states, not old ones. Many scholars have pointed to the fact that no significant interstate wars have occurred between democratic regimes. Some scholars have demonstrated that there have been no significant interstate wars in the last few years. This hypothesis says that a democratic zone of peace has evolved over the years. What is suggested, therefore, is that the furtherance of democracy will be the best insurance for peace. But what about wars between democratic and nondemocratic states? Are they not equally ferocious? Nothing in the literature suggests that there will not be wars between democratic and nondemocratic countries. An example was the brutal war between the United States (a democratic country) and Vietnam (a so-called nondemocratic country).

Interstate Conflicts

This is not to say that we may not witness a resurgence of interstate conflicts in the future. There are several intractable trouble spots with considerable war preparedness. The most dangerous arena and theater of war is the Middle East, with its particular focus on the Palestinian question. The Iran-Iraq War ended only to be replaced by Iraq's invasion of Kuwait and the ensuing Gulf War. There is no lack of instances of preparedness for war, as in the India-Pakistan conflict, or the recent conflict between Senegal and Mauritania.

Nuclear Proliferation

There is a greater diffusion of the nuclear arsenal to big and middle powers in the Third World and to so-called threshold countries (e.g., China and Iraq). As fears of superpower nuclear conflagrations recede, the specter of nuclear and conventional arms proliferation in Asia and the Middle East is growing. There are many disturbing examples. Saddam Hussein's belligerence and rhetoric to acquire nuclear capability is a very recent instance. There are continued efforts by Israel to develop an advanced nuclear capability. The rationale for the Pakistani, Indian, and Chinese bomb is still based on concepts of deterrence and nuclear terror. It is reported that North Korea is attempting to join the nuclear club. The various safeguards—safety and early warning mechanisms—are still at a primitive stage. Further, there is a greater demand for long-range ballistic missile technology. Most countries in Asia and the Middle East are seeking to acquire long-range ballistic missiles. Most countries are also acquiring combat aircraft that have a greater strike capability than ballistic missiles. Disarming and de-escalating the arms race in Europe has meant that some of these arms are being sold cheaply to Third World governments.[24]

Studies of war have tended, however, to ignore the significant increase and salience of internal wars, i.e., wars within a given nation-state. It is important not to confuse appearance with reality. Internal wars have led to massive civilian casualties and destabilized societies, and have created millions of displaced persons and refugees. Matthew Melko, for example, notes that while there have been only two major conflicts in the developed world since 1945 (the Greek civil war and the Hungarian revolution) there have been more than fourteen million people killed in the Third World, compared to fewer than 100,000 in the developed world.[25]

There is no evidence that internal wars are on the decrease; instead, all the evidence points to an increase in the scale, intensity, and frequency of such violent conflicts. Further, studies have not emphasized enough the increase in violence and criminality in many societies, rich and poor. In many Third World societies, violence has become endemic, along with militarization.

Although much has been said and researched on interstate wars, and on direct violence versus structural violence, there is still much to be done on the study of violence. Many of the indicators consist of quantitative figures related to numbers of deaths in a given conflict. What is more significant is the spread of violence as a phenomenon, and it is here that interdisciplinary work has only recently started. War has been given many definitions and has been the subject of many studies, but the conceptualization of violence and internal wars within the nation-state is still at an early stage. Galtung recently called attention to cultural violence, in which cultures legitimize structural violence and marginalize direct violence.[26]

ARMED CONFLICTS AND THEIR CHARACTERISTICS

Research on armed conflicts and their specificity may shed light on the types of conflicts we are witnessing today, and may also give us an idea of emergent conflicts in the future. The 1988 *SIPRI Yearbook* identified thirty-three contemporary armed conflicts—with armed conflict defined as a situation with over 1,000 casualties.[27] Thirty-two armed conflicts were recorded for 1989.[28] According to these estimates the total number of armed conflicts seems to be on the decrease. But if we also consider armed conflicts with less than 1,000 casualties, we get an increasing number of recorded conflicts. According to *SIPRI's* observations:

> The total number of ongoing armed conflicts in the world today is staggering. In some locations there are several destructive conflicts going on simultaneously.[29]

The yearbook suggests that the number of armed conflicts has increased to about seventy-five, and it is likely that more efficient reports would reveal that numbers would increase to about 150. Some interesting observations can be made, based on the empirical data available.

- Most of the armed conflicts take place in Third World countries.
- The basic issues in the armed conflicts of 1989 were related to internal matters.
- Interstate conflicts are currently on the decline—perhaps for the moment. This has inspired the media and others to talk of a grand peace settlement.
- In most of the conflicts that led to external intervention, either by the superpowers or by a major regional power, there have been military withdrawals or negotiations for phased withdrawals.[30]
- With regard to conflict management or resolution, the UN Security Council has rarely been involved; in some cases the good offices of the UN Secretary-General have prevailed, but most often conflict resolution has been the function of a big regional power. It is likely, however, that the United Nations, and in particular the good offices of the Secretary-General, will play a more active role in conflict resolution in the future.

• In most cases, the internal conflicts have been fueled by sales of arms and military equipment to combatants. Arms have been provided not only by the superpowers but also by some states in the Third World. Apart from arms there is evidence that chemical weapons are being used by both the state and the guerrilla.[31]

• There have been consistent and flagrant violations of human rights and no respect for the Laws of War. Gross abuse of human rights is evident on the part of both the state and the guerrilla movements. Civilians account for 74 percent of official deaths or almost three times as many military deaths.[32]

• In most cases, the conflicts have involved cross-border affiliations or networks, where a neighboring state provides sanctuary as well as arms and training to the guerrillas.

• Many of the conflicts listed are identity conflicts, most of which could be ended by granting substantial devolution of power or territorial autonomy.

These propositions raise a range of new issues that may bring about a significant shift in the paradigm of conflict research and international relations. First, there is the matter of building a sound comparative experience in internal conflict resolution. Here it is necessary to be able to identify the actors generally involved within the state, ethnic groups or religious groups, and particularly actors who are generally silent in the discourse. The Western liberal tradition has tended to ignore non-likeminded actors, particularly those belonging to fundamentalist religions or speaking minority languages.

TYPES OF INTERNAL CONFLICTS

We need to distinguish the various types of internal conflicts that generally result in serious or violent hostilities. From the data available on conflicts we may make the following classification with regard to internal conflicts:

• *Ideological conflicts* between the state and insurgent movements, in which the social inequality between classes is dominant.

• *Governance and authority conflicts* concerning the distribution of power and authority in society. Demands from the opposition are for regime changes and control over resources.

• *Racial conflicts,* including the conflicts in South Africa and Namibia and racial conflicts in the United Sates and Europe.

• *Environmental conflicts,* which are broadly resource-based conflicts, over land, water, the control of rivers, and the protection of forests. There are two categories of environmental conflicts: environmental conflicts between man and nature and conflicts between states and population groups caused or exacerbated by environmental problems. Resolving them requires different approaches.

• *Identity conflicts*, the dominant aspect of which is ethnic, religious, tribal, or linguistic. Often these conflicts involve a mixture of identity and the search for security, where the main contention concerns the devolution of power. This was the main type of war in 1987; such conflicts are likely to increase. Identity conflicts can be subdivided into territorial conflicts, ethnic and minority conflicts, religious assertions, and struggles for self-determination.

Various linkages may exist between the conflicts so defined, or we may find a mixture of types of conflicts. The above classification is, however, static, and what is required is to conceptualize the various interrelations between them. It may well be that several types of conflicts are being waged simultaneously or that a country faces two or more types of conflicts—for example, identity conflicts based on the demand for autonomy, and governance and authority conflicts. For example, in 1989 in Sri Lanka there were five armed conflicts waged simultaneously. In Colombia there were several armed conflicts being waged. In Lebanon several armed conflicts are being waged simultaneously. Given the analytical problems in defining the specificity of these conflicts, some have preferred to term these internal conflicts as protracted social conflicts or intractable conflicts.[33]

POTENTIAL CONFLICTS

If we examine the various types of domestic conflicts listed, we may speculate on the general trends and types of conflicts likely to emerge in the future.

Ideological Conflicts

Ideological conflicts have been and will be endemic in all societies where there are serious disparities in income and class stratification. However, it is likely that the traditional communist parties will no longer pursue armed guerrilla confrontations, except under very special circumstances. The ideological centers in Moscow and Beijing have discarded their leadership role as the vanguard of the international proletarian revolution. This does not mean that armed groups will not emerge in the future or will not persist, as the Sendero Luminoso in Peru or the Janatha Vimukthi Peramuna in Sri Lanka, but they will have to rely on their own resources to sustain a protracted confrontation with the state. Modern ethnopopulist movements and guerrillas seem to acquire not only a common ideology, but also common types of organization and politics. They tend to be military-politico movements with common features. There is some evidence that the guerrillas are involved in the drug trade and that this trade provides a source of funding for the purchase of arms. New tactics and methods of guerrilla warfare are also being adopted where civilians are increasingly becoming the victims. At least in some instances, destabilization and the collapse of a democratic alternative is the stated objective of the guerrillas.[34]

Governance and Authority Conflicts

Governance and authority conflicts are likely to become more salient in the future. These conflicts revolve around popular demands for democracy and political participation. The authoritarian responses to the demand for popular democracy in Romania is one example. The use of armed miners against demonstrators is another. The emergence of death squads and armed vigilante groups, mercenaries, commando units, and the increasing number of recorded "disappearances" and "extrajudicial killings" are indicators of the silent wars being waged today.[35] The transition to civilian governments in many Latin American societies is highly problematic and fragile. In many of these countries, the armed forces continue to retain significant autonomous power, and endemic forms of violence, such as police brutality, continue. In almost every country, civil rights are abused, various forms of discrimination are rampant, and economic and social conditions continue to deteriorate rather than improve. In countries such as El Salvador and Guatemala, grave violations of human rights continue under civilian governments. Severe violations of human rights, such as disappearances and assassinations, are more prominent in formal political democracies such as Peru and Colombia than in the last years of the military dictatorships of Chile and Paraguay. The situation is further complicated by the fact that several civilian governments face armed insurgent movements.[36]

The liberalization policies of regulated socialist societies have made new types of conflicts more visible. The process of democratization in these societies has revitalized sleeping conflicts suppressed earlier. In the Soviet Union, we are witnessing demands for greater independence for the various nationalities. This will be characterized both by armed conflicts with the central government and conflicts among the various nationalities. There will also be demands for greater autonomy for civil and political institutions. There is a serious possibility of fragmentation with competing powers struggling to assert control. There will be greater polarization on many fronts, such as ideological conflicts (both conservative and democratic), identity conflicts, religious conflicts, and conflicts over authority and governance. Conflicts over identity may take many forms, such as territorial conflicts leading to secession, as in Lithuania, Latvia, Estonia, Moldavia, and, potentially, Georgia. There will be heightened armed conflicts in

Nagorno Karabakh, Andizhan-Ost, Kirghizia-Uzbekistan, and Georgia-Abkhazia; perhaps another round of armed conflicts between Azerbaijan and other Islamic and Asian republics; and demands for autonomy for Turkish-Mischetints, Soviet Germans, and so on.[37] These conflicts are likely to be protracted and difficult to manage. It is obvious that the Soviet experiment in evolving a homogeneous communist Soviet citizen has been abandoned. But what will replace it? The ideological problem is not merely de-Stalinization but whether a revealed and absolute ideology can be replaced with liberalism. Could it not be that the Soviet Union may come to represent another case of Lebanonization, with different centers of power, greater use of extrajudicial methods of governance, the appearance of death squads, and the fueling of conflicts through arms? Could it not be the case that when the official ideology has been undermined and there is an increased sense of fragmentation, that communities will seek new identities or revive old identities as the only basis for security? These are questions that need to be asked about a period of transition. In China, the popular demand for democracy and participation was brutally suppressed, but we may expect the process to continue with greater vigor in the future.

The problems of governance in most parts of Africa will be turbulent. For instance, what would be the likely consequence of abandoning the one-party state and creating multiparty states? Events in the Soviet Union and Eastern Europe have encouraged debates in many parts of Africa. Several countries are already dismantling one-party rule, such as Côte d'Ivoire, Burkina Faso, Benin, and Algeria. Debates on multiparty systems are taking place in Tanzania, Zambia, and many other countries. In some cases, this has led to strong reactions by heads of state.[38] Arguments against establishing multiparty states have also been made on the grounds that it would lead to ethnic and tribal political configurations that would affect economic development and stability. There is currently a partial relaxation of the apartheid regime in South Africa. The transition to majority rule will be complex, and other conflicts between the various communities will emerge with greater salience. The region of Southern Africa, after many years of destabilization by the apartheid regime of South Africa, will face complex problems of governance.

Racial Conflicts

Of growing importance will be new types of racial conflicts that are likely to emerge, particularly in areas with large and growing numbers of new immigrants and refugees. These large flows of immigrants from the Third World to the West are already provoking intense debates in the United States and in Europe, with demands for various control policies to stem the tide of new arrivals. Characteristic of this new form of "racism" is that settled communities—large white populations—see a threat from the wave of Third World immigrants who refuse to adopt the cultural values of the white communities, wishing instead to bring their own culture into their new country. The insistence of immigrants on maintaining their religious, ethnic, and linguistic identities means that new tensions and conflicts will be created. These waves of migration are provoking ethnopopulist right-wing movements in many parts of Europe.

Environmental Conflicts

Disputes over the control of natural resources are likely to be a cause of war or a contributory factor. The boundaries between external and internal causes for environmental degradation and sustainability are disappearing. Clearly, environmental pollution will have global impact and be a serious threat to survival. Demands on land, fresh water, and other natural resources are growing rapidly because of increases in population and human aspirations, the latter in both the developed and developing nations. This dilemma suggests that natural resources have the potential for playing an even more important role as a cause of war in the future.[39]

There is a strong likelihood that states would resort to military action, or the threat of such action, to ensure continuing access to what they perceive as natural resources. This could be oil, but it could also be access to water, control of rivers, or disputes over mining and forests. Arthur Westing discusses the problems of the future:

> Of equal, if not greater importance is the extent to which the global natural resources can be managed and exploited in a way that: (a) will be in harmony with nature; (b) will avoid interstate conflict; and (c) will, in the case of the renewable ones, assure their long-term integrity.[40]

Identity Conflicts

Identity conflicts are the most pervasive and the most violent. Identity is defined as a sense of self and a sense of the relationship of the self to the world:

> Identity has been defined as an abiding sense of selfhood, the core of which makes life predictable to an individual. To have no ability to anticipate events is essentially to experience terror. Identity is conceived of as more than a psychological sense of self; it encompasses a sense that one is safe in the world physically, psychologically, socially, even spiritually. Events which threaten to invalidate the core sense of identity will elicit defensive responses aimed at avoiding psychic and/or physical annihilation. Identity is postulated to operate in this way, not only in relation to interpersonal conflict but also in

conflict between groups.[41]

William Bloom, in an interesting study, discusses the importance of identity to nation building. Identity is seen as a dynamic and ever-changing aspect of personality. As I have argued, it is in the interaction of state building and modernization that identity will play an important role.

> Identification is an inherent and unconscious behavioral imperative in all individuals. Individuals actively seek to identify in order to achieve psychological security, and they actively seek to maintain, protect and bolster identity in order to maintain and enhance this psychological security which is a *sine qua non* of personality, stability, and emotional well being.[42]

Little consensus exists in the literature regarding the terminology and basic concepts of ethnicity. *Ethnic group, minority, tribe, nation,* and *nationality* are used by different authors in different ways, which, of course, leads to analytical confusion.[43] Ethnicity is not a static concept but a dynamic one, in that ethnicity and ethnic boundaries can be continuously redefined, given certain factors. Politicization of ethnicity is a long historical process, where a crucial factor is center/periphery interaction. Polarization does not seem to take place until a certain point has been passed; before this point, there normally will be instances where conflict resolution can be achieved through compromise and accommodation.

The reasons for the ethnic revival have been fairly clearly identified. I will list below some of the important findings and existing knowledge regarding identity conflicts. A major reason for the ethnic revival is seen as the contradiction between state building and nation building, where the state, in its attempt to centralize resources, may come into conflict with the many nations that coexist within its borders.[44] However, some such center/periphery conflicts might well have been mediated through constitutional means (federalism) and other forms of devolution of power.

The distinction between "official nationalism" and "imagined communities" has brought about theoretical rigor in understanding postcolonial Third World nationalism. Here, some Third World states can be seen as artificial constructs not corresponding to the many coexisting nationalities. Imagined communities then are those that in turn create the myth of community as a strong force for identity.[45]

Considerable attention has been given to the tension between ethnicity and modernization. Here the argument has been that unreflected capitalism and modernization have created a sense of psychological deprivation (relative deprivation), which has led to a backlash in terms of a reawakening of fundamentalism.[46] Development strategies may have unintended effects on interethnic relations. Some scholars have advanced the concept of ethnodevelopment, arguing that development theories must be sensitive to cultural pluralities. This is particularly relevant to development strategies that ignore minorities and by which hegemonic elites and international donor agencies may concentrate on certain groups only.[47]

Many states have denied the existence of ethnic conflicts. In a recent study, Lawrence Barsh evaluates the extent to which international bodies responsible for the protection of human rights have recognized the significance of ethnic conflict as a destabilizing force in both developing and industrialized countries.[48] The study concludes that a surprisingly large number of states refuse to acknowledge the possibility of ethnic divisions. Examples of such denial can be found in all regions, but most frequently in Asia and Africa, where the evidence suggests that the contemporary threat from ethnic conflict is also the greatest.[49]

THE ROLE OF THE STATE

The role of the state is central to identity formations. The state creates and denies the identity of others. It is precisely here in this business of nation building and state formation that ethnicity assumes particular salience.[50] Together with the demands for democracy and participation, there are ethnic and religious minorities demanding greater autonomy, recognition, and identity. These problems and tensions will be a major focus of attention in the years to come. In the Third World, state formation will remain a complex problem, dealing as it must with concerns for general democracy, participation, and demilitarization. Ethnic and religious claims will become more urgent and more clearly articulated. These tensions are likely to be further compounded by severe poverty and unemployment in many parts of the Third World. The demand for identity and culture will be located within the framework of increasing gaps between the rich and the poor; language and culture may be the final focus of identity for the poor in a rapidly changing and modernizing world to which they are denied access.

State violence and counterviolence serve to exacerbate cleavages. The violation of human rights, including extrajudicial killings and torture, has produced a vicious cycle of violence and terror. State violence has brought with it a sense of insecurity; this then acts as a strong force of mobilization, which too often takes extraparliamentary or militant forms, leading to armed conflicts. In some cases, the misbehavior of the armed forces and police— often armies—has served to provoke guerrilla misbehavior.[51]

Further, the monopoly of physical violence is no longer the sole property of the state. According to Weber, the modern state must be defined as the societal institution that lays claim on the legitimate monopoly of physical violence. The essential attribute of the state creates a dilemma. On the one hand it has to protect its citizens against arbitrary violence of others, and for this purpose the state needs the monopoly on violence, or the means of using violence, respectively. On the other hand, by this very monopoly, the ruling group can use violence for its own interests against the people, even arbitrarily beyond accepted rules and laws. Other groups also have ready access to means of physical violence. These new actors tend to determine the direction of conflicts.

What is suggested here is that there is a global struggle for a redefinition of the state. The concept of the state and its role must be discussed within a changing global environment, where new actors and new initiatives challenge the ability of current state formations to resolve some of the most pressing problems of humankind. The "multiethnic state" is an organizing concept that can accommodate ethnic claims and demands in all parts of the world.

There is a growing awareness of the universality and complexity of ethnic problems and the need for concerted action to devise strategies, programs, and structures for managing these problems. Some multiethnic states have worked out federal forms of devolution. However, in the search for constitutional models there has been disagreement over unitary and federal efforts and the extent of devolution and autonomy. There is a need to reexamine the role of constitutions and similar mechanisms for conflict management.

Constitutions may, however, provide only de jure recognition of minorities, not de facto recognition. We need to identify cultural and social institutions within the countries concerned. There exist many mechanisms and religious and collective experiences that help to enhance cooperation and tolerance while respecting the positive aspects of ethnicity. They may be schools, places of common worship, trade unions, or various informal community organizations. School curricula, particularly as they interpret the country's history, are important in the decommunalization of the mind. More studies are needed on the role of curricula, particularly their impact on young people in the formative years. In some cases—perhaps many—history books will have to be rewritten to recognize the multiethnic character of societies. The role of the mass media is often crucial. Information, and the way it is handled, can exacerbate cleavages or help to enhance feelings of cooperation. All too often, disinformation campaigns and rumors serve to feed and excite tensions. The role of communication and information is an important aspect of research where more comparative knowledge is required.

GOVERNANCE AND CONFLICT MANAGEMENT

I have argued that although significant changes have occurred in the global situation, there is a gap between the international institutions created during the postwar period and the new problems that are emerging. Much has been written about the role of the United Nations and the role of the Secretary-

General in dispute settlement. Much has been said about the strengths and the limitations of the United Nations. An impressive record has been established in the operation of peacekeeping forces. Furthermore, equally impressive work has been done in mediation between states in many difficult circumstances. However, the mandate of the United Nations is basically to resolve disputes in the international arena. But what about violent internal conflicts that tend to destroy societies and cause untold human suffering? Would it be possible for the UN to revise its mandate regarding internal conflicts? Could it allow its good offices and its vast network of skills to be used to provide for timely intervention into conflicts internal to states?[52] Many proposals and recommendations have been made, and the current conjuncture enables the UN to review its mandate in conflict resolution and peacemaking.

Currently, there is a consensus on the need for preventative action, early warning, and problem solving in conflict situations. This work is still in its early stages, but a new coalition is likely to emerge. There is also increased cooperation among networks to create a wider forum for discussion on early warnings and conflict resolution.

A very significant and important instrument in conflict transformation has been the role of elections. International attention and monitoring can be strengthened to facilitate and ensure periodic elections. In many cases, transformation can be achieved only by insisting on regular elections.

Theoretical advances have been made concerning the role of third parties in conflict resolution, as well as in improving bargaining and negotiating strategies. New forms of conflict resolution have been suggested, from problem-solving approaches to professional facilitators. However, most of these theoretical advances have been made within stable democracies with a considerable tradition in conflict management. Further, such studies tend to focus on what happens once parties are brought to the negotiating table, whereas the real problem is often how to identify the actors and what can be done to get people to negotiate at all. Negotiations tend to imply equal partners, but domestic conflicts are often asymmetric or unequal conflicts between a powerful state and a weak internal opposition. Protracted social conflicts are generally not single-issue situations. They inherit a past that acts as a heavy burden on the future. Protracted social conflict involves questions of identity, symbolic meaning, control over resources, and a sense of meaningful security. More attention must be paid to conflict transformation. How can a framework be created for conflict resolution? How can the terms of reference and the constituency of the conflict be changed?

CONCLUSION

I have argued that new boundaries will appear as a result of the manner in which we conceptually define and analyze conflicts. The world is certainly becoming more violent, and for many people, more insecure. There is, therefore, a need to review existing global institutions and mechanisms for preventing and transforming conflicts.

The challenge will be to those who will capture the democratic space available. Will conflicts be transformed through collective forms of nonviolence, or will armed conflicts and criminality dominate the democratic space available? There is much to learn from the Intifada and from people's movements in Europe and elsewhere. There is much to learn about nonviolent social transformation.

NOTES

1. Internal armed conflicts are defined as intrastate conflicts that are generally conflicts between the state and the other party or parties who are either victims or unequal parties to the conflict.

2. "Five phases of international configuration of world power have been identified. The average duration of each phase has thus been about 35 years." Robert W. Cox, *Multilateralism and the United Nations System* (Tokyo: United Nations University, 1990).

3. For an interesting discussion of these issues see R. B. J. Walker, "Security, Sovereignty, and the Challenge of World Politics," *Alternatives* 15 (1) (Winter 1990): 3-29.

4. Defective states are those states that are controlled by a hegemonic ethnic group and bound by a network of patron-client loyalties that are incapable of transforming the states into multiethnic states that share power with other communities.

5. "Lebanonization" is used as a way of describing situations where the state has lost control of law and order and where many armed groups are contending for power.

6. Francis Fukuyama, "The End of History," *The National Interest* 16 (Summer 1989): 3.

7. Ibid., 4.

8. John Mueller, *Retreat from Doomsday: The Obsolescence of Major War* (New York: Basic Books, 1989), 3.

9. Ibid., 4.

10. The most important aspect of the new international division of labor is that characterized by the information revolution. The information revolution will lead to a new social stratification between those who control information and those who do not. Furthermore, the contradiction between classes based on industrialization will not be dominant.

11. Fukuyama's thesis does not belong to these crude versions of modernization, such as those by Rostow, but is an important philosophical discussion that must be given due consideration.

12. For an interesting discussion of Fukuyama's thesis, see also *The National Interest* 16 (Summer 1989) with responses by several American scholars.

13. The causal factors for the growth performance of NICs is highly controversial. Strong arguments suggest that it was state intervention and

protection of domestic markets that may have been important, at least for South Korea.

14. *Third World Guide 1989-1990: The World as Seen by the Third World* (Montevideo, Uruguay: Third World Editors, 1990), 17-18.

15. Johan Galtung, "Some Trends to Consider," paper presented at the Tenth World Future Studies Federation Conference, Beijing, 3-10 September 1988.

16. For an interesting discussion on this see "U.S. Intervention Thrives on Drugs," *South* (February 1990): 9.

17. Hugo Cabieses, *Lima Perú. Deuda Externa, Narcotráfico y Modelos de Desarrollo en América Latina* (unpublished, 16 October 1989).

18. Ibid.

19. R. T. Taylor, *Hot Money and the Politics of Debt* (London: Unwin & Hyman, 1987), 165.

20. For example, Burma is the source of much Asian drug trafficking. For a discussion on the links between drugs, arms, and the military see William H. Overbold, "Dateline: Drug Wars," *Foreign Policy* 77 (Winter 1989-90).

21. "Protest Against the Sale of Arms to the Drug Mafia," *Paz/prensa* no. 42, *La Epoca (Chile)*, 19 April 1990.

22. *Covert Action: Information Bulletin* 28 (Summer 1987). Special issue on the CIA and drugs.

23. See Mueller, *Retreat from Doomsday*.

24. Andrew Mack, "In the Third World, Nuclear Dominoes," *New York Herald Tribune*, 26 May 1990.

25. Matthew Melko, *Peace in Our Time* (New York: Paragon House). See especially chapter 3, "The Remission of Violence," 53-89.

26. See article by Johan Galtung in the *Journal of Peace Research* (March 1990).

27. *SIPRI Yearbook 1988* (Oxford: Oxford University Press), 285-301.

28. Ibid. See also *SIPRI Yearbook 1989*.

29. Karin Lindgren et al. "Major Armed Conflicts in 1989," *SIPRI Yearbook 1990*. (Oxford: Oxford University Press), 393–419.

30. For a discussion on the factors leading to military withdrawals, see Kumar Rupesinghe, ed., "Peace Building After Military Withdrawals," *Bulletin of Peace Proposal*, Special Issue (Spring 1989).

31. There was widespread allegation that Iraq used chemical weapons against the Kurds. Similar allegations were made by the Sri Lankan government that the LTTE has used chemical weapons.

32. Data from William Eckhardt, Lentz Peace Research Laboratory of St. Louis. See *Copred Peace Chronicle* (April 1990), 15.

33. Edward E. Azar, "Protracted International Conflicts: Ten Propositions," in *International Conflict Resolution: Theory and Practice*, ed. Edward E. Azar and John W. Burton (Hertfordshire: Wheatsheaf Books; Boulder, Colo.: Lynne Rienner Publishers, 1986). Also see Louis Kriesberg, Terrel A. Northrup, and Stuart J. Thorson, eds., *Intractable Conflicts and Their Transformation* (Syracuse: Syracuse University Press, 1989).

34. In some cases the objectives are not clear; there are no political programs, no manifestos, etc.

35. For an interesting discussion and review on gross human rights violations, see Alex P. Schmid, *Research on Gross Human Rights Violations*, 2d en. ed. (Leiden: University of Leiden, 1989).

36. New questions emerge in the agenda—issues in human rights, new challenges, new strategies, international human rights, and elected civilian

governments in Latin America.

37. Olga A. Vorkunova, "Some Root Causes of National and Ethnic Conflicts in the Soviet Union," paper presented at the International Peace Research Association conference, Groningen, Netherlands, July 1990.

38. For example, President Daniel Arap Moi has called an end to a short-lived debate on whether the country could afford to experiment with multiparty democracy. According to *The Economist*, those who persisted would be "hunted down like rats." See "Less Nice Than It Used to Be," *The Economist* 23 (June 1990): 23.

39. Arthur Westing, ed., *Global Resources and International Conflict: Environmental Factors in Strategic Policy and Action* (Oxford: Oxford University Press, 1986).

40. Ibid., 4.

41. Terrel A. Northrup, "Dynamics of Identity in Personal and Social Conflict," in Kriesberg, Northrup, and Thorson, *Intractable Conflicts*.

42. William Bloom, "Personal Identity, National Identity and International Relations," *Cambridge Studies in International Relations* 9 (1990): 53.

43. The International Social Science Council is attempting to restore some order in the confusion through the cooperation of the international disciplinary associations of the social sciences.

44. Walker Connor, "Nation Building or Nation Destroying," *World Problems* 24 (3) (1973): 319-355.

45. See Benedict Anderson, *Imagined Communities: Reflections on the Origin and Spread of Nationalism* (London: Verson Press, 1983).

46. Robert Norton, "Ethnicity and Class: A Conceptual Note with Reference to the Post-Colonial Societies," *Ethnic and Racial Studies* 7 (3) (1984): 426-434.

47. For an interesting discussion on this point see Rodolfo Stavenhagen, "Ethnocide and Ethno-Development: The New Challenge," *Development, Journal of the Society for International Development* (1987): 74-78.

48. Lawrence Barsh, "The Ethnic Factor in Security and Development: Perceptions of United Nations Human Rights Bodies," *Acta Sociologica 1988* 31 (4) (1988): 333-341.

49. There is also a view that the UN, specifically the Human Rights Commission, has been more open to discussing groups rights, particularly the rights of indigenous peoples.

50. Kumar Rupesinghe, ed., *Conflict Resolution in Uganda* (London: James Currey, 1989).

51. Kumar Rupesinghe, ed., *Ethnic Conflict and Human Rights: A Comparative Perspective* (Oslo: The United Nations University and the Norwegian University Press, 1988).

52. It is likely that the Secretary-General may seek a mandate from the United Nations General Assembly to provide for observer status in the negotiations on the conflict in Ethiopia. This initiative may provide the UN the occasion to play a role in other internal conflicts.

Part II
Reconceptualizing Security

If the term *security* is to be stretched to mean everything, is it in danger of meaning nothing? In part the debate in this section is a semantic one. Neither of the two authors who are using the narrower definition of security—as security from attack—would deny that there are many threats to human well-being besides military threats. What is important is to separate the strategy of warfare from the multitude of threats facing humans today, including those of ecological destruction and economic devastation. The authors arguing for the wider definition are basing their analysis on a model of interconnectedness of social and physical variables in a whole-system framework that their colleagues do not deny, and all agree that the real task is to eliminate destructiveness in all its forms and increase the level of human cooperation and environmental awareness as fast as possible.

—E. B.

CHAPTER 6

Security Through Military Defense?

RANDALL FORSBERG

This is a rare moment in history: a time when no great power threatens or feels threatened by another. This uncommon situation offers an extraordinary opportunity to develop an alternative security system that is safer than the current system, costs much less, and does more to promote democracy.

This new security system should be organized around the concepts of nonoffensive defense and international peacekeeping. At a minimum, this would require the governments of the large industrial nations to renounce unilateral intervention with their own armed forces, to strengthen international peacekeeping institutions, and to replace their large standing armies with small forces designed for territorial defense: a coast guard, an air defense system, a reserve-based home guard, and a border guard.

By adopting nonoffensive defenses and supporting international peacekeeping in place of unilateral intervention, the large industrial nations could begin the process of demilitarizing the international system. They could head off a renewed arms race later in the decade. They could lead the way in cutting world military spending by as much as $700 billion, including $250 billion in the United States alone. And they could lay the groundwork for a stringent nonproliferation regime, which would stop the spread of independent arms industries and encourage the adoption of nonoffensive defense in all parts of the world.

The idea that the world is ready for an alternative security system based on nonoffensive defenses and international peacekeeping bodies may seem far-fetched. But that is because we have not yet come to terms with the implications of the revolutionary changes in Eastern Europe and the USSR. Given the vanishing military "threat" and the establishment of pluralistic governments and civilian liberties in the East, a defense-oriented security system is entirely appropriate. This will become increasingly clear over the next decade, if East-West relations keep improving and the West focuses increasingly on steps to foster democracy in the East and to promote trade, investment, and exchange. In such a world, nonoffensive defenses make sense; large standing armed forces designed for preemptive attack, instant mobilization, and protracted conventional war do not make sense.

Naturally, it will take time for people to adjust to the idea that an alternative security system is possible. The risk is that unfounded fears, ignorance, and inertia may keep the old system going long enough for a new, economically based arms race to emerge. In the coming years, Japan and the European Community will be developing new arms industries. In Japan, this is the culmination of a program started in the 1950s aimed at gradually becoming independent in arms production. In Europe, nations that are reducing their military budgets and becoming more integrated economically will "rationalize" their arms plants, creating a powerful new, integrated European arms industry. When Europe and Japan begin to compete with the United States for technological superiority in weaponry and arms exports, the economic competition will take on military overtones. By the turn of the century, if great power leaders have not made a commitment to nonoffensive defense, the United States, the Soviet Union, Japan, and the European Community will almost certainly become entrammeled in a new four-way arms race. This will strain their relations and increase pressure for arms exports. As a result, independent arms industries will spread more rapidly, world military spending will rise again, and the risk of nuclear and conventional war will grow. Once this happens, shifting to an alternative security system will become much more difficult.

In sum, there are powerful reasons to replace the archaic postwar security system with an alternative system based on nonoffensive defense and international peacekeeping. In the mid-1990s, conditions for making this change will be more propitious than they have been before, or may be again for decades thereafter.

CONDITIONS RIPE FOR DEMILITARIZATION

Steps toward pluralistic democracy in Eastern Europe and the USSR have improved East-West relations. Now the United States and the countries of Europe are working with the USSR, although with setbacks and hesitations, to bring about the peaceful resolution of conflicts in the Soviet Union itself, in the Middle East, and elsewhere. For the first time since World War II, the UN Security Council and other UN agencies may be able to play their intended peacekeeping role.

In addition, the USSR may be prepared to make deep cuts in its nuclear and conventional forces. This was first suggested by the Soviet moratorium on nuclear testing, the generous Soviet approach to the INF treaty, and the withdrawal of Soviet troops from Afghanistan. Then in December 1988, President Gorbachev announced that in 1989-1990 the USSR would eliminate 500,000 troops and 10,000 tanks and make other unilateral cuts. In March 1989, the USSR entered talks on conventional forces that exclude US-based forces, and offered to destroy another 17,000 tanks, leaving one-third fewer than NATO has in Europe.

Early in 1990, we began to see signs of the dissolution of the Warsaw Treaty Organization (WTO), as the USSR agreed to withdraw all Soviet armed forces from Hungary and Czechoslovakia by mid-1991. (This timetable has been moved forward by recent events.—Ed.) The USSR has repeatedly called for even more far-reaching East-West arms reductions, including a further 50 percent cut in ground and air forces after the first treaty on conventional forces in Europe (CFE 1), cuts in naval forces, and the abolition of short-range nuclear weapons.

These actual and proffered steps of demilitarization have created the possibility for the United States, the other large industrial nations (the unified Germany, France, Britain, Italy, and Japan), and China to join the USSR in dismantling most of their standing nuclear and conventional forces.

Since Vietnam, most US nuclear and conventional forces have been maintained to deter another great-power war in Europe and the Far East, like World War II; and virtually all armed forces in Western Europe, Japan, and China are maintained to deter war with the USSR. Thus, if Soviet forces are sharply reduced, there will no longer be a military risk that justifies the huge expense of Western military budgets.

Conservative analysts have argued that terrorism and other Third World threats have created a new purpose for US military forces. The question is whether the US public will tolerate large-scale foreign military interventions like Vietnam, which last for years and incur tens of thousands of US casualties. Recent US interventions in Lebanon, Libya, Grenada, and Panama lasted only a few days or weeks and involved only a few thousand troops (20,000 in Panama). They were all objectionable on legal, moral, and political grounds. Attitudes toward war in the Persian Gulf have varied, but no scenario justifies keeping two million uniformed personnel under arms permanently in peacetime. (France, with a military budget one-tenth that of the United States, has repeatedly sent up to 10,000 troops to Chad to fend off incursions from Libya.)

Bush administration officials have proposed interdicting drugs as a useful role for the US military. But again, this would occupy no more than 10,000 troops; and few people consider such interdiction cost effective. Most believe that if a decision were made to devote a substantial fraction of the $300 billion military budget to the drug problem (over and above the $7 billion currently committed to the "war on drugs"), the larger sum should be spent on programs to end the demand for drugs, not on troops to intercept or destroy them.

Thus, for the foreseeable future, there should be no military requirement for the large, mobile, standing armed forces of the industrial nations. The world's largest and most modern oceangoing navies, long-range air forces, and mechanized armies are becoming superfluous. In this situation, stability and defense would best be served by a joint process of demilitarization in which the United States and the Soviet Union cut back to minimal nuclear forces, and all industrial nations reduced their conventional armed forces to territorial defense forces: a coast guard, an air defense system, a border guard, and a home guard. In addition to reducing the risk of war, converting to such nonoffensive defenses would strengthen security by releasing hundreds of billions of dollars for real security needs, heading off a new arms race, and creating conditions in which, for the first time, the industrial countries could establish a strict nonproliferation regime.

HOW A NEW ARMS RACE COULD EMERGE

Clearly, we are moving away from a bipolar world, organized around military strength, to a world with four leading economic powers: a unified Europe, the United States, the Soviet Union, and Japan. (In the next century, China, India, and Brazil may join this group.) What is not yet clear, however, is the military dimension of future relations among the world's major power centers.

Despite radically changed political conditions, it will be impossible to eliminate the old military order overnight. Because the long-lead-time weapon systems now in production were funded several years ago, because no plans exist to ease the transition for defense-dependent communities, and because our minds cannot adjust quickly to the disappearance of the threat images that have fueled the arms race for decades, it will be several years before the leaders of the United States and other Western countries consider the truly deep cuts in armaments that are now possible from a security viewpoint.

In the interval, unless there is a major public-interest campaign to promote demilitarization, the great powers are likely to develop a new *raison d'être* for their large military establishments—backing up their economic strength with allusions to military might and competing for world leadership in military technology and arms exports. The new version of the arms race is likely to emerge in the mid- to late 1990s, after the first major arms reductions (mainly cuts in the East) have been completed.

As things stand now, the great powers plan to continue developing and producing the full panoply of long-range, high-tech weapon systems: supersonic aircraft; ballistic missiles; cruise missiles; battlefield, naval, and air-launched missiles; intelligence-simulating computer control systems;

oceangoing naval vessels; and armored vehicles. Such systems are completely unnecessary in a world where no great power threatens another. Even worse, if not sharply reduced, standing armed forces constantly equipped with new versions of such weapons are likely to become an independent source of suspicion and tension.

US military planners, for example, will almost certainly come to see the Japanese navy as a potential threat in the Pacific. Japanese leaders will have a mirror-image concern about the US Navy. In the USSR, the joint chiefs will have to take into account the possibility that in some future crisis, the United States, Europe, and Japan might join forces against them. The integrated European Community, competing with the United States and Japan for technological superiority in the military aerospace and electronics industries, may increasingly perceive these competitors as potential enemies; and it may come to view the neighboring USSR as a potential ally. Thus, within a decade, the world's most powerful armed forces are likely to give rise to a new era of power politics, in which the arms race is linked to economic power rather than ideological conflict.

Absent serious pressure for change, the US government may actually invite a renewed arms race by resisting deep cuts in US, European, and Japanese military forces, spending, and industry. There are several reasons for this conservative US approach:

- Inertia, resulting from the psychic, bureaucratic, and political difficulty of imagining and creating a completely new security system
- Vested interests among military officers and defense industries
- Concern about a possible turnabout in the USSR
- Concern about the potential rearmament of Germany and Japan

The last concern is likely to be self-fulfilling. By resisting deep cuts in military spending, the United States may create conditions that support military buildups in the unified Germany and Japan. Left to their own devices, the European countries and the USSR might make deep cuts in military forces and spending. Soviet leaders, however, must take into account the forces based in the United States. As long as the United States maintains a large, deep-strike air force and an oceangoing navy, the USSR will do the same. The European Community, with heavily armed superpowers on both sides, will preserve comparable forces and industries. As a result, the unified Germany is likely to end up playing a central role in a militarized Europe; and the maintenance of high-tech arms industries in Europe, the United States, and the USSR will strengthen Japan's drive to establish an independent military industry and begin global power-projection forces.

THE STABILIZING EFFECTS OF NONOFFENSIVE DEFENSE

To avoid a new arms race, the industrial countries must do everything possible to eliminate armed forces that may not seem threatening in the current environment, but could be perceived as threatening at some future time when relations may be strained. If the United States and Japan maintain large, oceangoing navies, for example, then even if US-Japanese relations remain positive, sooner or later military planners will start thinking about how those naval forces could potentially be used against each other. However, if the United States and Japan cut back their naval forces to coastal patrol boats, then a naval war between them would be inconceivable. As a result, there will be much less peacetime inducement for leaders to slip into thinking about each other as potential military opponents. And this will be true in bad times as well as good.

The same reasoning holds for air forces and armies that are larger than needed for border patrol and can easily operate over long ranges and far from home bases. Air forces equipped with bomber, attack, and fighter-attack aircraft—especially great power air forces with mobile logistical support and aerial refueling—will naturally raise questions about their potential use in surprise attacks. In contrast, narrowly defensive air defense systems with antiaircraft missiles and short-range interceptors will not awaken fears of potential hostile use. Similarly, border guards with light equipment and no significant mobility will appear and be much less potentially threatening than large armored forces with mobile logistical support.

An especially attractive feature of nonoffensive defense is that it can be adopted unilaterally, but its benefits increase as more nations join in. In the unilateral case, relatively small, light, defense-oriented forces may be capable of defending against external attack by larger, heavier forces because the defense forces exploit the advantages of home ground. They can use local facilities for fuel and communications, they can employ deception and fortification, and they carry none of the baggage needed to undertake cross-border attack or distant intervention. When two or more countries adopt nonoffensive defenses, that greatly reduces the strength of a potential attack by either. From a wartime viewpoint, the effective strength of the defense against a less offensive opponent will be increased. From a peacetime viewpoint, the absence of any potential provocation or military threat will improve relations and help avoid the rise of new threat scenarios and enemy images. These sources of stability can be effective in all parts of the world; but they are likely to be especially useful initially in addressing the historically intractable problem of building trust and stability between the unified Germany and the USSR, and between each of those great powers and other countries in Central and Eastern Europe.

NONINTERVENTION AND INTERNATIONAL PEACEKEEPING

In order for the great powers to cut back to nonoffensive defense, their leaders must make a principled decision not to undertake unilateral military intervention in smaller countries. This principled choice, more than changing forces, is what will maintain the peace in times of stress. The decision that unilateral military intervention should end will not be made lightly; and once made, a thoughtful commitment to renounce unilateral military intervention will not be broken lightly. Cutting back to nonoffensive defense will raise a great practical obstacle to reverting. But even without such an obstacle, Gorbachev illustrated how a great power can stick by a principled decision to end intervention. Gorbachev announced at the UN in December 1988 that the USSR had rejected the use of force for any purpose other than defense and would pull out of Afghanistan. Then in 1989 and 1990, Gorbachev refused to intervene in Eastern Europe, where Soviet troops were still stationed, to stop the overthrow of communist governments.

In a world where the superpowers and other great powers have all made principled decisions to forgo unilateral intervention and cut back to nonoffensive defenses, two related questions may arise: Who will intervene in Third World situations that get out of hand, like the genocidal rampages in Cambodia and Uganda? And what is to prevent one of the great powers, or some other country, from reversing the decision to move to nonoffensive defense and rebuild more threatening forces?

The first of these questions is paternalistic. Situations have "gotten out of hand" at one time or another in all parts of the world. In any event, the great powers have neither the right nor the responsibility unilaterally to attempt to determine the future of a Third World nation. Moreover, in the past, when the United States could have intervened to try to stop genocide, it has not done so. Despite the rhetoric of bipolar "stability" and the Pax Americana, unilateral superpower military interventions have been used to achieve geopolitical goals, not for humanitarian reasons such as stopping bloodshed.

An alternative security system could, however, as a new and positive feature, include a provision for efforts to stop genocide, take action against other egregious violations of international law, and coordinate the response of the international community to steps by any nation to undertake a threatening military buildup.

As a preferable alternative to unilateral big-power intervention, the alternative system could provide for an international peacekeeping force designed specifically to conduct "humanitarian" interventions and to help keep or restore peace in cases of regional, border, or ethnic conflict. There would be two key differences between unilateral big-power military intervention in the Third World and intervention by an international peacekeeping force. First, use of a UN force made up of soldiers drawn from the smaller countries of East and West, North and South—but not from the largest and wealthiest nations—would tend to represent an international consensus. This would provide the intervenee due process, and remove the arbitrary character of unilateral great-power intervention. Second, the multinational, small-country character of the intervening force would help ensure that its role was restricted to humanitarian peacekeeping objectives.

If, after joining the alternative security system outlined here, one nation undertook a threatening military buildup, then other nations would be free to intervene with an international peacekeeping force or to respond with their own military buildup, or both. This freedom is the same as what exists today. Thus, the alternative security system will not make it *impossible* for nations to undertake threatening military actions; but it will create an environment in which, for many reasons, such actions are much less likely than they are today.

NONOFFENSIVE DEFENSE AND SPENDING CUTS

If the great powers shift to nonoffensive defense, this will be reflected in the magnitude of their military budget cuts. Cuts in military spending over the next decade that leave the industrial nations with military budgets 25 to 50 percent lower than they were in 1990 will allow military establishments to retain the core elements of their current long-range ground, air, and naval forces. These forces will, of course, be smaller; but they will still offer the economies of scale needed for the production of supersonic aircraft, oceangoing ships, and advanced conventional missiles. Military officers in the United States, the Soviet Union, Europe, and Japan will then argue, in a circular fashion, that the open production lines elsewhere make it imperative to retain them at home—not cut spending so deeply that entire sectors of military industry must be shut down.

Only if spending cuts in the major industrialized countries are much deeper—on the order of 75 percent or more, compared with 1990—will it be impossible to maintain traditional military forces with long-range, offensive capabilities. That is, only when US and Soviet military budgets decline from their current level of about $300 billion each (at comparable purchasing power) to the $50 to $75 billion range, can we expect to see a profound change not in just the size of the forces, but also in their character. With annual budgets limited to, say, $50 billion, military planners in the United States and the Soviet Union could not afford to do more than maintain an excellent global intelligence and communications network for verifying adherence to the nonoffensive-defense guidelines, in addition to the standard coastal defense, air defense, border guard, and national guard.

NONOFFENSIVE DEFENSE AND NONPROLIFERATION

An important benefit of deep cuts and defense-oriented restructuring of force in the industrial nations is that it will permit and even encourage them, for the first time, to establish a truly stringent international regime to stop the global proliferation of independent nuclear and conventional arms industries. Today, only four countries have industries capable of producing *all* of the essential parts and material needed for the production of the full range of modern, high-tech weaponry: the United States, the Soviet Union, France, and the United Kingdom. West Germany and Japan are close behind, but no other country even comes close to maintaining the range of industries and skills needed to produce the full panoply of modern weaponry. However, if the two superpowers, the integrated European Community, and Japan continue to produce such weaponry and compete to export it to the Third World, they will encourage the slow but steady spread of indigenous arms industries. Only if the large industrial nations shut down their own industries for producing nuclear weapons and high-tech aircraft, missiles, tanks, and ships will they be in a position to jointly commit themselves to stop exporting the essential parts, materials, training, and other forms of assistance that are still required to develop arms industries in the Third World.

Equally important, if the industrial countries shift to nonoffensive defense, they can join together to create a variety of powerful military, economic, and political inducements and sanctions—carrots and sticks—to encourage the Third World nations to adopt similar military postures, oriented strictly and narrowly to territorial defense. They can also cooperate in helping to resolve Third World conflicts; and in their own shift to nonoffensive defense, they would see a very different example regarding the usefulness and acceptability of threats to use armed force as an instrument of policy.

This combination of changes might not succeed immediately in eradicating all Third World ambitions to acquire sophisticated long-range weapon systems and industries to produce them. However, it would have a profound effect in slowing the pace of proliferation and would stop the process in many countries. Ultimately, success in regional conflict resolution, stronger international peacekeeping institutions, and pressure from the world community would be likely to complete the process of persuading all nations to limit their armed forces and industries to nonoffensive defense.

DECADE OF DECISION

The mid-1990s will be the optimum time for the governments of the large industrial nations to make a commitment to move toward an alternative security system comprising comprehensive nonoffensive defenses, deep cuts in military spending, stronger international peacekeeping institutions, and a stringent nonproliferation regime.

In 1991–1993, while the first CFE, START, and unilateral cuts are being implemented, policymakers are likely to establish the parameters for a second major round of arms reductions, to be implemented in 1994-1996. Then, around 1995-1996, they will set spending reduction goals for the last part of the decade. In those second and third rounds of cuts, great-power leaders will choose whether they want to make moderate reductions in spending and forces and retain offensively oriented arms industries, or make much deeper cuts and shift to nonoffensive defense.

After the turn of the century, it will be far more difficult to make this change. Once new arms industries are up and running in Japan and Europe— which will happen by the end of the decade unless there is a conscious decision to head in a new direction—it will be extremely difficult to shut them down quickly. In addition to strengthening vested interests in a continued arms race, the weaponry produced in the new West-West arms competition will generate new threat perceptions; the competition for arms exports will take on a life of its own; the number of countries with long-range nuclear and conventional forces will grow—and for all these reasons, demilitarization will be far more difficult.

Fortunately, many people in Europe and the USSR are now open to a historic change in security arrangements. Most Europeans feel that there is little risk of war and little need to sustain military spending, conscription, and arms production. Other concerns are far more important: the process of German unification and the concomitant need to raise the standard of living of the twenty million East Germans; working through the full economic integration of the European Community; the opportunity and need to establish a complex new web of relations between Eastern and Western Europe; and the transformation of the Conference on Security and Cooperation in Europe (CSCE) from a consultative body into a stronger, permanent institution.

Faced with massive demands for political and economic change, European governments could easily support truly deep cuts in armed forces and military spending undertaken jointly with the USSR. Within the decade, this process could well lead to the dismantling of the traditional arms industries—rather than the creation of a new, integrated European arms industry—and a shift in both Europe and the USSR to small, defensively configured armed forces.

Watching these developments, the US public and Congress would be unlikely to continue supporting costly, useless military forces and industries. In any case, US public opinion will undoubtedly demand much deeper cuts in military spending starting in 1991 when, under the terms of the CFE 1

Treaty, the USSR will begin visibly to destroy upwards of 100,000 major weapons systems (tanks and other armored vehicles, heavy artillery, and military aircraft).

If the United States joins Europe and the USSR in deciding to close down most traditional arms industries and to shift to nonoffensive defense, the Japanese government would experience tremendous internal and external pressure to abandon its planned buildup of power-projection forces. Japan would then be likely to revert to its long-standing self-defense limitation, which will have become the norm in all industrial nations.

By the mid- to late 1990s, under this scenario, the political leaders of the four economic power centers would be ready to make an explicit commitment to complete the process of converting to nonoffensive defenses over the next five to seven years. Then, instead of allowing military spending cuts to level off at 50 percent of the 1990 level, they would aim ultimately to reduce spending by 75 percent or more. This very deep reduction in spending would parallel the process in which they replace their oceangoing navies, long-range air forces, and mobile ground forces with coastal patrol boats, antiaircraft defense, and border guards.

CONCLUSION

The concepts presented in this chapter may seem too ambitious to be plausible. At the moment, it is difficult to imagine the large industrial nations cutting back to nonoffensive defenses and shutting down their major arms-producing industries by the year 2005. But I have not attempted to describe what is likely. I have set out policy goals that realistically *could* be implemented in the coming period. There are no real threats among the great powers that require or merit the maintenance of large-scale armed forces. However, if the great powers keep them, the forces themselves will eventually generate new threat perceptions.

It is essential for concerned observers to state clearly what reductions *are* reasonable—even if few voices join us initially—and what goals the world *should* aim for—even if they seem unlikely to be achieved in the near term. The single most important reason that a shift to nonoffensive defense seems unlikely is that the idea is new and strange. People have not heard about it or thought about it. They have not mulled it over and discussed it with their friends, family, and colleagues. They have not read about it in the newspapers or seen it on television.

Social change movements always start with a process in which a few people articulate ideas that most others find implausible or unsettling. They end when most people take those ideas for granted. The unsettling truth of this decade is that sophisticated, long-range, powerful military forces are archaic. They no longer serve a social function that bears any relation to their cost or danger. They place us in a position like that of the child who pointed out that the emperor had no clothes—except that in this case, the great powers' huge, costly standing armed forces are an empty suit of clothing, not animated by a worthwhile human purpose. We must make this shocking truth a commonplace. When it is, an alternative security system based on nonoffensive defense and international peacekeeping will seem perfectly natural.

CHAPTER 7

Security Through Defending the Environment: An Illusion?

LOTHAR BROCK

Only a few years ago, a major public concern in the Northern Hemisphere was the danger that a third world war might emerge from the renewed tensions between the two superpowers. Visions of a global holocaust captured the minds of many. No longer did the military destruction of civilization appear as remote as the biblical apocalypse: instead it seemed to have become a clear and present danger inherent in the day-to-day developments of nuclear confrontation.

Now these anxieties, it seems, have gone with the wind of change that has been transforming the political landscape of the Northern World since 1985. But even as fears of a third world war began to recede, a new global threat appeared, which has now become the object of private worries and public debate, nongovernmental action, and world conferences: the depletion of the environment.

Today, there is widespread fear that the natural basis of human civilization may be destroyed through the dynamic of this very civilization; that the biosphere may be thrown out of balance, with unforeseeable consequences for all existing social systems; that nondeliberate environmental destruction will darken the expectations of present and future generations just as much as the prospect of any deliberate war. Thus, one looming disaster has been replaced by another—with little time for relief in between.

On the other hand, environmental change—just like the nuclear stalemate between the superpowers—can give rise to new hopes. Precisely because it tends to affect us all (at least in the long run), environmental change may force societies to seek cooperation, and such cooperation may establish ties that could outlive acute crises and conflicts. "Through Hot and Cold Wars, parks endure," James Thorsell wrote in commenting on the international political role of border-straddling nature preserves.[1]

A global threat with mixed expectations as to possible outcomes constitutes an intriguing challenge for academic work. Peace research has readily taken up this challenge, and the environment has become a firmly established item on its agenda by now. However, unless we are content to define peace research as research on anything bad done by good people, we still have to ask which aspects of the wide array of environmental problems are of special interest to peace research, and what is the specific contribution peace research may hope to make to the analysis of environmental change.

The destructive use of natural resources by one country can do at least as much harm to the people of another country (or all other countries) as military aggression. Yet this does not necessarily imply that environmental destruction and military conflict amount more or less to the same thing. Does it make sense at all to talk about environmental matters in terms of aggression and security? Should peace research be concerned with "war on nature" just as much as with war against people? Are the patterns of agricultural and industrial uses of land, atmosphere, and water a legitimate and urgent concern of peace research? Should we shift our priorities and concentrate on ecological threats to the life and well-being of humankind, now that the East-West conflict has dissolved and the nuclear threat seems to be fading?

PEACE AND THE ENVIRONMENT—FOUR LINKAGES

The question of why peace research should deal with environmental problems may elicit quite different answers. It could be argued that

- Environmental depletion may lead to large-scale social conflict including war;
- Environmental modification can be used for hostile purposes in intersocietal relations;
- Environmental depletion constitutes a specific form of violence;
- Ecological cooperation may help to build confidence and trust in international relations;
- Countries or international organizations may resort to military action in order to enforce certain environmental standards or to ward off dangers to the environment; and
- A healthy environment may be regarded as an integral part of comprehensive security.

In sorting out these various statements, we can distinguish at least four different types of possible linkages between "peace and the environment." One concerns the *causal* relationship between the two issue areas. It emphasizes the importance of natural resources as a source of conflict and the environmental impact of violence as well as possible environmental restraints on war and other forms of collective violence. The second linkage may be termed *instrumental*. It points to the possibility of using the environment to broaden the options of warfare and also to the possibility of instrumentalizing environmental activities for peace building. The third linkage is *definitional*. It refers to the correspondence between environmental destruction and war (or other forms of social violence) and to the identification of nature as an object of peace. Finally, there is the *normative* linkage, which calls for a reorientation of security policies in the face of new nonmilitary threats to the life and well-being of humankind.

The first three linkages point to certain aspects either of war and conflict or of peace (building). In this sense we may group these as being either positive or negative. The normative linkage would then be located between the two since it transcends these categories (see Table 7.1).

Table 7.1   War/Peace and Environmental Concerns—Four Linkages

	Causal	Instrumental	Definitional	Normative
Negative Linkage	War over resources Environmental impact of war	Environmental warfare	Environmental depletion as war and violence	Environmental security
Positive Linkage	Environmental pressures against war and other	Environmental cooperation as a means to build peace	Nature as an object of peace	Environmental security

A closer look at these linkages may help to indicate the relative importance of environmental problems to peace research and of peace research to the solution of environmental problems.

CAUSAL LINKAGES

War over Natural Resources

The term *environment* may refer to nature as an antithesis or a balancing force to civilization, or to creation as a challenge to an anthropocentric interpretation of the world. But it may also refer to the natural resources that serve the human economy. Natural resources, in turn, can be understood as encompassing primary goods (living and nonliving) as well as land, water, and atmosphere. To these can be added genetic diversity, which is a precondition for the adaptation of all life forms to change in the overall ecosystem. If we regard these resources as a continuum of life-sustaining conditions, then the ozone layer constitutes just as much a natural resource as a fish in the water.

From this perspective, the causal linkage between the peace problematique and environmental questions becomes quite evident: Throughout history, the utilization of natural resources by humans has meant not only hard work but also fighting between social entities—clans, tribes, states—over access and distribution.

In addition, control over natural resources has always been important in enabling a country to wage war. An extreme example is the War of the Pacific between Peru and Chile (1879–1884). Disagreement over guano deposits caused this war because the saltpeter that was extracted from the guano was necessary to produce gunpowder, i.e., to wage war. Later, the substitution of the guano product by a synthetic equivalent proved decisive for German fighting capacity in World War I.

Among the natural resources that have been the object of wars or conflicts involving military threats, we may cite land, timber, minerals, fuels, and fresh water as of special importance. Conflicts over land probably have been most frequent and most violent, since land is also a symbol and an instrument of power. Forests have played an important role in enhancing the armament process in Europe and in the European conquest of the world. Timber was cut in huge amounts, with grave ecological consequences, to build the military fleets with which the Europeans fought each other and which later on were used to protect the economic penetration of overseas territories.[2] In turn, the resources brought back from these territories helped to spur the process of capital accumulation that formed the basis for the establishment of the "industrial system."[3] This system, originating in Europe, set the pace for the systematic worldwide valuation of natural resources, a process still accompanied by considerable collective violence. The present struggle in the Amazon region between the people of the forest, small farmers, Garimpeiros, politicians and their bureaucratic clientele, large landholders, and industrial interests is one case in point.

Oil provides the most dramatic linkage between the scarcity of natural resources and intersocietal conflict. However, the gravity of international conflict over the sources and the circulation of oil also demonstrates that scarcity of natural resources cannot be regarded simply as a special feature of nature. Before World War I there was no scarcity of oil, even though very few wells had been drilled by that time and very little oil was pumped up and processed. Scarcity grew with the increasing output, because demand outpaced supplies. But such oil demand was not determined by nature, and even the supply was very much a function of cost-benefit considerations rather than of absolute scarcity. In other words, there is no "scarcity" as such; it exists only in specific political, socioeconomic, and cultural contexts. For another example we may refer again to the Amazon region. Here, the abundance the forest provides for its peoples is now being defined by outside interests in terms of scarce resources that supposedly have to be opened up (through roads, power plants, mines) for the sake of macroeconomic development. As a result, the peoples of the forest also may come to regard their environment as a scarce resource and may take part in turning it into a market product.

Furthermore, it is easy to exaggerate the importance of natural resources as an object of conflict. Militant conflict over natural resources seems so frequent that it can become tempting to regard competing demand for resources as the single most important cause of war.[4] However, a militant conflict that involves resources is not necessarily a struggle over resources. As Ronnie Lipschutz and John Holdren have pointed out, the need for specific resources (including oil) more often serves the rationalization of militant state behavior than it is actually the cause of war.[5] Hitler's *Lebensraum* policy—the justification of aggression as being a (legitimate) quest for land—may be remembered as one of the most cynical attempts to define political ambitions in terms of scarce resources.

So the question arises whether peace research should pay more attention to the nature of societies than to nature itself when dealing with conflict over natural resources. In line with this question, Third World criticism of the first Club of Rome report insisted that the core of the problem lay not in the physical limitations of natural resources but rather in the lack of distributive justice.[6]

This aspect of the great North-South debate of the 1970s should not be entirely forgotten as peace research tries to define its stand on environmental questions today. True, we may all be in the same boat as far as world climate or ozone protection from ultraviolet radiation are concerned. But ecological interdependence still goes hand in hand with massive economic disparities between societies; it is linked with vastly differing capacities to externalize the ecological costs of economic activities or to construct and apply new protective devices—for instance, dykes against the effects of global warming. In the future, such disparities are likely to become more important as a source of conflict over environmental issues than the relative scarcity of nonrenewable resources.

The same is to be expected of the vastly disparate pollution per capita that each society contributes to the depletion of global resources. Third World countries have already begun to demand for themselves higher quotas of long-range transboundary pollution. In all likelihood, conflict over these issues will increase. Of course, it is hardly conceivable that in the future the

European Community or any other group of states would fight a war against the United States (or other states) because of disproportionally high emissions of carbon dioxide. However, it is conceivable that states could use military force to protect themselves from such social consequences of global environmental decay as large-scale migration. In addition, within the framework of international organizations, states may agree on collective action to enforce international environmental law or treaty obligations.[7]

The Environmental Impact of War and the Military

Wars are fought over natural resources and with the help of natural resources (minerals, energy sources, etc.). Wars also devastate natural resources. Battlefields always have been sites of intensive man-made destruction, which affects the environment like anything else. As war activities are no longer confined to any particular battlefield but may be spread over the entire territory of the adversaries, they also may cause increasing environmental destruction parallel to their growing impact on the civilian population. As long ago as the Thirty Years War of 1618–1648, which depleted the population by two-thirds in the area immediately affected by the war, more people were killed by the starvation that followed military destruction of crops and means to work them than through direct violence.[8] Today, in countries like Ethiopia or Mozambique we witness the close interrelationship between environmental degradation and war, resulting in chronic famine among the local populations.

The environmental destruction caused by the two world wars was considerable. And yet, it did not overtax the ability of the natural environment to renew itself. In a nuclear war this would be different. In all likelihood, nuclear war would constitute a deadly manipulation of world climate, the result of a sudden fall in global temperatures due to the absorption of sunlight by dust and black soot thrown up through nuclear explosions. The ensuing "nuclear winter" might cause the extinction of human life as we know it today. In addition, ionizing radiation set free through a nuclear war would affect the conditions of all forms of life on earth for a time span transcending the past history of the human being.

Nuclear weapons aside, even the application of conventional weapons (not to speak of chemical and biological warfare) could contribute considerably to environmental degradation. The military also contributes to environmental stress during times of peace. Depending on the size of the military system, land is used for military infrastructure, maneuvering, and testing grounds.[9] In the case of nuclear testing, the latter covers huge areas and the testing has produced considerable global fallout. The military also consumes energy resources and contributes to pollution of air, land, and water. The sinking of a Soviet submarine with nuclear weapons on board off the Norwegian coast in 1989 and the mass destruction of sea fauna in the White Sea in 1990, presumably caused by leakages in military installations, may serve as cases in point.

Military outlays have contributed considerably to public debt in developing countries.[10] Growing public debt has in turn accelerated the reckless depletion of natural resources in these countries. Conversely, in an analogy to the debate on disarmament and development, funds spent for the military may be regarded as funds lost for financing environmental protection.[11]

Furthermore, the military may play an important role in decisionmaking on the use of natural resources. Thus, infrastructural penetration of the Amazonian rain forest began as a "national security" project under the military government of Brazil that came to power in 1964. After the return of government to civilian rule, the military insisted on continuing and even intensifying its presence in the Amazon region. For this purpose the Calha Norte project was invented. It implies large-scale military penetration of the Amazon region along the border between Brazil on the one hand, and Guyana, Venezuela, Colombia, and Peru on the other.

Environmental Pressures to Avoid War and Reduce "Structural Violence"

The disastrous environmental effects of war point to a positive aspect of the causal linkage between the peace problematique and environmental matters: If the environmental repercussions of military activities cannot be confined to the war area, international pressure may mount to avoid wars, for ecological reasons. Those who have stressed the danger of a "nuclear winter" have done so in order to persuade decisionmakers to refrain from a policy of nuclear brinkmanship. Also, with a view to conventional wars, the argument has been made that the international community simply cannot afford a war because of its adverse environmental effects. King Hussein of Jordan argued at the Geneva World Climate Conference of October/November 1990 that an international war over Kuwait would be intolerable for environmental reasons. In such a war, a substantial part of the local oil fields would go up in flames releasing a hundred times more carbon dioxide in weeks than worldwide economic activities would do in the course of a whole year. This argument was taken up in the Western prewar debate and helped to arouse considerable public concern and even resistance against the war. During the war, the oil fields of Kuwait did go up in flames, but contrary to the apprehensions voiced in the prewar days, the ecological damage seems to be confined, for the time being, to the region. The ecological damage in the region, however, is considerable though probably not devastating enough to deter the various conflicting parties in the area from another war.

The argument that there are environmental pressures to avoid war may also be applied to the "structural violence" of incomplete or deficient modernization in most Third World countries; it suffices to throw the traditional social orders out of balance but lacks the dynamics to establish new viable orders. Incomplete modernization goes hand in hand with high pressures on the natural resources of the respective countries—whether as a strategy for sheer survival (on the part of the poor) or for extensive growth (on the part of the bureaucracy), or simply as a strategy to make as much money as possible in the face of mass poverty (on the part of national and international economic interests). To the extent that the ecological consequences of incomplete modernization cannot be confined to their place of origin, we may expect mounting pressure at both national and international levels to redefine present programs for structural adjustment in socioecological terms.

Of course, we cannot realistically expect any sudden change of world (or local) politics from new ecological insights. The countervailing interests are still far too strong. But if we tune down our expectations, we may find that environmental concerns have some importance for building peace after all. If despite the Gulf conflict we do witness an "erosion of military power in modern world politics,"[12] this will be the result of a long process of accumulation of many different factors. Among these factors, environmental concerns may become more important in the future—despite, or perhaps even because of, the fact that environmental modification can broaden the options of military warfare.

As far as nonmilitary conflict is concerned, environmental problems again have to be seen in close interrelationship with other factors such as the breakdown of Third World societies, resurgent regional conflict, and increased North-South tensions. In connection with these other factors, environmental concerns could act to increase the pressure that has accumulated to overcome existing disparities in the world economic system. It is certainly too early to decide whether the world is already on the way toward "a new political dialectic between human betterment and environmental protection," as envisaged by Sverre Lodgaard;[13] but there is ample evidence that environmental stress not only causes political conflict but also creates pressures toward cooperation.[14]

THE INSTRUMENTAL LINKAGE

Environmental Warfare

The environmental impact of military activities mentioned above may be considered an unintended consequence of such activities. However, the military can also aim at altering the environment as a means of warfare.[15] In recent history, such environmental warfare was practiced by the United States in the Vietnam War (Second Indochina War). One-third of the total wooded area was treated with chemicals to denude trees so that the Vietcong would lose their cover against airborne combat action by the United States. The United States also apparently tried (without much success) to manipulate cloud formations to enhance target performance in air raids and to cause floods.[16]

Such environmental manipulation is of special interest for the "counterinsurgency" type of warfare.[17] But it can also be an instrument of mass destruction. The dynamiting of the Huayuankow Dike of the Yellow River in 1938 during the Second Sino-Japanese War (1937–1945) may have been "the most devastating single act in all human history, in terms of numbers of lives claimed," as Arthur Westing points out.[18] Today, besides dikes that protect low-lying areas (as in the Netherlands), there are more than seventy major dams in some twenty countries, the bombing of which could cause immense damage. With much longer lasting effects, the same would hold true for the bombing of any of the nearly 300 nuclear energy installations around the world, or the release of microorganisms—as demonstrated by the British when they set free the *anthracis bacillus* (causing anthrax) for testing purposes on the Scottish island of Gruinard during World War II. The island will remain uninhabitable for years to come. Environmental modification as part of warfare lends itself to speculation. Up to now, capacities to control clouds; to cause tsunamis, earthquakes, or even volcanic eruptions; to influence the acoustic or electromagnetic properties of water and the atmosphere for hostile purposes; and so on, seem negligible.[19] However, the 1977 Environmental Modification (ENMOD) Convention prohibits only the actual use of environmental modification techniques for hostile purposes, not their development. "What is [already] militarily attractive remains permissible, or at least not explicitly prohibited."[20]

Environmental Cooperation as a Means to Build Peace

In sharp contrast to environmental modification for war purposes, there exists the possibility of environmental cooperation as a means to build peace. For example, East-West cooperation for the protection of the Baltic Sea was relevant not only for environmental reasons but also as an instrument to bridge the East-West conflict and to maintain functional communication even in times of high political tension. Actually, environmental cooperation among Western European countries for the protection of the North Sea lagged behind East-West cooperation for the protection of the Baltic Sea. This may indicate that there was special interest in environmental cooperation in the East-West context for the very reason that such cooperation could also do more than handle specific environmental problems. Environmental cooperation in this case helped uphold the Conference for Security and

Cooperation in Europe (CSCE) process and demonstrated the possibility of international regime building even across the dividing lines of global conflict formations.[21] This way, environmental cooperation on the Baltic Sea not only served the ecology, but it also functioned as an instrument for improving overall East-West relations.

We may assume that ecological interdependence, like the nuclear stalemate, played a certain role in justifying the "new thinking" in the socialist countries vis-à-vis orthodox opposition to perestroika and glasnost. From this viewpoint it is hardly surprising that both Mikhail Gorbachev and Eduard Shevardnadze, in statements to the forty-third session of the UN General Assembly in 1988, forcefully called for global collective action for environmental protection.[22]

A functional spillover may also be expected from parks that straddle existing borderlines.[23] Such parks are in the interest of environmental protection; at the same time they can serve as buffer zones between conflicting parties, they can help to demilitarize sensitive border areas, and they can function as a vehicle for the establishment of lines of communication between conflicting parties. For example, it may be of some importance for future relations in Southeast Europe that Turkey and Greece are considering the establishment of an international peace park along both sides of the Evros River boundary. To quote Thorsell once again: "In seeking policy areas for collaboration, the presidents of both countries have indicated that the conservation of nature in this locality may pave the way towards settlement of more contentious issues."[24]

In accordance with this line of argument, Reidulf Molvaer describes environmental cooperation among the nations of the Horn of Africa as a confidence-building measure. He reports on "a firm belief that [environmental] cooperation could set the stage for greater dialogue amongst the nations of the Horn, possibly leading to increased political and diplomatic contacts."[25]

This is David Mitrany's "working peace system" at its best. However, the experience with "technical cooperation" in the context of the international division of labor suggests we should keep our expectations within bounds when it comes to the possible spin-off effects of ecological cooperation for peace. Peace through functional cooperation has been just as much a disappointment as the older ideas of the free trade pacifists. As yet it remains an open question whether environmental issues are better suited for a functionalist approach to international peace building than the supposedly unpolitical regulation of international economic relations. Perhaps ecological cooperation can succeed in impressing the minds of people and their attitudes toward one another more than rule making in the realm of international trade. It may therefore become an independent variable of world politics with increasing influence on the overall relations between states. But this would be something to be hoped for in the future—if at all. At present, ecological cooperation is a dependent variable that reflects the state of overall relations more than it influences these relations.

THE DEFINITIONAL LINKAGE

Environmental Degradation as War

We may identify two distinct traditions in the history of thought on war. One has its roots in the idea that war is a natural and necessary attribute of human existence (Xenophon) and may be regarded as a dynamic force underlying all human progress (Heraclitus). The other stresses the tragedy of war, the suffering and destruction that war brings about. The latter may be called the Erasmus perspective on war, because after Euripides and Aristophanes no one has lamented the destructive nature of war as eloquently as Erasmus of Rotterdam in his *Querela pacis* (1517). In the value system of the United Nations, the Erasmus perspective on war is clearly dominant.

In this perspective, it seems logical to compare military wars with environmental destruction. If war kills people and destroys their means of reproduction, so does environmental degradation. If war negates the claim of national integrity and self-determination, so does transboundary environmental pollution. Its effects are longer lasting and more encompassing than those of (conventional) wars. Even the possible effects of a nuclear war can be matched by environmental destruction. The massive increase of carbon dioxide in the atmosphere over the past 200 years may lead to a disruption of the long cycles of warm and cold periods in the history of the earth, causing a dramatic change in global climate with unforeseeable consequences for human life everywhere.

The destructiveness of war has grown tremendously since the first industrial revolution because of the development of ever more powerful weapons and of the tendency of wars to inflict more and more damage on the civilian population in comparison to total losses. Environmental degradation has developed along the same lines. Over the past 200 years, the process of environmental degradation has experienced a tremendous acceleration. In addition, the number of people affected by environmental degradation is increasing rapidly. This reflects not only a growing world population but also the technological advances in environmental destruction. More and more people are suffering under transboundary or global environmental degradation that does not originate in the area where they are living.

Thus, it seems that the intra- and international consequences of environmental degradation can well be compared with those of war. This functional equivalence of war and environmental depletion could lead us to conclude that the possible "erosion of military power" referred to above would be a sign not of the "obsolescence" of war,[26] but rather of the changing face of war. Military destruction would be simply replaced by transboundary pollution. Thus, we could define the continued attempts to externalize the environmental costs of production on the international level as "aggression," and the competing efforts of two or more countries in this respect as "war." Defining transboundary pollution as "aggression" would have grave consequences: Article 51 of the UN Charter could then be invoked to justify countermeasures as an expression of the right of each country to its individual or collective self-defense.[27]

Such a move would not be quite as revolutionary as it may appear at first sight. Throughout history, war never has been the sole way to inflict damage on another country—only the most dramatic one. Other ways include unequal economic relations, through which countries can exploit each other, and the destruction of cultural identities through the nonmilitary penetration of other societies. In the 1970s, the plea for a new international economic order was dramatized by referring to the economic policy of the North vis-à-vis the South as "economic aggression." As we enter the 1990s, it may seem appropriate to stress the need for a change in the dominant patterns of exploitation of natural resources by branding these patterns as "ecological aggression" or "war on nature." In this perspective, it would become self-evident that peace research should deal with ecological degradation. However, some counterarguments may be made:

• We should be careful not to gloss over the difference between war and conflict.[28] War involves conflict but is not identical with conflict. It rather signifies a violent approach to the solution of conflict or a violent outcome of conflict. Peace research deals with the question of which conflicts are likely to lead to war and under what conditions. It cannot and should not try to evade this task by simply labeling all social conflict as "war." Often the term *war* is applied to emphasize that a certain conflict is carried out with great vigor and could have repercussions on the general relationship between the entities involved. (Thus, we have witnessed the "chicken war" or the "steel war" among OECD countries.) For peace research, the important thing is not that these conflicts exist but rather that they are not being fought out in wars. Past and present patterns of exploitation of natural resources may be as destructive as war, and they may generate international conflict that in turn could lead to war. They do not, however, in themselves constitute war. Our task is not to redefine the meaning of war but rather to analyze the conflict potential deriving from environmental degradation and the conditions under which such conflicts may lead to war.

• Environmental degradation lacks an important feature of military aggression. The latter can be defined as hostile action designed to force the will of the adversary, to take something away from him, or to destroy him.

There is a desire to exert violence in order to affect the adversary against his will. This *dolus malus* is missing in ecological destruction, with the exception of environmental warfare. Except for the latter, environmental degradation does not take place in order to harm someone else. The damage done comes as an unintended consequence of economic activities. This is reflected in the ENMOD Convention of 1977, which prohibits environmental manipulations carried out with a deliberate hostile intent.

There are good reasons, of course, to discard this restriction and to prohibit any environmental modification that has "wide-spread, long-lasting and severe" effects on human life (ENMOD Convention, Article 1). This would be quite in line with general criminal law, which does not confine its sanctions to cases of hostile intent. However, such a general prohibition again would have to distinguish between environmental modification in the context of interstate conflict on the one hand and "normal" economic activities on the other. In interstate conflict, the subjects are states; in the case of "civil" environmental depletion, most actors are nongovernmental, ranging from the landless poor to large transnational companies. These actors cannot all be treated in the same way and subjected to the same administrative regulations simply because the result of their respective economic activities (e.g., deforestation) is comparable. While the big commercial exploiters of natural resources may be appropriate objects of administrative restrictions, the poor, who have no maneuvering room for environmental adjustment, can hardly be subjected to the same restrictions, unless we want to solve environmental problems through more social injustice.

A more radical approach to interpreting the similarities between the effects of war and the effects of environmental depletion would be to define the entire process of industrialization as a functional equivalent of war or even as a form of (protracted) war.[29] Such an approach not only would blur the distinction between war and economic activities, it would consciously discard this distinction in order to stress the destructive character of the industrial system. This would leave us but two options: either to stop industrialization or to return to the old social Darwinist proposition that to sustain life means to destroy life.

The latter choice is unacceptable for peace research; the former seems impracticable. So we will probably have to follow a pragmatic course and concentrate on how to prevent violent clashes over environmental issues in order to create or stabilize the conditions conducive to substantial conflict resolution (i.e., the reduction of existing and the prevention of new environmental destruction).

To sum up, if we do not wish to abandon the task of differentiating human behavior analytically that we can understand it better, we must be careful not to gloss over the specificities of war on the one hand and environmental depletion on the other. Tempting as it may be to brand environmental depletion as war in order to mobilize counterforces, this would cloud the issue and distract our attention from the danger that environmental depletion may lead to war, and how war in turn contributes to environmental depletion.

It remains to be asked whether environmental degradation may be defined as a form of "structural violence." This question is difficult to answer. On the one hand, structural violence also lacks a *dolus malus*. Thus, the arguments forwarded against the use of the term *aggression* in connection with transboundary pollution would also apply against the whole concept of structural violence. On the other hand, the merits of the concept of structural violence may be a strong argument for playing the *dolus malus* argument down. But if we did so, this would not solve the conceptual problem. In a country in which practically every family owns a car or a refrigerator it would not make much sense to brand driving automobiles or refrigeration as a form of structural violence, because those from whom the structural violence emanates would also be its victims. In this context the concept of structural violence would lose whatever merits it has.

The case may be different if we refer to the uneven international distribution of pollution per capita in connection with the uneven distribution of gains from pollution. In this case, the application of the term *structural violence,* at first sight, would make more sense. But here, too, we get into problems by applying the concept of structural violence. If we do so, leveling pollution ratios could lead to contradictory consequences. It could reduce the structural violence inherent in the uneven distribution of pollution ratios without necessarily reducing the structural violence inherent in pollution as such; the former may even be attained at the price of more pollution (i.e., more structural violence). This danger looms large in the debate on the distribution of pollution ratios in North-South relations. Also, bringing down worldwide pollution may solve the global environmental problem (in the interest of every human being) without necessarily reducing the inequality of pollution ratios. So, for reasons of consistency it would probably make more sense to speak of injustice rather than structural violence in this case.

Peace with Nature

A positive aspect of the definitional linkage could be seen in the call for *peace with nature.*[30] This term points to the need to transcend a strictly anthropocentric reading of environmental degradation. Churches have taken up this idea by referring to the integrity of creation and not just a healthy environment for humans (Seoul Declaration of the World Assembly of Churches, 1989; also the World Charter for Nature, Article 1). But thinking in terms of "peace with nature" (and the negative equivalent of "war on nature") creates the impression that people could do something to nature without at the same time doing it to themselves.[31] This assumption contradicts ecological interdependence.

The most important argument against continued attempts to externalize the environmental costs of production and consumption is that environmental degradation, no matter where it takes place, interacts globally, because all local and regional ecosystems are indissolubly interlinked on the global level. In this respect, nature does not confront the realm of human life: human life is part of nature. All our advances in protecting ourselves against wind, weather, rain, cold, and heat—the so-called "forces of Nature"—by well-insulated houses and warm clothing have not made us any more autonomous vis-à-vis nature. In no way have we become the masters of the laws of nature: we have only learned to apply them. We are still the objects of these laws. We have the freedom to ignore the laws of nature, but not to escape them. In talking about "peace with nature," we may create the misunderstanding that we are dealing with a segment of creation of which we are no part. In reality, there is no conflict of interest between nature's right and the right of humans to exist. Peace with nature implies peace among people. In this sense "ecology can be defined as the study of the balance of *all* life on Earth"[32] (emphasis added).

THE NORMATIVE LINKAGE

The Concept of Environmental Security

The interrelationship between ecological issues and those issues that peace researchers and analysts of international relations in general are concerned with may be highlighted by the concept of environmental or ecological security.[33] This concept is based on the assumption that there are increasingly nonmilitary threats to the territorial integrity of a state, its right to self-determination, and its economic well-being. Environmental degradation is seen as one such threat.[34]

The concept is being discussed not only in academic circles. It has also been taken up by international organizations (especially the UN General Assembly and UN Environment Programme) and national governments. In this respect, the present Soviet government has been especially responsive. Thus, former Soviet foreign minister Eduard Shevardnadze contributed to the clarification of the concept by defining environmental security as a state of international relations, "in which the maintenance, rational use, reproduction and qualitative improvement of the environment in the interest of a stable and assured development of all states and favourable living conditions for each person are being guaranteed." In this sense environmental security calls for "a system of normative, organizational and economic measures within the framework of comprehensive international cooperation based on international law."[35]

The notion of ecological security takes up some of the more recent developments in scientific and political thinking on security. Especially relevant is the concept of common security,[36] which is centered on the observation that traditional security policy enhances overall insecurity and that this contradiction can be overcome only by pursuing a policy that defines the security needs of the one party in terms of the security needs of all parties. Cooperation and reciprocity are key elements of this concept. By stressing ecological interdependence, the concept also underlines the necessity of thinking in global terms and of abandoning the idea that security—with whatever connotation—can be attained on a national level.

The concept is clearly normative in that it pleads for a reorientation of security policy under the impact of environmental threats and especially the depletion of global commons like climate, atmosphere, fresh water, and oceans. According to Lodgaard,

> the concept of environmental security challenges established frames of mind and political conduct. It conveys the message that environmental problems have a legitimate claim for status at the level of "high politics," just as much as military problems have.[37]

Despite these features and claims, the concept of environmental or ecological security invites some second thoughts; it is not necessarily to be discarded but perhaps to be used with some caution.[38]

Environmental Security and Sustainable Development

Security policies are essentially status quo oriented. The most common argument against change is that it might jeopardize security. "Don't rock the boat!" is the central message of security thinking. With this connotation of security, the term *environmental security* would become a contradiction in itself, because ecological thinking is dynamic and global, whereas security thinking is static and particularistic. The one stresses adaptation, the other enforcement and control. This contradiction can be overcome by redefining security to make it conducive to ecological thinking as stated above. But why need we stick to the term *security* at all; why not refer to *sustainable development*—a term that would much better signify what is now being labeled as "environmental security?" As I see it, the central explanation must be seen in efforts to instrumentalize the high standing that security has in the realm of "high politics" for environmental purposes.[39] But trying to claim the term *security* for environmental matters, it seems to me, may go off in the wrong direction. Here we should recall the experience with another attempt to define nonmilitary aspirations in terms of security—the experience with "economic security."

In the 1970s, when détente went through its first phase, preoccupation with military security was modified by concerns over "economic security." To my knowledge, this concept was first used by the Latin Americans in their post-World War II negotiations with the United States. At that time, the United States called for inter-American cooperation in the field of security in order to transform the all-American front against fascism into an all-American front against communism. Against this quest for political and military cooperation, Latin American nations stressed that their real problems were of an economic nature; they were not concerned with military but with "economic security."

This attempt to characterize the needs of the developing countries did not impress the United States; it also failed to move the economically most potent industrialized countries to make any substantial concessions to the Third World in the debate on the New Economic World Order some twenty-five years later. Instead, the industrialized countries of the West were to take up the term *economic security* to defend the existing international order. They argued that any attempt on the part of the developing countries to put pressure on the industrialized countries by threatening to disrupt the free flow of strategically important raw materials would be considered a threat to the security of these countries. In other words, the status quo of the international economic order was defined as a security matter for the industrialized countries.

In the light of this experience, we should realize that the concept of environmental security—regardless of intent—may be invoked to defend the status quo of the present world ecological order, in which the distribution of benefits from environmental degradation is clearly in favor of the highly industrialized countries.

Rationalization of Traditional Security Thinking

The term *security* refers to a universal aspiration to live in the expectation that life and physical integrity will not be threatened by any other person, group, or society. Security involves existential interests. The protection of existential interests, however, can be used to legitimize the use of force as a last resort—regardless of the fact that this, in turn, may jeopardize the life and integrity of others. Article 51 of the UN Charter guarantees to every state the right to individual and collective self-defense, despite the prohibition of war and the obligation to pursue peaceful conflict resolution.

Defining environmental degradation as a threat to the security of societies may help to legitimize the use of force when it comes to protecting certain economic and ecological interests, or warding off negative consequences of environmental degradation. In this context we could recall the argument of Lipschutz and Holdren: references to the need to acquire natural resources have quite often "served as rationalizations, for consumption by publics and legislators, in support of policies with much more elaborate origins."[40]

With the demise of the East-West conflict, the armies in all Northern countries stand ready—though perhaps with reduced numbers—to serve new tasks as the old ones are fading away. Protection of certain features of the global environment or of the controlling power exercised by the industrialized countries over the use of natural resources may be regarded by the military as such a new task. In this way, defining ecological interests in terms of security needs could contribute more to the militarization of ecopolitics than to a demilitarization of traditional security thinking. Indeed, as early as 1969, NATO took up ecological questions to give the alliance a role to play in this issue area. It remains to be seen whether this will contribute more to a transformation of NATO than to a symbiosis of military and environmental politics.[41]

Such a symbiosis has recently been suggested by Senator Sam Nunn, chairman of the US Senate Armed Services Committee, who proposed that substantial Defense Department and intelligence resources be shifted to solve ecological problems through a "Strategic Environmental Research Program." According to Senator Nunn, some data gathered by the armed services and intelligence agencies could be opened up to nonmilitary scientists, and military aircraft, ships, submarines, and satellites could collect information on air and water quality and on global climate. The powerful computers used by the Defense and Energy departments could also be made available to civilian researchers. As reported by Philip Shabecoff in the *International Herald Tribune*, a Defense Department spokesman said that the plan "sounds good," though "we have to see what the specifics are before we can embrace everything he has proposed."[42] This positive reaction is hardly surprising, since the idea behind the proposal was to combine environmental concerns with the interest of the defense establishment in retaining research and technological capacity for the military, at a time when military budgets will be shrinking substantially due to changing international threat perceptions after the demise of the East-West conflict. The Gulf War has taken away some of the pressure from the military to look for new assignments, but it remains to be seen whether the postwar situation will leave the military satisfied with what it can hope for in the future if disarmament should proceed.

Environmental and Comprehensive Security

One other possible pitfall of "environmental security" should be mentioned here. Environmental security is to unfold in the context of "comprehensive security," which stresses the interrelationship between military, economic, social, cultural, and ecological factors. However, in a programmatic report formulated in December 1988 and issued by the USSR Academy of Sciences, the International Peace Research Institute in Oslo, the United Nations Environment Programme, and the Ecoforum for Peace (Sofia), environmental security together with politico-military security was given priority over economic and social concerns. The report states:

> It is clear that politico-military, environmental, economic, and social problems are all interconnected. Thus, it makes good sense to include all of them in the concept of comprehensive international security. However, the primary security issues—those upon which the very survival of humankind depends—are the politico-military and the environmental ones.[43]

It follows, as indeed spelled out in this report, that "new opportunities for shifting attention and resources from the military sector" should be used in favor of the environmental sector. However, if we are serious about the interrelationship between economic, social, ecological, and politico-military factors, then there is no reason to single out one or two of these aspects for special treatment. Of course, a third world war would make all other considerations obsolete. Likewise, a collapse of the biosphere would affect everything else. In this sense, politico-military and environmental aspects of security are of special importance to the well-being of humankind. But the thesis that all the various aspects of security are linked up with each other implies that ecological problems can be solved only in connection with the solution of economic and social problems. As a matter of fact, if we define environmental security as being in the interest of "stable and assured development of all states" and of "favorable living conditions for all persons," we are contradicting ourselves if we give environmental security priority over economic or social aspects of security.

Furthermore, such priority of environmental aspects over economic and social aspects exists only on a high level of abstraction. The poor in many countries deplete the natural resources in order to survive. Protecting the resources against them would speed up the deterioration of their living conditions. There are obviously conflicting security interests that cannot and should not be solved without due regard for the concrete economic and social contexts in which they develop. Categorically establishing a priority of environmental security over economic and social considerations would contradict precisely the dynamic features that "environmental security" is to display.

CONCLUSION

Environmental depletion constitutes a legitimate and necessary concern of peace research. However, we need further clarification of the underlying issues and the concepts that have been developed so far to deal with them.

Central to the entire debate on the interrelationship between the peace problematique and environmental issues is the assumption that transboundary environmental pollution and the depletion of the global commons constitute a nonmilitary threat to the security of societies. While there are good reasons for this approach to environmental problems, the following caveats should be kept in mind:

• In referring to nonmilitary threats to the life and well-being of societies we are talking of nothing new. Time and again the identity of societies has been destroyed through their economic, political, and cultural penetration by others; their economic well-being has been harmed by international exploitation; their right to self-determination has been rendered obsolete by one-sided dependencies; and so on. The debate of the 1970s on economic security is an expression of these nonmilitary threats to the security of societies. Concern for environmental security should not replace the task of dealing with economic and social aspects of the security of societies, lest "environmental security" should deepen structural violence and pave the way for continued recourse to direct violence in intra- and intersocietal relations.

• When we are talking of increasing nonmilitary threats to the life and well-being of societies, this does not imply that military threats are automatically lessening in importance. As the above observations on the causal and instrumental linkages between "peace and the environment" show, environmental depletion can constitute a new source of military conflict. In addition, military activity can contribute to environmental degradation, and the conscious manipulation of the environment can be used to broaden the options of military warfare.

• Defining environmental issues in terms of security risks is in itself a risky operation. As pointed out above, we may end up contributing more to the militarization of environmental politics than to the demilitarization of security politics. Negative causal linkages are quite strong, and it may be just as tempting for the military to embrace environmental concerns as a fashionable field of activity as it is for peace researchers. On the other hand, if the military is tempted to take over environmental tasks, then, of course, peace researchers should formulate some counterclaims. Whether this can be done by first referring to environmental problems as security issues and by then trying to give the security issues a meaning conducive to the values of peace research remains an open question.

Much will depend on positive causal and instrumental linkages. Here the question arises whether environmental concerns are better suited to fulfill the promises of interdependence and functionalism than economic matters. With a view to ecological interdependence, Klaus Michael Meyer-Abich stated that "changes in world climate will do as little to compel us to live in peace as nuclear weapons did. To the contrary: peace will be further threatened because there will be losers and winners [of the climatic change]."[44]

This is exactly the point; the degree to which social groups, societies, or geographical regions are affected by global environmental degradation still differs widely. Before the effects of environmental degradation can become globally more homogeneous, further differentiation is most likely. For example, the depletion of the ozone layer may proceed with highly different repercussions on the polar areas, the adjacent areas in the North and the South, and the regions close to the equator. Another example is global warming, which would lead to even more dramatic disparities: low-lying countries would be affected especially severely through flooding caused by rising sea levels (e.g., the Netherlands and Bangladesh), while other countries of the Northern Hemisphere might well profit from climatic change.

Such local and regional disparities are accentuated by economic disparities. The combined disparities modify the meaning of ecological interdependence. States and groups of states will seek alliances as they try to exploit or to escape these disparities, and they will try to find partners in doing so. Therefore, antagonistic ecoalliances may develop despite ecological interdependence.

On the other hand, ecological interdependence has already led to some cooperation. In the course of only a few years a huge body of international environmental regulations and principles has evolved that is slowly but steadily acquiring the character of international law. Of course, international law in itself is weak; however, the difference from national law is not quite as great as it appears at first sight. National law, too, depends largely on its norms being internalized by the citizens. Enforcement has only a marginal regulating effect. This is, perhaps, where functionalism comes in; environmental problems may contribute to the establishment or expansion of routine international communication and cooperation, thereby helping to marginalize the acceptability of the use of force in international conflict resolution. More importantly, environmental cooperation and networking on a transnational level, including the communal level, may help to develop a public awareness of national, regional, and global environmental problems in their specific economic and social contexts; this in turn could have a considerable influence on the formulation of national or regional politics. It could also influence the degree to which internationally agreed regulations are actually put into practice.

In this respect, "peace parks" may serve as a symbol for what can be done. They "offer alternative visions for the border regions that hitherto have been military staging grounds and fields of battle."[45] On the other hand, the delineation of nature preserves usually goes hand in hand with the practice of opening up the adjacent territory to commercial exploitation. In this sense, the idea of peace parks in regions of conflict like Central America, the Horn of Africa, or Southeast Europe could become a trap—as a practice of confining peace to parks. This only shows the functional ambivalence of environmental problems. The problems are real, but they can also be used to distract attention from other equally real problems.

NOTES

1. James Thorsell, "Through Hot and Cold Wars, Parks Endure," *Natural History* 99 (6) (June 1990): 56-58.

2. Alexandre Moreau de Jonnès, *Premier mémoire en réponse à la question . . . quels sont les changements que peut occasionner le déboisement de forêt . . . , etc.* (Brussels 1825).

3. Martin Jänicke, *Wie das Industriesystem von seinen Misständen profitiert* (Opladen: Westdeutscher Verlag, 1979).

4. P. Colinvaux, *Fates of Nations: A Biological Theory of History* (New York: Simon & Schuster, 1980); Robert C. North, "Integrating the Perspectives: From Population to Conflict and War," in *Multidisciplinary Perspectives on Population*, ed. Nazli Choucri (Syracuse: Syracuse University Press, 1984), 195-215; Arthur H. Westing, ed., *Global Resources and International Conflict: Environmental Factors in Strategic Policy and Action* (Oxford: Oxford University Press, 1986); Marcel Leroy, "Human Population as a Factor in Strategic Policy and Action," in Westing, *Global Resources and International Conflict*, 159-182.

5. Ronnie D. Lipschutz and John P. Holdren, "Crossing Borders: Resource Flows, the Global Environment, and International Security," *Bulletin of Peace Proposals* 21 (2) (June 1, 1991): 121-133.

6. Amílcar O. Herrera, Hugo D. Scolnik et al., *Grenzen des Elends: Das Bariloche-Modell* (Frankfurt: Fischer, 1977).

7. Nico Schrijver, "International Organization for Environmental Security?" *Bulletin of Peace Proposals* 20 (2) (1989): 115-122.

8. Harald Müller, *Umwelt und Konflikt* (Frankfurt: Peace Research Institute Frankfurt, 1990), 30.

9. Arthur H. Westing, "The Military Sector vis-à-vis the Environment," *Journal of Peace Research* 25 (3) (December, 1988): 257-264.

10. Michael Brzoska, "The Military Related External Debt of Third World Countries," *Journal of Peace Research* 13 (3) (September 1983): 271-277; Saadet Deger and Ron Smith, "Military Expenditure and Development: The Economic Linkages," *IDS Bulletin* (Brighton) 16 (4) (1985): 49-57; Robert E. Looney and Peter C. Frederiksen, "Defense Expenditures, External Public Debt and Growth in Developing Countries," *Journal of Peace Research* 23 (4) (December 1986): 329-338.

11. Gro Harlem Brundtland et al., *Our Common Future* (Oxford: Oxford University Press, 1987), ch. 11.

12. Evan Luard, *The Blunted Sword: The Erosion of Military Power in Modern World Politics* (London: Tauris, 1988).

13. Sverre Lodgaard, *Environmental Conflict Resolution*, paper delivered at the UNEP meeting on "Environmental Conflict Resolution," Nairobi, 30 March 1990.

14. Lester R. Brown, *Redefining National Security*, Worldwatch Paper 14 (Washington, D.C.: Worldwatch Institute, 1977); Norman Myers, "The Environmental Dimension to Security Issues," *The Environmentalist* 6 (4) (1986): 251-257.

15. Arthur H. Westing, ed., *Environmental Warfare: A Technical, Legal and Policy Appraisal* (London: Taylor & Francis, 1984); Knut Krusewitz, *Umweltkrieg. Militär, Ökologie und Gesellschaft* (Königstein: Athenäum, 1985); Ulrich Albrecht, "Wetter-Rüsten," *Natur* (8 August 1983): 50-59, 102-103; Frank Barnaby, "Environmental Warfare," *Bulletin of the Atomic Scientist* 32 (5) (May 1976): 36-43; Richard Falk, "Environmental Warfare and Ecocide," *Bulletin of Peace Proposals* 4 (4) (1973): 1-17; Jozef Goldblat, "Environmental Weapons," in *World Armaments and Disarmament: SIPRI Yearbook 1978* (London: Taylor & Francis, 1978).

16. Horst Siebert, *Die vergeudete Umwelt* (Frankfurt: Fischer, 1990); Arthur H. Westing, *Ecological Consequences of the Second Indochina War* (Stockholm: SIPRI, 1976).

17. Richard A. Falk, "Environmental Disruption by Military Means and International Law," in Westing, *Environmental Warfare*, 33-52.

18. Westing, *Environmental Warfare*, 6.

19. Ibid.

20. Falk, "Environmental Disruption by Military Means," 33.

21. Martin List, "Cleaning up the Baltic: A Case Study in East-West Environmental Cooperation," in *International Regimes in East-West Politics*, ed. Volker Rittberger (London: Pinter, 1990), 90-116.

22. Alexander S. Timoschenko, "International Environmental Law and the Concept of Ecological Security," *Breakthrough* 10 (4) (Summer/Fall 1989): 22-24.

23. James Thorsell, ed., *Parks on the Borderline: Experience in Transfrontier Conservation* (Geneva: International Union for the Conservation of Nature, 1990).

24. James Thorsell, "Through Hot and Cold Wars," 58.

25. Reidulf K. Molvaer, "Environmental Cooperation in the Horn of Africa: A UNEP Perspective," *Bulletin of Peace Proposals* 21 (2) (1990): 135-142; Lodgaard, *Environmental Conflict Resolution*, 19; Michael Renner, *National Security: The Economic and Environmental Dimension*, Worldwatch Paper 89 (Washington, D.C.: Worldwatch Institute, 1989), 43.

26. John Mueller, *Retreat from Doomsday: The Obsolescence of Major War* (New York: Basic Books, 1989); Evan Luard, *War in International Society* (London: Tauris, 1986).

27. Peter C. Mayer-Tasch, *Die verseuchte Landkarte* (Munich: Beck, 1987), 113.

28. Daniel Deudney, "The Case Against Linking Environmental Degradation and National Security," *Millennium: Journal of International Studies* 19 (3) (Winter 1990): 461-476.

29. Mathias Finger, *Can Peace Research and Ecology Be Linked? An Epistemological Approach*, paper presented to the Thirteenth General Conference of the International Peace Research Association, Groningen, Netherlands, 3-7 July 1990.

30. Klaus Michael Meyer-Abich, *Wege zum Frieden mit der Natur:*

Praktische Philosophie für die Umweltpolitik (Munich: Piper, 1984).

31. Cf. Lodgaard, *Environmental Conflict Resolution*, 1, who speaks of "man versus nature" types of conflict; *Environmental Security: A Report Contributing to the Concept of Comprehensive International Security*, from a conference in Moscow, 28 November–1 December 1988, cosponsored by the USSR Academy of Sciences (Moscow), the International Peace Research Institute (Oslo), the United Nations Environment Programme (Nairobi), and the Ecoforum for Peace (Sofia) (Oslo/Nairobi, 1989), 16, refers to "security of the biosphere"; cf. in this context also Wolfgang Huber, "'Nur wer die Schöpfung liebt, kann sie retten' Naturzerstörung und Schöpfungsglaube," *Frieden in der Schöpfung*, ed. Gerhard Rau, Adolf M. Ritter, and Hermann Timm (Gütersloh: Mohn, 1987).

32. Birgit Brock-Utne, "Formal Education as a Force in Shaping Cultural Norms Relating to War and the Environment," in *Cultural Norms, War and the Environment*, ed. Arthur H. Westing (Oxford: Oxford University Press, 1988), 88.

33. Both terms are used in the literature. Cf. Pat Mische, "Ecological Security in an Interdependent World," *Breakthrough* 11 (4), 12 (1) (Summer/Fall, 1989): 7-17; Timoschenko, "International Environmental Law"; *Environmental Security*; Lodgaard, *Environmental Conflict Resolution*.

34. Richard H. Ullmann, "Redefining Security," *International Security* 8 (1) (Summer 1983): 129-153; Harald Müller, *Security and the Environment: Report on the International Workshop on Security and the Environment* (Royal Norwegian Ministry of Defense in Support of the World Commission on Environment and Development, 1987), 20-41; Westing, *Global Resources and International Conflict*; Johan J. Holst, "Security and the Environment: A Preliminary Exploration," *Bulletin of Peace Proposals* 20 (2) (June 1989): 123-129; Mische, "Ecological Security"; Norman Myers, "Critical Link Between the Environment, Natural Resources, and War," *Second Biennial Conference on the Fate of the Earth*, ed. A. S. Kelly (San Francisco: 1985), 47-53; Renner, *National Security*; *Environmental Security*; Lodgaard, *Environmental Conflict Resolution*.

35. *Literaturnaja Gazeta* 47 (1989), cited after the German text in Brigitte Stepanek, "Ökologieproblematik als Aufgabe der Friedenspolitik," in *Friedensforschung in Deutschland*, ed. Dieter Senghaas and Karlheinz Koppe (Bonn: Arbeitsstelle für Friedensforschung, 1990), 88.

36. Olof Palme et al., *Common Security* (London: Pan, 1982).

37. Lodgaard, *Environmental Conflict Resolution*, 18.

38. Deudney, "The Case Against Linking Environmental Degradation."

39. Lodgaard, *Environmental Conflict Resolution*, 17.

40. Lipschutz and Holdren, "Crossing Borders," 123.

41. Krusewitz, "Umweltkrieg," 166-171.

42. Philip Shabecoff, *International Herald Tribune*, 30 June–1 July 1990.

43. *Environmental Security*, 12.

44. Klaus Michael Meyer-Abich, "Im Treibhaus der Konflikte: Politische Krisen durch die Klimaänderung," *Bild der Wissenschaft* 27 (1) (1990): 70.

45. Renner, *National Security*, 44.

Other references for this chapter are: Günther Bächler, "Ökologische Sicherheit und Konflikt," *Dialog* 18 (1-2) (1990): 231-261; Malin Falkenmark, "Fresh Waters as a Factor in Strategic Policy and Action," in *Global Resources and International Conflict*, ed. Arthur H. Westing (Oxford & New York: Oxford University Press, 1986), 85–113; and Harald Müller, "Internationale Ressourcen—und Umwelt problematik," in *Einführung in die Internationale Politik*, eds. Manfred Knapp and Gert Krell (Munich & Vienna: Oldenbourge, 1989), 324–349.

CHAPTER 8

Security Through Defending the Environment: Citizens Say Yes!

—————————————— PATRICIA M. MISCHE

ENVIRONMENTAL THREATS AND
THE NEED TO REDEFINE SECURITY

Heated debate occurred over the use of the phrase *ecological security* at the International Peace Research Association (IPRA) in Groningen, Netherlands, in July 1990. Understandably, much of the argument took place in the meetings of the Ecological Security Commission, which uses the phrase as its very title. This is a newly created commission within IPRA, and there are still many questions about what assumptions and core concepts should guide its work. The different views made our sessions exciting and stimulating.

The phrase *ecological security* was also challenged by Lothar Brock in his paper for the panel. Because I am among those being taken to task, I feel the need to share why I consciously and deliberately chose to use *ecological security* in past writings and why, after hearing and reading some of the criticism, I remain convinced that the merits outweigh the objections.

Objections by some peace researchers spring from their associations of the word *security* with the military. Concern grew when some US political and military leaders recently proposed that the US defense establishment should play an important role in responding to global environmental problems. Those proposing this military involvement were seeking ways to keep military funding intact at a time when the Cold War and military threats were declining and cuts in the military budget were being debated in Congress. Thus, peace advocates were concerned about the manipulation of the phrase *ecological security* for military means.

It is premature to evaluate the validity of these concerns, although they merit continued attention and research. The relevant policy decisions have not yet been made, and if there is to be military involvement, its precise nature is not yet clear. Possibilities recommended by Senator Sam Nunn, chairman of the US Senate Armed Services Committee, included: using military aircraft, ships, submarines, and satellites to collect information on air and water quality and on global climate; making the powerful computers of the Defense and Energy departments available to civilian researchers; and devoting research money and equipment now used for military programs to develop energy technologies for civilian use.

Some of these proposed military contributions might actually benefit the environment and should not be summarily dismissed simply because they are associated with the military. Some military technologies are more advanced than anything available in the civilian sector and could improve civilian capabilities for environmental protection. Furthermore, where multiple applications or civilian adaptations are possible, using such technologies for environmental protection could be a positive step toward economic and technological conversion.

On the other hand, some proposals require more caution. For example, in the matter of research, what biases would accrue under military auspices? The US military establishment has been a major source of environmental damage and has not been made to comply with the same environmental protection requirements that bind the private sector.[1] In the matter of energy alternatives, would military researchers be biased toward nuclear energy because of its linkage with nuclear weapons production, and because of a historical desire to offset the public image of the destructive potential of nuclear weapons through promotion of the "peaceful uses of the atom"?[2] Another question might be, has the fact that the US Department of Energy is linked with nuclear weapons production been a factor in the poor progress to date in the development of adequate energy alternatives in the United States?

My real point here is neither to defend nor criticize proposed military involvement in environmental security. Rather it is to defend the use of the phrase *ecological security* by peace and environmental advocates regardless of whether or not it is used by the military. Whatever motivations or biases are involved in US political and military leaders identifying the environment as a national security issue, does not make it less a *real* security issue—one that vitally affects the future prospects of war or peace—indeed, the very survival of future generations.

When I first coined the phrase *ecological security* in 1986, I thought I was alone. Later I discovered like-minded people in other parts of the world who also were using this or similar phrases to express their concern about threats to the environment.[3] As far as I know, none of these people were in the military or influenced by military objectives. On the contrary, most of us were deeply involved in peace or environmental research, or both. Our reference to *ecological security* predated its use by US political and military leaders.

I cannot speak for others, but I can tell you why I first began using this phrase and why I still continue to do so. First, words are important; and words that convey the deep feelings, concerns, anxieties, hopes, needs, and meanings of a people are especially important. The word *security* is a power word. It is related to the primary need to survive. The peace movement has made a mistake in avoiding it in the past. In the 1960s, some in the peace movement questioned the word *security* because it was used by military and political leaders to justify the Vietnam War and the arms race. In the dualistic, polarized thinking of the time, use by the military made the word itself suspect. Being for peace meant being antiwar, and being against war meant being against the military and "hawks." By association, if the military professed to be protecting security, then being antiwar and antimilitary meant being anti-the-language-of-security. This polarizing logic was also adopted by some "hawks": *peace* was for "peaceniks" or "pinkos" and naive, mushy-minded, and cowardly "doves"; *security* was the language of realpolitik and "real" (i.e., loyal, freedom-loving, and courageous) Americans. The peace movement also gave away other important words and symbols. The Bible was ignored and the American flag was burned. By default, these deep cultural symbols were then identified with, and gave moral legitimacy to, military escalation.

Second, the need for security is intrinsic in all human beings, indeed all species. Human infants, for example, need some physical and psychological security in order to survive, grow, and become fully human. At the same time, complete security is probably not achievable or even desirable. A certain amount of risk is necessary to growing, learning, and becoming mature human beings. There is a need for some balance between risk and security, and the effort to arrive at some balance implies activity and change in response to changing conditions. Within living systems, including human social systems, security is not a fixed or steady state, but functions more like an organizing principle stimulating and steering a dynamic, evolutionary process. That plant and animal species—indeed, whole ecosystems—have evolved in particular ways with particular characteristics, has been greatly affected by their struggle to survive under different or changing environmental conditions. So, too, some of the physical and cultural variations among different human groups have been influenced by their struggle to survive under different or changing environmental, historical, economic, technological, political, or other conditions.

Third, security systems are total systems. The ways human societies organize for security involves and affects the whole fabric of society at conscious and unconscious levels. The guiding myths, religious and identity systems, structures of thought, gender roles, and leadership requirements, as well as political and economic systems, are all affected. So is social status— i.e., who is valued and who is marginalized, who will lead and who will follow, who will rule and who must obey. Status and leadership are greatly affected by a society's perceptions of who can make the most important contribution to group security, and who is a burden, liability, or threat to it.

Fourth, security systems historically preceded the rise of the war system. In the millions of years of human evolution, organized warfare is a relatively new social invention. Many historians date its emergence somewhere between 5,000 to 10,000 years ago in the Bronze Age. Only relatively recently in history, then, has the concept of security taken on a narrow, military character. We are now at a new place in history where it has become imperative to reconceptualize security along more holistic and comprehensive lines.

Major Periods in the Evolution of Concepts and Systems of Security

Humans' perceptions of the primary threats to their survival, and the systems they have developed to meet these threats, have varied over time and in different geographic regions. In general, however, there have been two major historical periods, and we may now be entering a third.

In the first and longest period of human history, concepts of security centered primarily on *nature*, including (a) the life-giving, nurturing, aspects of nature; (b) the life-threatening capabilities of nature in the form of earthquakes, volcanoes, hurricanes, tornadoes, floods, droughts, blizzards, and changing food and water supplies; and (c) the sense of mystery, awe, surprise, power, and beauty aroused by nature. Clearly there were powerful forces beyond human control within nature. Early human societies developed whole social systems related to their experience of these life-giving and life-threatening powers of nature, including religious, economic, political, and social systems. Leadership went to those—male or female—who seemed most skilled in mediating or protecting a group from the more threatening forces and/or who symbolized or seemed best able to secure the life-giving and nurturing forces. Over time, humans learned to protect themselves from the more threatening forces of nature and so came to fear nature less.

In the second period, the primary locus of threats shifted from nature or the biosphere to the sociosphere. Over time, intergroup conflict and hostilities, fear and enmity, were institutionalized in a war system, given political content (e.g., "Better Dead than Red"), and built up until they constituted megathreats that were met by megaweapons and megamyths so pervasive and destructive that the whole world hung on the verge of Armageddon.

Some historians now believe that environmental degradation may have contributed to the rise of organized warfare in the Bronze Age. When deteriorating environmental conditions—whether from natural or human causes—led to food shortages, some groups resorted to raiding and plundering from their neighbors. Over time, where this plundering paid off in the form of food, material goods, and increased power and prestige for the plunderers, whole social systems began to develop around it. However the war system originated, it eventually became a total system affecting the structures of thought, religious beliefs and myths, culture, economic and political structures, leadership requirements, gender roles, and social status within warring societies. The groups that were invaded, raided, and conquered, if not killed or enslaved, gradually developed their own systems to defend against such aggression. Ultimately, the war system spread worldwide until it was nearly universal. By the twentieth century, only a few isolated human groups were not affected.

Although the Cold War is over, the underlying world system is still largely a war system. However, the war system is a human invention. We can invent new systems to replace it. This will not be easy, but it is within the realm of possibility. The end of the Cold War has opened a window of opportunity for developing a global peace system as the basis for a new world order. But this will not be automatic. Social systems, and the habits of mind that go with them, tend to reproduce themselves. Systemic change requires a conscious, continuous effort; systemic change of a global order requires a global effort.

In the meantime, a new class of threats is emerging that requires a whole new way of thinking and organizing for human security. Once more the threats have to do with nature, but this time not what nature can do to humans, but rather how human activities may be damaging nature, and in turn, the way this damage may diminish the prospects for future human survival, security, and peace. Humans have been benign, sometimes beneficial, and sometimes destructive. But now the capacity for destruction has reached an unprecedented scale and complexity. We have new powers over life and death never dreamed of by our ancestors. We can intervene in the DNA, the delicate genetic coding that has built up through eons of natural selection. We can create new species in test tubes. We can alter the earth's climate. We can poison the soil, food, air, and water on which our lives depend. With our weapons of mass destruction, we can render the earth uninhabitable for future generations. We can cause millions of plant and animal species to go out of existence, and if we do this, not even God will be able to bring them back; a part of the earth, a part of ourselves, will be lost forever.

There is only a limited amount of time in which to develop global systems of ecological security to overcome the threats to humanity powered by new threats to the environment. Like the war system, wide-scale environmental damage is a product of human volition. But unlike the war system, which can be reversed by human choices, if damage to the earth's life system goes beyond a certain point, the climatic and other changes set in motion may take on a life of their own and may not be humanly reversible. The question is not whether the earth will survive, for the earth will adapt and survive in some fashion.[4] The question is whether humans will survive the adaptations that the earth makes.

Unlike threats in the social sphere, human threats to the earth cannot be defined ideologically. Neither Adam Smith nor Karl Marx provide solutions to the environmental challenges we face today; both capitalism and communism have failed in this regard. Threats to the environment cannot be solved through conventional competition for power; more powerful arsenals are no added advantage. Domination will not bring salvation. John Wayne and Rambo machoism provides no protection against environmental threats.

Furthermore, the transboundary and interdependent nature of environmental threats defies existing concepts of state sovereignty. The earth does not recognize sovereignty as we now define it.[5] The sovereignty of the earth is indivisible; the earth is one, interdependent system. This is true not only spatially, as a view of the earth from outer space makes evident, it is also true temporally. Future generations will be dramatically affected by the decisions we make today related to environmental security.[6] The earth has its own laws, which precede and are more binding and sovereign than human laws.

Thus, threats to the environment challenge the very foundations of modern thought structure—the myths, beliefs, and philosophical premises on which the war system has been built and maintained. Ecological security requires a new cosmology[7]—a whole new world view and new approach to security. It requires moving from a homocentric to a biocentric view of the world. The earth is like a single cell in the universe, and humans do not control the cell but are part of it. We will live or die as this single cell lives or dies.[8] Our common survival requires new identity and loyalty systems. All our separate past histories are now converging toward one shared future history. We will either learn to live together or we will die together. Our sense of community needs to expand to include the whole human community; and the community of humans must learn to live in concert with the larger community of all beings. This requires a new social contract based on new understanding of our relatedness in one life system. It also requires the development of global systems of peace and ecological security capable of managing conflicts and preventing wars and environmental devastation.

Obstacles to New Systems of Security

There are contradictions and very intricate and difficult problems of transition from a war system to a global system of peace and ecological security. On the one hand, the continuation of the war system is inimical to ecological security. Warfare and preparation for warfare (including the production, testing, and stockpiling of nuclear, chemical, biological, and other weapons) has been devastating to the environment. According to United Nations data, by 1980 the nuclear powers had conducted some 1,233 nuclear tests globally, destroying desert ecosystems, vaporizing some Pacific islands and rendering others uninhabitable, and contaminating oceans, marine life, and human populations. Untold numbers of people have suffered cancers, birth defects, and other related ill-health effects. In some cases, whole family lines have died out from the effects of radiation exposure from nuclear testing.[9] The Kwajalein Atoll in the Marshall Islands was a target for US intercontinental ballistic missiles aimed from Vandenberg Air Force Base in California. Although not carrying nuclear warheads, the missiles came crashing in at 8,000 miles per hour, destroying coral reefs and lagoons. The ecological damage resulted in toxin-carrying fish and subsequent food poisoning among the people, who could then no longer eat what had been a staple food.[10] None of the nuclear powers factored such damage to environmental and human health in their national security budgets. It was simply written off as "collateral damage."

The nuclear powers are not the only countries of concern. Currently some twenty-four countries, most in the Third World, have or are developing long-range rockets that can be used as ballistic missiles armed with nuclear, chemical, or biological warheads. Six of these countries presently have, or are on the threshold of having, nuclear weapons capability.[11]

Even "conventional" military activity is damaging to the environment. The military has consumed inordinate amounts of nonrenewable resources and national monies and coopted the scientific and technological research and development that could have been used to advance ecological sustainability. As already mentioned, often the military has not been bound by the same environmental protection requirements as civilian populations. In the United States, for example, there are some 15,000 suspected hazardous waste sites on active and former Department of Defense properties. But, according to the Center for Defense Information, "the majority of US military facilities do not meet federal and state hazardous waste control requirements."[12] Recent disclosures have exposed environmental contamination at seventeen nuclear warhead factories in twelve states. "Hundreds of billions of gallons of extremely toxic radioactive, chemical, and mixed wastes have been discharged into the soil and air in violation of federal hazardous waste disposal laws."[13]

Thus, *the advancement of world peace is essential to ecological security.* On the other hand, the paradox is that increasing environmental degradation may further entrench the war system. Although environmental insecurity has played a role in past conflicts and wars (e.g., over resources, land, food, and water rights), this may be minor compared to what can be expected in the coming century when strains on the environment will reach an unprecedented scale and complexity. The anticipated doubling of the world population from five billion in 1990 to ten to twelve billion sometime in the twenty-first century is only one indicator of the stress to come. Immense ethical issues are involved. The planet cannot support more than about 2.5 billion people at the economic level now enjoyed by the twenty-four most developed countries; yet most of the world's people aspire to this standard of living.[14] "Already there are more than ten million environmental refugees."[15] Increased environmental degradation will produce increased numbers of refugees, increased economic and political instability, and increased strife within and between countries. National governments may then resort to increased use of military power to protect or seize vital resources or to quell rebellion and maintain law and order. Lacking effective international systems to protect countries against environmental aggression, or assure them equitable access to resources in an environmentally deteriorating world, it is unlikely that countries will disarm. Thus, the other side of the paradox is that *ecological security is essential to world peace.*

Economic pressures seriously compound and intensify the problem, increasing the probability of environmental degradation and conflict. In the poorer countries poverty has been a cause as well as an effect of environmental degradation.[16] Confronted with debilitating foreign debts, rising interest rates, interrupted financial flows, and adverse terms of trade, many poorer countries have tried to rectify a bad economic situation by overusing their resource base and exporting precious natural resources, while ignoring the resulting environmental damage. The long-term effects are likely to include further erosion of economic, human, and ecological health and increased social unrest.

Although their GNP scores may be higher, the richer countries also feel pressed by increasing global economic competition to sacrifice longer-term environmental security for the sake of immediate survival in the global marketplace. Even conscientious governments and corporations will tend to resist environmental protection standards and costs unless their international competitors accept the same requirements. Faced with a choice between being environmentally correct or economically at risk of bankruptcy, plant closings, and unemployment, they opt for economic survival. Or, as is already happening, corporations in countries with higher standards of living, such as Western Europe, Japan, and the United States, may export their toxic wastes, or the polluting aspects of production, to countries with lower standards of income, who may be unaware of or willing to overlook the threats to the environment or health in return for foreign currency.[17] Universal standards of environmental protection are needed so that countries and corporations are not unfairly advantaged or disadvantaged by differing national policies.

In an interdependent world, few, if any, countries are self-sufficient enough to extricate themselves from global economic competition. Thus, local and national solutions alone, or even environmental solutions alone, are inadequate. The transboundary and interactive nature of peace, and environmental and economic security, necessitates developing cooperative global systems that effectively advance all these dimensions of security. Peace, economic well-being, and ecological sustainability are all part of one seamless fabric of global security.

Challenge to Peace Research

Peace research has traditionally focused on such areas of inquiry as conflict analysis and resolution, arms control and disarmament, causes and prevention of war, and the history and strategies of nonviolent action. In this new era, further work in these areas can contribute important insights for global peace and security, but researchers also need to go beyond them to give increased attention to economic and environmental aspects of peace and security. These areas pose new challenges and opportunities for peace research. Most importantly, they require an increased emphasis on peace itself (i.e., concepts, conditions, paradigms, history, dynamics, causes, and structures of peace, not just conflict and war). They require that peace and security be viewed as a total system. Peace research needs to do much more to increase an understanding of the ecology and economy of peace—i.e., of the conditions and interactive and interdependent dynamics of peace as a total system—and of how to advance and sustain a global peace system.

We are at a critical point in history. Even conservative heads of state speak of major changes in world order. The question is not whether there will be a new world order, but rather what kind of world order, based on what values, with what outcome for the world's peoples and the life of the planet? Will it be an order of greater peace and economic and environmental well-being, or of ever greater military, economic, and environmental insecurity? The answer lies in human perceptions of the meaning and scope of security in this new era, and of the best means and systems to promote and sustain it.

INTERGOVERNMENTAL AND CITIZEN INITIATIVES

The development of a world order of greater peace, economic well-being, and ecological sustainability requires initiatives at both intergovernmental and citizen levels. Both deserve the attention of peace research.

Intergovernmental Initiatives

At the intergovernmental level, this era of increasing global interdependence and transboundary environmental threats requires strengthened international law and more effective regional and global arbitration, juridical, and compliance systems. "There has been substantial development of international law in this century. Most of this development has come in the latter half, and especially the latter third of this century, indicating a rising trend. Currently there are more than 140 multilateral treaties that are partially or wholly related to the environment and more are being negotiated."[18] But most of these have been too little, too late, and are too limited and too lacking in compliance mechanism to be effective guarantors of global ecological security.[19] There is still a long way to go.

Recently the international community and some national leaders have given increased attention to international law, including international environmental law, and to the need for more effective global structures for global peace and ecological security. The United Nations declared the 1990s as· the Decade for International Law. In speeches at the United Nations, Mikhail Gorbachev[20] and Eduard Shevardnadze[21] called for a new world order based on strengthened international law. Among other measures, they proposed making the International Court of Justice and the UN Security Council more effective and establishing international systems for monitoring and verifying arms control and disarmament agreements. They also advocated that, where necessary, new global structures be created to enhance the prospects for world peace and for economic and ecological security. George Bush has also espoused a new world order, although he has not fully defined what he means by this in practical terms. However, the use of world order language by the leadership of both powers in the dying days of the Cold War suggests their growing recognition that national policies alone, and even bilateral agreements, are insufficient guarantors of peace and security in an increasingly interdependent world.

The growing recognition in high-level circles of the need for global systems to resolve global problems was also evidenced in a meeting sponsored by the Inter-Action Council (an organization of former heads of government chaired by the former chancellor of West Germany, Helmut Schmidt). The topic of the three-day meeting, held in Lisbon in March 1988, was "Global Interdependence and National Sovereignty: In Search of a New World Order." Invited to give expert input into the deliberations, I found these former heads of government seriously concerned about and receptive to recommendations regarding new conceptions and practical policy proposals for advancing peace and security in a new world order. At the end of the meeting they issued a statement in which they declared:

> The world is at a crucial turning point in its history. Behind us: forty years of cold war, superpower confrontation and ever-burgeoning military arsenals. Before us: the chance to move towards a new era of peace, cooperation and dialogue. . . .
> The management of this era will require new instruments, new forms

of leadership and a new definition of the interrelationship between national and global interests.[22]

The former heads of state went on to make specific recommendations related to peace, the economy, the environment, and human rights. There was clearly a consensus that national and global security encompassed much more than military security. Regarding ecological security, they proposed a number of international initiatives, including: establishing a high authority to set an internationally binding policy framework with regulatory powers; creating regional institutions to manage specific environmental issues such as deforestation and shared water resources; strengthening international environmental law and adopting a convention on transboundary cooperation in environmental matters; establishing a monitoring system related to global environmental protection; and creating a global facility to assist developing countries to establish and implement environmental programs.

Citizen Initiatives:
Toward a Global Culture of Ecological Responsibility

Developing more effective intergovernmental systems is important, but in the case of ecological security, citizen initiatives may be even more important. In questions of war and military security, governments have a monopoly on decisionmaking, but in questions of ecological security, governments alone have not caused all the problems. Many environmental threats originated in the private sector—in our consumer habits, modes of production, and wasteful or negligent behavior. Stronger environmental legislation and enforcement at local, national, and global levels will help but will not in itself be sufficient. There are currently more than 140 international treaties related to environmental protection. But few people know about or pay attention to them. Even if they were made stronger and more effective, it would be almost impossible to enforce these treaties on a global scale unless human beings everywhere adopted the laws in their own hearts, minds, and actions. In short, we need to develop a global culture of ecological responsibility.

A global culture of ecological responsibility requires global civic literacy.[23] This includes understanding human interdependencies and the global institutions and systems people have created. Global civic literacy also requires a deep understanding of the earth system on which our lives and economies depend, and of the ways our human activities affect this life system. It also includes a deep awareness of the effects of our activities on future generations. The choices we make today will affect the earth and human generations far into the future, and we need to choose the future we want for our grandchildren and great-grandchildren. Our new powers over life and death require that our choices be guided by greater moral maturity and wisdom than at any time in past history because the consequences of our choices are so far-reaching.

Around the world many ordinary people are already altering their behavior and undertaking initiatives aimed at advancing ecological security. In many cases citizen groups are leading the way, with governments following far behind. Examples of citizen initiatives include the hug-a-tree movement in India; the Greenbelt movement in Kenya; the movement in the Philippines to create a seat for nature in the legislature; the international rain forest network, through which thousands of people from many different countries are working to save the world's remaining tropical forests; and the Environmental Sabbath, an effort of the world's major religious networks, in collaboration with the United Nations Environment Programme, to help people relate environmental concerns to their respective religious beliefs and practice. Everywhere around the world there are groups of people dedicated to cleaning up rivers, to planting trees, conserving topsoil, preserving biodiversity, and protecting air and water from pollutants and poisons. Many of these projects are being undertaken internationally, with people working across national lines on behalf of their common future.[24]

To illustrate the potential of citizen initiatives, I would like to describe in greater detail two projects with which I am familiar: (1) The Earth Covenant: A Citizen's Treaty for Common Ecological Security and (2) Project Global 2000, in which IPRA is a partner.

- The Earth Covenant:
  A Citizens' Treaty for Common Ecological Security

In this initiative ordinary people from around the world and all walks of life are entering into a covenant to accept responsibility in their personal, occupational, and community lives to protect the integrity of the earth. It is aimed at helping shape a global culture of ecological responsibility.

More than 200 individuals and organizations from forty countries sent written input for the text of the Covenant. In September 1989, eighteen individuals from nine countries met to draft the Covenant based on this input. It is a *covenant* made by and among ordinary people around the world to adopt environmentally safe practices in their personal, civic, and occupational lives. It is also

- A catalyst in the creation of a global culture of ecological responsibility;
- A stimulus for governmental action;
- A springboard for worldwide citizens' action; and
- A global educational tool.

The Earth Covenant has already been

- Translated into over a dozen languages;
- Adopted for use by the United Nations Environment Programme and by Earth Day 1990;
- Used to launch a radio series on the earth, and featured on several other radio and television programs;
- Signed by a number of heads of government as well as thousands of ordinary citizens;
- Included as part of religious worship services and in the final religious vows of one group of Catholic Sisters; and
- Used by civic groups to organize environmental activities in their communities.

Why a "citizens'" treaty?

The Earth Covenant is not a petition to governments. Nor is it antigovernment. It represents a new, more mature stage in democratic participation. We do not need to wait for government legislation to force us to be more environmentally responsible. We can take responsibility for our own actions in the laws we establish in our own hearts and minds. The covenant is an agreement by citizens around the world to join with governments in creating a more ecologically secure future.

When people sign the Earth Covenant, they make a commitment to use whatever talents or resources they have to put the principles of the treaty into effect in their own lives and their own communities. The Covenant is a *process* in which citizens can begin to link together, exchange ideas, and formulate strategies for specific change efforts. In creating a global culture of ecological responsibility, we help to create the political space for governments to be more responsive and effective in protecting the earth.

Why call it a "covenant"?

The word *covenant* reminds us that we are seeking more than just legislative change. On a deeper level, we are establishing laws in our own hearts and minds, and in relationship with one another—laws by which we bind ourselves to be more responsible for the state of our neighborhoods and the state of the earth. We link ourselves with people of different cultures, lifestyles, professions, and histories in a growing global partnership to care for the earth. In light of the fragmentation and alienation of our fast-changing, technological society, there is a spiritual element of renewal in this relationship. We are healing ourselves as well as the earth by recognizing our interconnectedness with one another and with the life systems of the planet.

What makes the Earth Covenant different?

The Earth Covenant takes people into areas not always considered in the environmental debate. The "Four Principles" of the Covenant stress the connection between the protection of nature and of human life. Creating a healthy environment also means making the earth a more just and habitable place for human beings. The Covenant states that we are responsible not only to the earth, but to each other (and the "other" here means those in other cultures and parts of the world, as well as our immediate families and neighbors). If we are aware of our relationship with others, then we have to recognize that protecting the environment means addressing economic and social injustices around the world.

The Earth Covenant helps to go beyond some of the narrow divisions within the environmental movement. It stresses the need for economic and governmental changes on a global as well as local level.

Another distinctive feature of the Earth Covenant is that it does not tell people what to do. Environmental problems and needs vary in different world regions. The Covenant encourages people to find creative ways to respond to the most pressing needs in their local area. Through a newsletter and related educational projects, the Covenant also sets in motion a process of follow-up for local communities and a way for them to hook into an international network of people and organizations. This gives the Covenant flexibility for mobilizing diverse groups on a range of social and environmental issues. It can help such groups renew their commitment to the now popular slogan, "Think globally, act locally."

Restoring the health of the earth requires a cultural transformation of values. If Earth Day proved a spark, then the Earth Covenant provides a continuing fuel in developing a global culture of ecological responsibility. With its attempt to integrate the many dimensions of the environmental struggle, the Earth Covenant can be a rare tool for overcoming divisions and making new alliances in the search for alternatives to social and ecological destruction.

• Project Global 2000

This project will involve teams of scholars, policymakers, and leaders of diverse constituency groups in some fifty countries in research, analysis, and policy development aimed at more effective global systems for common economic and ecological security. IPRA is one of seventeen organizations that has joined in partnership with others to sponsor and implement this project. A primary goal is to develop a transnational forum and process in which the world's peoples can participate in shaping our common future.

The project will involve a broad cross-section of the world's peoples in the *redefinition of security and sovereignty* within a context of global interdependence—a fundamental step toward developing institutions capable of managing threats to common human security. Special priority will be placed on understanding the *interface between economic and ecological systems,* and on policy and institutional changes that would enable these systems to be mutually supportive.

Together, the teams and the partner organizations will

- *Produce national and regional monographs* that examine linkages between economic and ecological security and propose policies and systems that promote equitable and sustainable development;
- *Disseminate these monographs* through the global and national networks of the partner organizations to develop programs to generate wide public understanding and political will to work for those policies and systems; and
- *Build an ongoing global movement* of organizations, institutes, and individuals who can translate the proposals presented in these monographs and programs into concrete policies and systems at local, national, regional, and global levels.

The challenge of creating a cooperative world order cannot be left to governments or political leaders alone. Historically, only during times of cataclysmic world crisis have government leaders engaged in cooperative planning for the restructuring of international relationships and systems. In more normal times, a preoccupation with immediate problems of governance tends to preclude such long-term planning. Moreover, government leaders are often constrained by political, cultural, and ideological considerations from taking positions at variance with long-held assumptions and world views. This is especially true with regard to the need to delegate a degree of sovereignty to create institutions for economic and ecological security. Such political considerations deter most government leaders from providing the vision and leadership needed today.

International nongovernmental organizations (INGOs) can transcend many of the above constraints.[25] They can contribute relevant expertise, institutional linkages, and worldwide networks for research, policy formulation, and public education on global economic and ecological interdependence. Equally important, many INGOs have competence in critical economic, social, and cultural areas that often lie outside the domain of governments.

The task of researching the complex interrelationships between economic and ecological security—and then formulating realistic policies and systems options for coping with this complexity—and, finally, developing national, regional, and global strategies for implementing the policies and creating the systems—requires a global partnership. This is what Project Global 2000 provides.[26]

NOTES

1. Center for Defense Information (CDI), "Defending the Environment: The Record of the US Military," *The Defense Monitor* 18 (6) (1989).

2. Rosalie Bertell, *No Immediate Danger: Prognosis for a Radioactive Earth* (Summertown, Tenn.: The Book Publishing Co., 1985).

3. See, for example, *International Peace Research Association Newsletter* 27 (1) (January 1989), Special Issue on Ecological Security; A. Timoshenko, "International Environmental Law and the Concept of Ecological Security," *Breakthrough* (Summer/Fall, 1989); and Arthur H. Westing, "The Environmental Component of Comprehensive Security," *Bulletin of Peace Proposals* 2 (2) (June 1989): 129-134.

4. J. E. Lovelock, *Gaia: A New Look at Life on Earth* (Oxford: Oxford University Press, 1979).

5. T. Berry, "The Cosmology of Peace," *Breakthrough* (Spring 1984); Patricia Mische, "Ecological Security and the Need to Reconceptualize Sovereignty," *Alternatives* 14 (1989): 389-427; Patricia Mische, "Ecological Security in an Interdependent World," *Breakthrough* (Summer/Fall 1989).

6. L. Timberlake and L. Thomas, *When the Bough Breaks: Our Children, Our Environment* (London: Earthscan Publications, 1990).

7. Berry, "The Cosmology of Peace."

8. T. Berry, "The Ecological Age," in *The Whole Earth Papers* (New York: Global Education Associates, 1979).

9. Rosalie Bertell, "Early War Victims of World War III: Rosalie Bertell Testifies at 1983 Nuremberg Tribunal," *Breakthrough* 5 (4) (Fall 1983); Rosalie Bertell, "The Health of the Oceans," *Breakthrough* 5 (4) (Summer 1984); Rosalie Bertell, *No Immediate Danger*; Rosalie Bertell, "An Appeal for the Marshall Islands," *Breakthrough* 7 (3) (Spring 1986); E. Billiet, "Hibakusha: A Survivor Speaks," *Breakthrough* 7 (3) (Spring 1986).

10. Bertell, "The Health of the Oceans."

11. Admiral Roche in CDI, "Defending the Environment."

12. CDI, "Defending the Environment. "

13. Ibid.

14. Arthur H. Westing, "Constraints on Military Disruption of the Biosphere: An Overview," in *Cultural Norms, War and the Environment*, ed. Arthur H. Westing (New York: Oxford University Press, 1988).

15. J. Jacobsen, *Environmental Refugees: A Yardstick of Habitability*, Worldwatch Paper 86 (Washington D.C.: Worldwatch Institute, 1986).

16. World Commission on Environment and Development, *Our Common Future* (New York: Oxford University Press, 1987).

17. J. Brooke, "African Nations Barring Foreign Toxic Waste," *New York Times*, 23 September 1988; P. Diven, "Our Newest Hazardous Export," *Christian Science Monitor*; "The Global Poison Trade," *Newsweek*, 7 November 1988; D. Pletka, "Developing Nations as Dump Sites," *Insight*, 15 August 1988; Third World Network, "Report on Toxic Waste Dumping in Third World Countries" (Penang, Malaysia: Third World Network, August, 1988).

18. "Special Issue on Ecological Security," *Breakthrough* (Summer/Fall 1989); United Nations Environment Programme (UNEP), *Register of International Treaties and Other Agreements in the Field of the Environment* (Nairobi, 1985); United Nations Environment Programme (UNEP), *Supplement 1 to the Register of International Treaties and Other Agreements in the Field of the*

Environment (Nairobi, 1987).

19. Mische, "Ecological Security and the Need to Reconceptualize Sovereignty"; Mische, "Ecological Security in an Interdependent World."

20. Gorbachev, 1988.

21. Eduard Shevardnadze, "Address to the United Nations," *Provisional Verbatim Record of the Sixth Meeting*, A/43/PV.6, 1988.

22. Inter-Action Council, "Global Interdependence and National Sovereignty: Towards Global Order," statement for the meeting in Lisbon, 9-11 March 1990. The Inter-Action Council has offices at 821 United Nations Plaza, New York, NY 10017.

23. Elise Boulding, *Building a Global Civic Culture: Education for an Interdependent World* (New York: Teachers College Press, Columbia University, 1988; and Syracuse University Press [paperback], 1990).

24. These and other examples of citizen initiatives for global ecological security are described in the Summer/Fall 1989 and Spring/Summer 1990 issues of *Breakthrough*.

25. Elise Boulding, "The Rise of INGOs: New Leadership for a Planet in Transition," *Breakthrough* (Spring 1988).

26. For more information regarding these initiatives, write to: Global Education Associates, Suite 456, 475 Riverside Drive, New York, NY 10115.

CHAPTER 9

Ecodevelopment: What Security for the Third World?

URSULA OSWALD

On the threshold of the twenty-first century, it is important to reflect on the past three decades of development in terms of peace and active nonviolent conflict resolution. What has development achieved—and what effects has it had on the environment, on the world society, and in particular on the Third World?

The first section of this chapter critically reviews the past three development decades and analyzes the repercussions of the global policy in terms of ecology and quality of life. The second section reviews the development myths and explores possibilities for a peaceful postdevelopment utopia.

DEVELOPMENT AND ECOLOGY

After World War II, the United Nations implemented three decades of development, based on Truman's doctrine of developing the world through international help and the transfer of technology and capital from North to South. Development, a new philosophy, was understood to be a holistic concept of world integration—replacing the old paradigm of colonialism— bringing First, Second, Third, and Fourth Worlds into a relationship of more freedom and more equality. The new paradigm was disseminated with vigor and was implemented by United Nations organizations, governments of the First World, the World Bank, the International Monetary Fund, commercial banks, private and public aid agencies, churches, and multinationals. All sent experts, technology, and money to the Third World. The initial exuberant reports of rapid improvement within the underdeveloped countries were gradually overshadowed by the undeniable realities of poverty, hunger, ecological destruction, and other conflicts. Development had become myth.

In 1990, more than three billion human beings were living in poverty—37 percent of those in extreme poverty.[1] For children this means perverse poverty; because of permanent malnutrition they will be limited in their futures both physically and mentally, and they will be unable to achieve an integrated and healthy development of their bodies, personalities, and mental capabilities.

Malnutrition is interrelated with social, agricultural, economic, and ecological phenomena. As an example, 49 percent of the basic corn in the world is used to feed cattle, chickens, and other domestic animals.[2] If this corn were used as human food, 3.6 billion more people could be fed. Corn from the United States alone could feed another 816 million people, and from the Soviet Union, 734 million.[3] The low fifty-four-day world reserve of grain of 1990 was, in part, the result of speculative practices by North American farmers, who reduced cornfield acreages by more than 20 percent, creating an artificial scarcity to improve the international price. Hunger persists also as a result of monopolized commercial structures, worldwide change from basic production to cash crops, ecological destruction, and extremely low purchasing power in the Third World. For all these reasons, malnutrition is not a problem of real scarcity but of structural misspending, monopoly, poverty, power management, and gender- and culture-based oppression. Malnutrition is an integral part not only of the development myth, but also of ecological destruction, as will be shown.

There is no doubt that the green revolution bears a heavy responsibility for the vulnerability and destruction of the ecosystem. At the same time, the green revolution and biotechnology have not brought about the eradication of hunger within the existing socioeconomic and political structures. Besides a large number of landless peasants and unemployed (because of mechanization) rural people, the modernization of agriculture through the green revolution has also brought a significant increase in the use of chemical fertilizers and pesticides—practices that are not linked with improved production. The combined effects of the modernization of agriculture and livestock production have brought desertification and salinization, the so-called *paya-dune* phenomenon. About three billion hectares, or one-quarter of the earth, are severely damaged. Each year we lose more than 200,000 square kilometers of agricultural land; this erosion is an ecological time bomb. Annually, the world is deprived of twenty-five billion tons of humus.[4] This is a severe problem when we realize that the earth needs a minimum of 100 years just to create 2.5 cubic meters of humus.

Finally, we cannot criticize the development myth without including the debt problem and the resulting deep socioeconomic crisis. As Raúl Prebish pointed out, the decade of the 1980s was not only a "lost decade" for Latin America, but for the entire Third World.[5] The external debt expected for these countries in 1990 was about $1,200 billion. In the 1980s, $181.1 billion was bled from Latin America in the form of negative capital flow to the North. Capital flight and the internal transfer of money within multinational corporations are not included in this figure and are difficult to estimate.

Other phenomena that indicate structural violence against the South are commercial transactions, terms of trade, low salaries, foreign assistance, food aid, industrialization, transportation, service sectors, and knowledge and technology transfer. The important question to answer is: Why and how do increasing conflicts in the Third World stemming from social, ecological, cultural, and human destruction affect the whole world and not just the Third World?

The answer can be summarized as follows. There are at least eight major mechanisms for extraction from the South, all of which are linked to the myth of development and ecological abuse. The Third World is

- A backyard *market* where industrial and agricultural overproduction is placed
- A backyard for production in which the North exploits the *cheaper labor force* existing in the South
- For some countries still a cheap source of *raw materials*, especially oil and minerals
- A backyard for *tourism and exotic sex*
- An important *ecological reserve* for the earth—the green lung of the planet because of the tropical rain forests
- A backyard for *human, technological, and military experimentation*
- A backyard for depositing *toxic waste,* such as nuclear or chemical junk
- A backyard to *extract money* through interests, patents, royalties, regalia, unequal terms of trade, multinationalization, and poorly paid labor forces

Faced with worldwide disaster and well-implemented extraction mechanisms from the North, the South must find a way, after a diagnostic phase, to stop this vicious cycle. Is there any chance for the South to shake off this development myth?

STRATEGIES TO OVERCOME THE DEVELOPMENT MYTH AND ENTER PEACEFUL POSTDEVELOPMENT ECOTOPIA

At the present time there are three courses proposed to overcome the poverty and structural mechanisms of violence:

- The integration of liberal and neoliberal economies and the formation of huge economic blocs such as the European bloc joined with an Eastern

European and African backyard; the North American bloc joined with a Latin American backyard; and the Japanese bloc joined with an Asian, perhaps a Pacific, backyard. This course offers little opportunity for the dependent countries. Commerce and production are fundamentally carried on among the industrialized countries, with less and less interaction with the South. In this case, the backyards could lose their future importance to the economic powers. At the same time, this could be an opportunity for them to develop their own forms of organization, interaction, and life.

• The New Economic Order, in which the international relationship would be changed, but without touching the internal social structure and social polarization. This is still a hypothetical proposition.

• An autonomous development with some temporary, sectoral, or regional delinking from the world economy. These autonomous forces would come from below and are based on ecological and nonviolent criteria.

The first model means greater integration into the existing unjust and predatory world order, which has produced so much violence and destruction in the past. Economic development through organizations such as multinational corporations, the IMF, the World Bank, and multilateral organizations with bilateral agreements in the Third World only create an elite in the Third World. This elite serves as a base for establishing expensive, Western-oriented patterns of consumption and culture. As the gap between the elite and the popular sector increases so do violence and ecological destruction increase—in response to the excessive consumption of the rich and the extreme and perverse poverty of the poor. Within this model, Third World countries lost during the last two decades of development $241 per capita in real terms, while Western countries gained $2,711 per capita; that means the Third World went from $731 to $490 and the First World from $7,558 to $10,209.[6] In other words, the gap between the poor and the rich, both between countries and within the poor countries, grows.

A similar process could occur in the second case with the New Economic Order, because only the political and economic elite would have access to the development benefits, and the North would not provide investments or privileges if it could not take advantage of the situation. Unfortunately, economic power corrupts so quickly that the new political elite would soon forget their regional interests. As we can see in a comparative study of China and Saudi Arabia, the increase in GNP will not automatically mean better social and living conditions for all people. The poor nation of China, with a per capita GNP of $290, has an infant mortality rate of 3.2 percent and an illiteracy rate of 13 percent, while rich Saudi Arabia, with a per capita GNP of $6,200, has an infant mortality rate of 7 percent and an illiteracy rate of 49 percent.[7]

There is no chance to achieve a peaceful and ecologically sound future with either of these approaches. What about the third solution: temporary, sectoral, and regional delinking? This strategy would induce many decentralized and diversified processes at local, regional, and national levels. If these processes reinforce local interests and efforts, without any pretension of hegemony, they could permit a different, nonviolent, and postdevelopment course. But, to obtain this utopia, certain basic propositions need to be understood, accepted, and acted on as follows:

• We have to shift from a capitalistic logic of maximization of profits to a productive logic of use. This should be oriented to satisfying basic human needs and security and to respecting the environment and society. Free market ideology that did not improve civil society and democratic participation would not only increase the existing disaster, but would also create a new elite, with more personal than social interests.

• Only by recycling waste and abolishing toxic materials, together with adopting a rational process of horizontal and vertical productive integration in accordance with the environment, can we avoid starvation, famine, poverty, and violence for future generations.

• Individual profit-making ideas have to be replaced by individual and collective self-sufficiency logic, where modern, nondestructive techniques are combined with traditional ones, directed toward increasing environmental recovery and socioeconomic improvement. The basic paradigm is social solidarity and hospitality based on diverse and decentralized cultural experiences.

• Peaceful development is oriented toward conflict resolution, and its starting point is a pluralistic world where ethnic, social, economic, and ecological differences combine in a complex and interdependent relationship, but without exploitation, hegemony, or paternalism.

• There is no peaceful, ecologically sound postdevelopment without personal, family, social, and national security. It cannot be based, as before, on mutual terror and arms; it must be based on the replacement of military industries by human ones oriented toward economic, social, and cultural identity and diversity.

• The only possible way to change, recycle, recover the environment, and facilitate postdevelopment is through integral education and collective consciousness practices.

• Only the integration of women and ethnic, social, and religious minorities into the total life of a society—as spelled out in ecofeminism—can open the way for a democratic and pluralistic world society and participation without paternalism.

The ideas presented here point the way to a peaceful, sustainable green alternative path that could change the nature-society relationship, permit a future for our children, and produce an ecologically viable, nonviolent beginning of the next century: a postdevelopment era of peace.

NOTES

This chapter was translated by Joy Olson.

1. UNICEF, *Informe Sobre el Desarrollo Mundial, 1990*, charts 1 and 6 (Barcelona: UNICEF, 1990), 76-77, 86-87.

2. FAO, *Informe Anual* (Rome, 1988).

3. Rudolf Strahm and Ursula Oswald, eds., *Por esto somos tan pobres* (Cuernavaca, Mexico: CRIM/UNAM, 1990), 63.

4. *Worldwatch Institute Report 1990*, chart 2.3 (Washington, D.C., 1989), 84; *Business Week*, 3 April 1989, 66-68.

5. Raúl Prebish, as quoted by the Comisión Económica para América Latina y el Caribe; México (CEPAL), "Transformación Productiva con Equidad," *Comercio Exterior* 40 (7) (July 1990): 648.

6. Strahm and Oswald, *Por esto somos tan pobres,* 30, 31.

7. UNICEF, *Estada Mundial de la Infancia, 1990*, chart 1, (Barcelona: UNICEF, 1990), 76.

PART III
NEW SECURITY TECHNOLOGIES

Is it possible to reduce threat levels and increase feelings of security—in the sense of feeling safe from harm from outside sources—in situations where there is a long history of hatred, violence, and wanton destruction between parties to a conflict? The answer is yes, given the will to reeducate and strengthen the civil society as distinct from its armed forces (although reeducated armed forces may also have a part to play in societal rebuilding). Two dramatic stories from Africa and one from the UN, covering three continents, tell how the beginnings of trust can be developed in the most unpropitious settings. The closing chapter reminds us of the omnipresence of militaristic elements in every part of culture in most contemporary societies. Part and parcel of the creation of new security technologies is the development of a peace culture in which new ways of dealing with conflict can thrive.

—E. B.

Chapter 10

How Guerrillas Became Peace Builders

Winifred K. Byanyima

In the twentieth century, the East African country of Uganda underwent massive upheavals, from colonization by the British to independence, followed by several brutal dictatorships, to a five-year civil war, and recently, attempts at reconstruction. The dream of self-determination after sixty-eight years of colonial rule was soon shattered by the unspeakable injustices of the primitive fascist dictatorships that followed independence. When all forms of peaceful resistance had been exhausted, the majority of Ugandans saw no alternative but to join an armed struggle to end the years of atrocities and to regain human dignity. An armed resistance aimed at restoring human rights, introducing meaningful democratic rule, reconciling and ensuring the equality of all groups—religious, ethnic, and political—and most important, bringing peace met the basic interests of the masses of suffering Ugandans. By the 1980s, it was clear there was no alternative to the official or state-inspired violence except to resist it in an organized armed struggle.

I will begin by advancing a brief explanation of the sources of conflict that led to twenty-one years of violence and war in postcolonial Uganda. The resistance to and wars against colonialism are beyond the scope of this chapter, but provide a good background for the problems. I will then trace the evolution of a national resistance against dictatorship. The main focus, however, will be on the political struggle of the National Resistance Movement (NRM), which can be called the most important and certainly the latest phase in the Ugandan people's struggle for human rights and democracy. I will attempt to explain the movement's strategy to bring peace and reconciliation among the various political, military, ethnic, and religious groups and to "grow" a new political culture where conflicts and problems are resolved peacefully through negotiations in a broad-based parliament supplemented by a grassroots popular democratic process. I will conclude by assessing the results achieved thus far and the movement's vision of a Ugandan nation of the future.

THE SOURCES OF CONFLICT

The Colonial Legacy and the Distortions Introduced

The area now known as Uganda has for many centuries been inhabited by several different groups of peoples whose customs and traditions go back to diverse roots in the past. Before colonial rule, these groups lived as separate and independent states with different forms of political organization. The kingdoms of Bunyoro, Buganda, Toro, Nkore, and others had clan systems based on lineage and blood kinship. There also existed "segmentary" societies where the elders had most authority, such as the numerous states of the Luo-speaking people and the Bakiga. Migrations of the different groups sometimes brought about a blending of kinship concepts and segmentary politics of consensus of the elders.[1]

The precolonial states often emerged as powerful states trying to establish a pan-Ugandanism. The Bunyoro Empire, for example, had stretched to the far northern border of modern Uganda, and in the south it covered part of northern Tanzania. To the west it covered a large area of modern Zaire. However, these states were not permanent because of their low scientific and technological base. To take the example of Bunyoro again, the ruling Babiito dynasty began to decline in power, and other kingdoms rose at its expense, particularly Buganda, Toro, and Nkore.

The struggle, therefore, of uniting Uganda politically and evolving lasting institutions that would end recurrent upheavals started well before the Europeans drew the borders of Uganda. The Ugandans then had not yet succeeded in these political tasks and were therefore vulnerable to colonization. Because of scientific, technological, and organizational superiority, the colonizers were able to impose order and fragile peace in Uganda by eliminating intertribal wars; but they did very little to consolidate national unity, as this was not in their interest.

The colonial authorities found it useful to divide in order to rule. Uganda was divided into a society of contradictory and mutually suspicious interests. For example, they made central and, to a lesser extent, eastern and western Uganda areas for growing cash crops for export, while making sure that some parts of Uganda, such as the northern region, had no cash crops. One part of the country therefore became the lucky producer of cash crops, and the other became the unfortunate reservoir of cheap labor and of recruits for the colonial army. These inevitable inequalities led to intense and disruptive conflicts of rivalry over access to resources and opportunities between the various ethnic groups concerned. Such resulting inequalities gave rise to perceived superior and inferior ethnic division.

In the precolonial societies, there were, in most cases, no clear-cut distinctions between political, economic, and religious power, as these were usually fused. It was common to find the whole or most of an ethnic or clan group owing allegiance to a particular spiritual/political ruler. The penetration of foreign religions into indigenous political and social systems introduced a new source of conflict in Uganda. The very important contribution that missionaries have made toward development is undeniable. However, it must also be admitted that the new religions in Uganda were used to pursue other interests, causing conflict, disruption, and upheaval. In the last quarter of the nineteenth century when the scramble for Africa began, missionaries became active agents of imperialism. In many parts of Africa the new religions brought with them rivalries, competition, and conflict. In Uganda, religious rivalry between the White Fathers from France and the Anglican missionaries from Britain, on the one hand, and Christians and Muslims (the latter having arrived in Uganda many years before the former), on the other hand, influenced greatly the political developments that followed. When the diplomatic efforts by King Mwanga of Buganda to play one group against the other in order to resist encroaching foreign domination failed, a civil war based on religion ensued; the real war was between France and England, and to a much lesser extent Egypt, for colonial control over Uganda. Even after the British had secured control over all of Uganda, the religious competition for converts and influence among local indigenous leaders continued to give rise to religious antagonism and chauvinism among the African converts.

The new religions sometimes worked against national integration, as in the case of the formation of political parties in the 1950s. The Democratic Party became a party for Catholics, and the Uganda People's Congress was largely a party for Anglicans. The religious polarization had surfaced in the new political parties, which were preparing for independence. Ugandan elites were involved in and continued the old English/French conflict even after taking political power. The new national rulers were neither interested nor able to correct the colonial distortions in the economy and politics. Instead, they mishandled those problems and created new sources of conflict.

Postcolonial Uganda: Other Sources of Conflict

The colonial period lasted sixty-eight years, after which a constitution was hastily drafted, discussed (at the inevitable Lancaster House), and passed by the British Parliament in June 1962, ensuring that power was transferred to those elite groups that could best be trusted to serve British interests in Uganda after independence. The majority of Ugandans did not participate in the constitution-making process. In fact, the constitution was mainly concerned with protecting the interests of the elite who were represented in London at the Lancaster Conference and with rewarding the allies of the departing colonial rulers.

The British government made sure that Uganda was to continue to provide a market for British manufactured goods and to be a source of raw materials and primary commodities such as copper, coffee, tea, and cotton. The British found collaborators in a new class of Ugandans who wanted to maintain the old system in order to inherit the privileges of the departing colonial administrators. In 1962, the British withdrew, having secured Uganda's neocolonial state, leaving its predominantly peasant population vulnerable to, yet heavily dependent on, the international coffee market with all its vagaries.

Upon independence, a parliamentary structure based on the Westminster model was adopted. This system, apart from being new and not well understood even by the elite themselves who were the actors, was not truly representative because it did not allow the majority to participate in decisionmaking for their communities. The reality that soon became evident was that parliamentary democracy was a mere disguise; actual power remained firmly in the hands of foreign nations and their Ugandan allies holding high public office.

The first civilian government after independence did not enjoy popular support. It had been brought to power by Britain as preferable to the more internally popular, predominantly Catholic party. Lacking a political base, the leaders tried to remain in power by whipping up the already existing ethnic differences, especially in the armed forces. Unable to articulate a development program that could meet the national expectations characterizing the struggle for independence, they became absorbed in maintaining power by promoting factional interests. To remain in power they found that the political distortions introduced by colonialism served them well. Fostering wider national interests was not only beyond the capacity of these elites but was seen to contradict their own personal or group interests. The new leadership lacked a national vision, had a limited outlook, and was undisciplined. Therefore, the absence of an ideologically competent political force aimed at independence and capable of harmonizing the existing contradictions was a major cause of the growth of internal conflicts.

Economic factors also had a bearing on the problem of national unity. There were parasitic economic interest groups in the country that have been mainly responsible for the perpetuation of sectarian politics in Uganda. These interest groups used ethnic groups, which are in themselves harmless and form the basis of Ugandan society, as cheap political platforms to unfairly get into positions of power or influence, then used that power and influence to gain personal economic advantage.

Modern religions were used in the same manner. (I call these groups parasitic because they acquired power and positions that they did not use to benefit the country; they took from the public but could not or would not reciprocate.) These parasitic groups developed a stake in the bad type of politics prevailing in Uganda after independence. The Civil Service, parastatal organs, public institutions, and industry recruited personnel on the basis of ethnicity, nepotism, and similar harmful criteria. The effect of these practices not only increased conflict and tension by excluding certain groups from participation, but also immobilized the potential of a large number of Ugandans who could have made substantial contributions to the country.

A narrow economic base that could not accommodate the competing interests of different social groups was also a major source of conflict. The elite, who competed ferociously for the facilities of the semimodernized, but hardly expanding, economy, were, to a large extent, responsible for the internal conflicts after independence.

Other factors contributed to the sharpening and increasing number of conflicts in Uganda. For example, certain external interests whose prosperity depended on Uganda's weaknesses allied themselves to the sectarian politicians and other elites. But the major sources of conflict were the inherited colonial distortions in the economy and politics, the absence of a competent political force, the exploitation of religious and ethnic loyalties by parasitic economic interest groups, and the narrow economic base that was not expanding and was unable to satisfy the growing interests of different social groups.

THE EVOLUTION OF A NATIONAL RESISTANCE MOVEMENT

Within three years of independence, the British-style parliamentary democracy had collapsed, and by the fourth year, the constitution was abrogated. The right to vote was meaningless, not only because "parliamentary democracy" in Uganda had never been democratic, but also because elections simply were not called when they were due. As external exploitation increased (infiltration of the army, police, and intelligence services by foreign powers, fluctuating international markets, institution of trade barriers, etc.) and internal contradictions deepened, the elite leaders continued to compete among themselves for the privileges of official positions. The people's discontent was met with coercion, and for this purpose a brutal and repressive machinery was developed.

The first civilian dictatorship of Milton Obote was brought to an abrupt end by Idi Amin's military coup d'état in 1971. It is estimated that 500,000 women, men, and children were killed during the eight years of Amin's fascist regime. Yet, in essence, Amin's regime was similar to the one it had replaced; both were, as it became increasingly clear, agencies of one or several foreign powers.

It was during the repression of the first civilian dictatorship of Obote that some Ugandans first organized—under the student movement of the sixties; then, during Amin's rule, they joined together under FRONASA (Front for National Salvation). Later, during the interim period following Amin's downfall in 1979, they expanded under the movement of the broad UNLF (Uganda National Liberation Front), which eventually became the NRM (National Resistance Movement) after the rigged elections of 1980. The young leaders understood very clearly that the colonial instruments of power, like the army and the police, had been handed over to protect the agents of colonialism against the people. It was not possible to achieve real independence when these agents were perpetuating the divisive and oppressive tactics the colonialists had used to subjugate the African people. The civilian dictatorship of Milton Obote and the military dictatorship of Idi Amin had developed a primitive fascism that could only be overthrown by the suffering Ugandans organizing an armed struggle.

To understand the reasons for the war of resistance, it is important to understand that at this stage war was not seen as one of several alternatives to solve Uganda's problems. It was the last resort of women and men who had suffered for nineteen years the excesses and atrocities of three violent dictatorships. The people had tried to resist nonviolently but without success. Parliamentarians who, in the 1960s, had spoken against the first regime had been imprisoned without trial under emergency laws, and demonstrators had been shot. In the 1970s, peasants cut down their coffee trees in an attempt to stifle Amin's coffee-for-arms deals, but Amin borrowed money from keen foreign lenders for more weaponry. Politicians, journalists, academics, preachers, lawyers, judges, and other protesters were killed openly or disappeared forever. Exiled Ugandans urged governments and international organizations to ostracize Amin's regime; they campaigned for an economic blockade, but received no response. Only Tanzania rejected Amin's government and consistently opposed it.

The Guerrilla War, 1981–1985

The two years after Amin's fall were marked by a growing power struggle between the old politicians (heavily backed by their foreign sponsors) and the young and relatively unknown leadership of the nationalist and antifascist movement. In 1981, after a massively rigged election, the NRM, led by the now mature student leaders of the sixties, declared a protracted people's war on the second, foreign-backed civilian dictatorship led by Obote. The struggle against Amin from 1971 to 1978 had been hijacked by the old agents, but this time able and competent Ugandan leadership organized the armed resistance against another dictatorship (1981 to 1985).

Before explaining the broad strategy for peace within the context of a guerrilla war and later for a broad-based government, I should emphasize that whereas conflicts are characteristic of all groups and societies, it is misleading to lump all conflicts into one category. A conflict can be healthy and justified or it can be unjustified and illegitimate. Conflicts between Ugandan traditional rulers against colonial occupation forces were justified. It is not correct to say that Ugandans should have accepted colonial rule without resistance simply to avoid conflict. However, the conflicts that have followed have been unprincipled and unnecessary, arising from the mishandling of political and economic problems by the interest groups in leadership, which Ugandans had eventually to challenge and remove from power.

The conflict that led to the two wars mentioned above (the struggle against Amin, 1971–1978, and the resistance war against Obote's regime, 1981–1985) was unavoidable. It was a conflict between primitive neocolonial forces on the one hand and nationalistic and modernistic forces on the other. It was a conflict between the humiliation of the Ugandan people and their struggle to assert their dignity and humanity.

War is not the desirable way to resolve conflict. Ugandans had attempted peaceful resolution of their conflict with the dictators, but had failed. Even the OAU and the UN had failed to intervene when there was not a shadow of doubt about the genocide that was taking place during the dictatorships. When some people are pursuing illegitimate interests, peace cannot be achieved. Through a very painful process, women and men of all classes and backgrounds acknowledged the fact that peaceful means had failed to end the aggression of dictators and to bring Uganda to democratic rule. Instead, violence had escalated to horrendous levels. The situation left people with one option: the support of an armed struggle to defend their families and homes against the violence meted out to them by the government that was supposed to protect them.

A STRATEGY FOR PEACE AND RECONCILIATION

The strategy for peace can be seen within the context of the protracted people's war, the formation of a broad-based government, and the implementation of the ten-point program since the NRM took power in 1986.

The Protracted People's War

We have already seen that some form of organized violence was the only option left for Ugandans to resist state-sponsored violence against them. The violent situation pertaining in the country left no social group unaffected. That is why it was not difficult to mobilize people from different classes, ethnicities, and religions in the resistance. At this stage in 1981, the NRM leadership had to decide on a strategy to adopt for the struggle. The choice of strategy depended on the movement's mission, which was perceived to be that of changing the political system through the involvement of people in a struggle for democracy, human rights, peace, and development. The change had to be organic, beginning from the bottom and moving upward. The choice of strategy also depended on the means available to make war. A Protracted People's War (PPW) was declared on 6 February 1981. The strategy of PPW was not a new one; the NRM had not created it. It had been used in Vietnam, China, Cuba, Mozambique, Algeria, and other countries. However, in all these cases the enemy was easily identified as the foreign power trying to occupy the indigenous people's country or actually doing so.

In the case of Uganda, identifying "the enemy" was not as simple. To understand and define to people "the enemy" was a delicate yet very important task. The struggle could easily have failed if at any stage there had been ambiguity on this question, especially on the part of the leadership. So, who or what was "the enemy" to be fought?

Because of the history of violence and repression, the people mobilized in the resistance, who were from different social groups, were able to easily identify their common interests: human rights, democracy, peace, and better living conditions. An analysis of the obstacles to the attainment of these objectives was followed. Through a process of political education, resistance fighters and supporters were able to understand that "the enemy" was, first and foremost, a series of attitudes and perceptions: primitive fascism, superstition, ethnocentricity, and religious bigotry—all these and other backward attitudes were the enemy to be eliminated. As long as these attitudes remained among the leaders and the people, there would be no peace, and foreign interference in the affairs of Uganda would remain.

The means to destroy these attitudes were both political and military. Politically through mass mobilization and education, the people would learn to articulate their interests, see through the divisive tactics of the dictators, and value the unity of the country. Militarily, the resistance, refusing to accept dictatorial rule, would defend the population against the army of the dictator. It was always emphasized that a soldier fighting on the side of the dictator was not an enemy but a misguided Ugandan and the resistance fighter had a duty to try to win him or her to the people's side. When captured, therefore, government soldiers were well treated and well fed, and the wounded were given whatever medical treatment was available. They were all given a choice: to observe and learn about the goals and methods of the NRM, and to join if they wished, or return to their homes. This practice, which was derived from the movement's political analysis and strategy of struggle, was crucial in dismantling the ethnic suspicions that had been created in all the Ugandan government's armies after independence.

The first reason for the choice of a Protracted People's War was to involve the majority of Ugandans in the struggle against primitive dictatorships and neocolonialism. For this reason, among others, strategies like urban terrorism, and the assassination of political leaders were ruled out. These strategies were viewed as not empowering the people and were therefore in contradiction with the movement's primary objective.

The second reason for choosing this particular strategy was related to the movement's perceived mission. Given that the forces of foreign domination (which always allied themselves with the dictators) were superior to the nationalist forces, technologically and organizationally, it was essential to evolve a leadership group that could stand the test of time in national liberation. In order to cut off external influence to resist neocolonialism, an ideologically well-trained leadership that thoroughly understood the politics of nationalism was required. It was necessary for leaders to acquire organizational skills and learn about resolving conflict, harmonizing contradictions, and cooperating with and/or coopting other groups resisting the undemocratic regime in power without compromising the movement's primary goals.

To oppose better-organized and well-entrenched forces, the NRM recognized the need to evolve a culture of resistance among its leaders. There are many examples in history of struggles that collapsed because of the lack of resilience. A capacity to surmount hardship was required in the situation of war and after. Suffering hunger in the bush, for example, could be necessary preparation for accepting a poor wage after the war of resistance. Even after overthrowing neocolonial forces, the Ugandan nationalists realized that they could not survive alone. The process would continue in a struggle for Africa. Therefore, the length of time and the tough conditions associated with the chosen strategy were seen as advantages for forming future leaders.

Although the main reasons for the war declared by the NRM in 1981 were clear, it was necessary that at every stage of the war the principles being fought for were being practiced by the NRM fighters and leaders themselves. Most important, the NRM relied, both as a means and an end, on mobilizing the people of Uganda as a whole, rejecting factionalism and emphasizing the independence of political processes in Uganda as the only way to solve national problems. The NRM was able to show that it is possible to defeat repression through self-reliance and, therefore, to lay the foundation for the peaceful resolution of internal conflicts without any external interference.

The movement brought together peasants and intellectuals; monarchists and republicans; Marxists, socialists, and supporters of the free market; Catholics, Protestants, Muslims, and spiritualists to struggle for peace, human rights, and democracy. The merging of different social classes and strata in this common struggle has in itself been a major factor in building peace. A new leadership with shared goals and working methods has developed and is still growing. Working together both during the war and in government is helping to break down, among the leaders from different backgrounds, the harmful barriers that have existed for decades. For the first time, too, the peasant majority have been organized and empowered to influence Uganda's political direction, and they continue to be represented in the government.

During the war, it was found necessary to articulate a minimum political program that would form the basis for a national coalition of democratic, political, and social forces after the war. The ten-point minimum political program summarizes the basic points of agreement within the NRM and also sheds some light on the common vision of what the nation of Uganda should be. Briefly, the points are: democracy; security of person and property; consolidation of national unity and elimination of all forms of sectarianism; defense and consolidation of national independence; building of an independent, integrated, and self-sustaining national economy; restoration and improvement of social services and the rehabilitation of the war areas; elimination of corruption and misuse of power; and the redressing of errors that have resulted in the dislocation of sections of the population. Additional points include cooperation with other African countries in defending human and democratic rights of the African people throughout the continent and developing a mixed economy strategy. The implementation of some of these points to achieve peace and reconciliation will be discussed later. It is around this political program that the NRM has formed a broad-based interim government that represents all political parties, ethnic groups, religions, sexes, and age groups.

The Politics of the Broad Base

The principle of achieving the broadest possible unity for the people of Uganda by operating through popular committees and utilizing a broad-based national government is regarded by the movement as the most effective way to achieve unity. A lack of unity was one of the main reasons why the Ugandan precolonial states were conquered and ruled for nearly seventy years. It is also the reason why after independence incompetent, intellectually inadequate, brutal dictators were able to take and hold state power for a long time. National unity is a primary objective of the movement. But the concept of a broad-based government is being discussed nationally within the framework of drafting a new constitution. Whereas the interim government formed by the NRM in 1986 and still in power today is broad-based, the movement accepts that it is the people who must decide, by participating in the formulation of the new constitution, what kind of government they will have. And this they must do before the next elections, due in 1995.

The implementation of the broad base can be said to have been successful in that a government of diverse political tendencies has been able to work together for four years. Despite all the bitter divisions of the past, all political parties agreed to take part in the National Resistance Council (NRC)—parliament—and in the election of the grassroots Resistance Committees. The parties fielded candidates who stood not on partisan lines, but as individuals. Despite the successful implementation of the movement's ideal, the imposition of broad-based politics would contradict the basic goal of empowerment. Should the people decide to tackle national problems in separate political forums, the NRM is prepared to accept that choice because of its historical mission to empower Ugandans.

The broad base also ensures the inclusion of all social and political groups and thereby enhances peace. In a country where discrimination and exclusion from decisionmaking has been the constant practice, the need for all to share power is great and urgent. The resistance itself was broad-based; it had been supported by people from different political parties, members of the national army, and others; as such it was imperative for the NRM to form a broad-based government when it took power in 1986. Not doing so would have caused disappointment and feelings of betrayal and resentment among many supporters of the war of resistance. The formation of a broadly based government was therefore a strategy to satisfy, through inclusion in decisionmaking, not only all those who supported the resistance but also representatives of all socio/political/military groups in Uganda.

The Ten-Point Program and Its Implementation

As a matter of illustration, it is important to explain how some points of the program are being implemented to achieve peace and reconciliation and to introduce a new, civilized, and modern political culture.

Democracy. For the NRM, democracy has to consist of three elements to be meaningful: parliamentary democracy, popular democracy, and a decent living for every Ugandan. It is significant that the war of resistance was declared soon after a parliamentary election had been rigged by Obote. The movement believes that it is the right of Ugandans to elect a parliament at regular intervals and that these elections should be free of corruption and manipulation. To supplement parliamentary democracy there should be people's committees at the village, parish, subcounty, and district levels. This allows the majority of Ugandans to participate actively in decisionmaking for their communities. Democracy in politics, however, is not possible without a reasonable standard of living for the people. Illiterate, sick, superstitious Ugandans do not actually take part in the political process of the country even if the structures exist. They are easy prey for the elite to manipulate by taking advantage of their ignorance. The NRM, therefore, views democracy in a total context of emancipation. What did the movement do during and after the war to realize the people's expectation of democratic rule?

During the war, popular democracy was not merely promised by the NRM; it was established in the war zones through cells with Resistance Committees (RCs or Bukiiko). To be able to choose leaders and to participate in decisionmaking in their communities was a completely new and liberating experience for the people. People in the war zones could sit on the Bukiiko and choose their representatives—dismiss them if they failed in their duties or were corrupt or unfair. Since the war ended, the system has spread throughout the country. A five-tier system of administration based on councils and committees of citizens has been established. Two statutes have been passed by the NRC (parliament) giving judicial and political powers to the citizens through these councils and committees.

In 1989, the NRC, which consisted of the founders of the movement, was expanded through a new process of voting leaders into office. The elections promoted unity because they enabled the electorate to choose representatives who would articulate the interests of the people rather than base their decisions on their own partisan, ethnic, or religious interests.

To be truly representative the movement considers that women should participate at all levels in the political structure. Therefore, each district has a woman representative in the NRC, and at all the grassroots levels every ten-member committee has one guaranteed seat for a women's representative. Apart from the district-level women's representatives, the NRC also has some women who contested and won constituencies like their male counterparts. There are still many questions being asked as to whether this system satisfactorily includes women and takes their interests sufficiently into account, but at least it is a beginning. Fourteen percent of the parliament are women and, more important, at the grassroots level many Resistance Committees have an even higher rate of participation by women.

Youth and workers also have guaranteed seats in the NRC. The National Resistance Army, which was initially the armed wing of the NRC (also the founder of the NRC) is now the National Army, having integrated into itself the defeated soldiers of the last dictatorship.

The interim government has the duty to put into place structures and institutions to ensure the development and protection of a democratic process. Elections are to be held in 1995. The government is expected, among other things, to formulate, discuss, and enact a constitution; reinforce the judiciary; develop police and prisons services; and develop a reliable civil service.

Security. The war of resistance was ignited by the rigging of a national election, but the underlying cause—the denial for twenty-one years of human rights to life and honestly earned property—was the real catalyst for the guerrilla war. The movement vowed to end state-inspired violence and to be on the side of the people against terror and bad leadership. The leaders in power and their armies abused the human rights of the people because, having no mandate to rule, they could do so only by coercion. It was a case of the rulers against the people, and the NRM saw as its duty the liberation of the people from bad leadership. However, the question of violence and abuse of human rights was closely linked and could not be separated from the absence of a democratic culture and democratic structures. It is why democracy comes first on the minimum political program.

Apart from evolving a popular democratic system, the movement built a politically conscious and highly disciplined guerrilla army. A high level of discipline was also maintained by political leaders in the movement. The guerrilla army would replace the criminal army of the regime in power. Moreover, the strategy of Protracted People's War required that the guerrillas win the people on their side in order to be successful. The human rights record in the war zones was exemplary, while on the other hand the civilian dictator had to depend more and more on coercion and repression as the war spread. As a result, the NRM became the unchallenged champion of human rights in Uganda. Political education in the guerrilla army played an important role here. Discipline, honesty, humility, and self-sacrifice were rewarded. Nondisciplined behavior, intrigue, cliquishness, and arrogance were discouraged. The Resistance Committees were also forums for education—political, human rights, people's rights—with their concomitant responsibilities. This was a very important stage in the political development of Uganda, as it had almost become accepted that the leaders, and particularly the army, must be criminal and unaccountable to the people. Restoring people's faith in leadership and in the army was important.

To restore security and the rule of law, the NRM government needed to reestablish the structures and institutions of state eroded by past regimes, in particular the local government structure, the judiciary, police, prison services, and the army. After the war, the government recruited a nationally balanced army with a professional code of conduct. Every nationality in a district was given a quota to fill within the national army. The same system has been used to recruit for the police and prison services. The code of conduct lays emphasis on cooperation among soldiers of all ranks, democratic methods in decisionmaking, mastery of military science, and political education. It condemns sectarianism, corruption, intrigue, and clique formation within the army.

When the movement took power in 1986, it had defeated all other military groups existing in Uganda, as they all had joined the last military government of Tito Okello (which succeeded Obote's dictatorship and was in power for six months). The reorganization of defeated forces (political and military) and their integration into the national political process was a major component of the movement's short-term and long-term strategy for building unity and peace. All defeated soldiers were given the choice of being integrated into the NRA; this was important because some districts of Uganda had become the recruiting ground for the army, and those districts offered few other possibilities for earning a living. Resettlement programs for those soldiers not integrated were started, and they have also received technical and financial assistance from international agencies.

A national amnesty was declared to all who had been involved in the war, and this amnesty is still valid. It covers institutional crimes but does not protect those who committed personal crimes from being prosecuted under the law. Most of the soldiers who were not of the NRA have now been integrated, and the political preparatory schools that were set up for their integration have now been closed.

Changes of government in Uganda had in the past been followed by revenge massacres of innocent people from the ethnic group of the deposed leader. Amin eliminated all soldiers in the National Army who belonged to Obote's ethnic group, and his soldiers committed genocide in the districts of Lango and Acholi, the home base of Obote. When Amin was overthrown, forces loyal to Obote also waged a war of revenge on the people of the West Nile and Madi districts, Amin's ethnic group. As far as the NRM was concerned, the question of revenge did not arise; its army did not represent the interests of any one ethnic group, and its aim was to unite, not to further divide. For the people the example of "no revenge" was particularly reassuring. Half a million refugees who had escaped from the vengeful wars of the past (300,000 of these were from the Sudan) were peacefully repatriated. The government appealed for and received substantial assistance for their resettlement.

Ugandans had suffered at the hands of criminal armies. Twenty thousand soldiers could terrorize a population of fifteen or sixteen million people. People were weak and frightened of the "armed men." It was therefore necessary to demystify the gun. By involving many people in the security system through local defense forces, the fear of a few "armed men" would be dispelled; villages and towns would be more secure, since a police force barely existed in 1986, and Ugandans would be mobilized to protect and defend, if necessary, the democratic system they themselves were evolving.

A human rights commission was set up to investigate past violations. As new cases come up, the commission continues to confirm the movement's commitment to respect human rights, and it also serves as a balm for the pain borne by many Ugandans. Its proceedings are followed very closely and reported in detail in the daily newspapers.

National unity. Lack of unity was a principal cause of strife in Uganda. It enabled foreign powers to colonize Africa and allowed colonialism to continue. Lack of unity in Uganda enabled incompetent dictators like Amin to take power illegally and retain it. For too long the people of Uganda were fragmented by opportunistic politicians and could not, working through such leaders, unite to confront the common problem of underdevelopment stemming from foreign domination.

From the earliest stages of the resistance, sectarianism, with all its permutations, was rigorously opposed. Unity was in the interest of the people, so that whoever impeded unity was an enemy of the people of Uganda. Sectarianism fragmented the people's efforts toward emancipation and encouraged fratricidal conflicts.

The broad-based government is a major component of the process of building nationalism. The coalition nature of government is reflected not only in the NRC and cabinet but also in the lower levels of government such as the leaders of Ugandan foreign missions, parastatal bodies, companies, and financial institutions.

Regional political schools for the army and civilians were established. The objectives of the schools are to develop Ugandans' sense of national identity and pride in their culture and heritage. Political education will also be introduced into school and college curricula.

The process of formulating a new constitution, that would be widely accepted, is also a part of the process of unification. For the first time in the country's history, the majority of people are actively involved in deciding on the laws that will govern them in the future. Peace cannot be achieved when the operational constitution protects the interests of only a few people.

A law prohibiting discrimination based on ethnic or religious considerations has been enacted. The issue of building one nation has assumed importance because of these steps. The movement believes that by uniting people through these laws, it is tackling the source of Uganda's internal conflicts.

National independence. The NRM acknowledges the failure of national independence in Uganda and attributes blame for this to the leaders since independence—9 October 1962. Decolonization, although tactical, was nevertheless a retreat resulting from the worldwide transformation of relations between the masters and the subject people. It would have been possible for Uganda to exercise independence if the leaders had not been intellectually, ideologically, politically, and morally inept. Uganda's struggle for democracy and human rights illustrates very clearly the problems associated with a national condition of dependency. Idi Amin was originally courted by the Western countries, and when he fell out with them, he quickly joined the Soviet camp. The Soviets and African left-wing governments that had hitherto supported the people's struggle against Amin then changed their minds and asked the nationalists now to work with Amin. The West denounced him but continued to supply him with weapons for his reign of terror. Obote in the late 1960s had been rejected by the West because they erroneously thought he was a socialist. When he returned to power through a rigged election and began another violent dictatorship, the West wanted Obote to be given "a chance," since he had now become a convert of the IMF. If the movement had not pursued its own independent line in the struggle, Uganda would still be swapping one fascist dictator for another, depending on the interests of other countries in Uganda's future. For there to be peace and development, the people working through their democratic institutions must be in control of their economy, politics, and culture. The movement, therefore, maintains an independent line in economics, politics, culture, and foreign relations. Relationships with other countries are judged according to how they interact with Uganda's interests, irrespective of the social systems obtaining in them.

The interim government's foreign policy has been nonaligned. The mixed economy being pursued consists of values from both the Eastern and Western social systems. The government also aims at achieving both regional and continental integration of Africa.

CONCLUSION

Although the National Resistance Movement has been in power for only four years, its leadership has been engaged in the struggle for democracy, human rights, and independence for more than twenty years. There are still many problems to solve, especially that of liberating the country from its underdeveloped economic and technological position. However, the main problem that had plagued Uganda since independence—the problem of inadequate and illegitimate leadership—has largely been resolved. The foundations for building a democratic, united, and peaceful nation are being laid in a careful and systematic manner. Ugandans are learning to trust their leaders and, more important, to practice democracy. A peaceful culture and civilized political behavior, it is hoped, will emerge from the long and courageous struggle of the nationalists of the NRM.

NOTE

1. A. R. Dunbar, *A History of Buyoro-Kitara* (Nairobi: Oxford University Press, 1965).

CHAPTER 11

From Confrontation to Mediation

HENDRIK W. VAN DER MERWE
ANDRIES ODENDAAL

The almost exclusive concern with the Cold War on the part of some peace researchers has led to suggestions that now, with the end of the Cold War, there is no further need for peace research. In the same spirit people have asked: Now that apartheid in South Africa is being phased out and the white government and the black opposition are talking to each other, is there any further need for mediation?

The end of apartheid, like the end of the Cold War, does not mean the end of conflict and violence. In his opening address of the Twenty-fifth Anniversary Conference of the International Peace Research Association, Hylke Tromp argued that everybody lost the Cold War. Both leading world powers in the post–Cold War era are faced with problems such as "stagnation, pollution, corruption, organized criminality, unemployment, alcoholism, drug-abuse and scandals in government agencies."[1]

The end of apartheid marks the end of colonial rule. But the end of colonial rule does not mark the introduction of utopia. Birgit Brock-Utne of the University of Dar-es-Salaam quoted Issa G. Shivji, who complained, after three decades of independence, that the national liberation movements rule through the barrel of the gun and that mass parties are "riding on the backs of the masses and presiding over authoritarian legal and political systems."[2] She also quoted Ben Turok, who talked about "the false assumption that the removal of colonial rule would usher in democratic government."[3]

In Africa, as in Europe, new problems and new forms of conflict and violence emerge as old problems diminish. Continued and renewed conflict and violence also occur in South Africa.

THE SHIFT FROM IDEOLOGICAL RACISM TO PRAGMATISM

The unbanning of the African National Congress (ANC) and the Pan-African Congress (PAC), and the drastic steps taken by the de Klerk government to break down apartheid even before negotiations began, did not come as a complete surprise. For a number of years it was evident that the basis of the political conflict in South Africa was shifting away from the commitment to maintain white racial purity and privilege.[4] With this shift, new emphases and new political dynamics came into play, influencing the prospect of a peaceful negotiated settlement. Apartheid has lost its ideological character for a significant part of the white establishment. It is only in right-wing circles that the vision of people like the late Hendrik Verwoerd still survives.

An important factor that contributed to the shift away from ideological apartheid to greater pragmatism was the erosion of the moral base of apartheid. With the development of the ideology during the 1940s and 1950s, Afrikaner politics was slowly, but fatally, theologized. The National Party (NP) became imbued with a secular religion.[5] During the 1970s and 1980s, however, the theological basis of apartheid came under attack, not only from the worldwide Christian community, which reached almost complete consensus that apartheid should be viewed as a heresy, but also from inside the Afrikaner churches. A growing number of theologians, pastors, and members of the Afrikaner churches identified with the view that apartheid is a fundamental contradiction of the Christian gospel.[6] A process of theological retraction became clear, for example, in the Dutch Reform Church, with the General Synod of 1986 almost admitting that its justification of apartheid was a major blunder.

With the acceptance, at least intellectually, by Nationalist leaders that the removal of apartheid was inevitable, came the realization that if whites wanted to retain any political power at all, they had to share it. Power sharing became an option as distinct from majority rule. Majority rule, at least according to the Westminster model, means that the winner, in this case inevitably the blacks, will take all—leaving virtually no possibilities for meaningful participation in political decisionmaking for minorities such as the whites. Power sharing, however, means steering away from the adversarial approach and inventing a form of majority rule in which minority groups are assured of meaningful participation. De Klerk's concept of power sharing is, therefore, in no way meant to ensure white domination.

An interesting example of the shifting alliances in South African politics is the fact that whereas the concept of power sharing between the NP and, for example, the ANC became a strong possibility, no power sharing is possible between the two major white parties. It is unthinkable that either the NP or the Conservative Party (CP) will appoint members of the opposite party in its cabinet. It is, however, a strong possibility that a future ANC government of national unity may have people like F. W. de Klerk, Pik Botha, and Barend du Plessis in its cabinet. De Klerk can share power with Mandela, but not with Treurnicht, leader of the CP.

It is not only in white politics, however, that the basis of conflict is shifting. Simmering differences and conflicts among black opposition and liberation groups have burst into ferocious violence in various parts of the country. Disagreements about the models of society—capitalist, communist, socialist, africanist, etc.—and methods used to attain these goals—incremental change, working within the system, violence, democratic means, etc.—have been the causes of extensive violence and the loss of hundreds of lives. Whereas the ANC has demonstrated its own shift toward greater pragmatism, the PAC and the Azanian People's Organisation (AZAPO) have picked up the ideological torch and are attracting increasing numbers because of their unbending stand on ideological issues.

FREE MARKET VERSUS A CONTROLLED ECONOMY

The idea has generally been accepted within government circles that the economic cake of South Africa should be cut in a much more equitable way and that socioeconomic backlogs should be addressed. The remaining problem relates to the way in which wealth has to be redistributed. Van der Merwe has identified an emerging process in the 1980s of the reformulation of interests away from racist economic policies toward a (nonracist) divide between free-market and controlled economic systems.[7] In favor of a free market are the parties currently represented in parliament and Inkatha. In favor of a controlled economy are the ANC/UDF, AZAPO, and the PAC, which show a strong ideological commitment to African socialism. *Nationalization* and *privatization* have become catchwords that are dividing the players.

"Nationalization," however, is more than just a rational statement of economic policy. "Ideologies fulfill basic human needs and the development of conflicting ideologies around perceptions and models of the socio-economic system is inevitable."[8] W. Thomas gave an explanation of some of the basic needs symbolized by "nationalization."[9] The concept is a powerful symbol of participation and co-ownership to the millions of South Africans who have not yet participated in the economic decisionmaking process in the country. It is the lever that black leaders hope to use to, inter alia, create job opportunities (over against the rationalization/mechanization process), redistribute ownership of the economy (with 90 percent of ownership of shares currently in white hands), address the issue of land ownership, and so on. In short, the outcry from the free marketeers that socialism has proved itself a failure is unlikely to impress those in favor of nationalization unless convincing alternatives can be found that address the same needs. The call for nationalization served the same needs among Afrikaners when they first gained political control in the 1920s and again in 1948.

PROSPECTS OF A PEACEFUL NEGOTIATED SETTLEMENT

The prospects of a peaceful negotiated settlement depend on (a) the extent to which the major contenders, the National Party and the ANC, can come to terms; (b) the extent to which other political actors can be assured of full and meaningful participation in the process of a negotiated settlement and in the government that will emerge; and (c) the extent to which the leaders will be able to sell to their followers whatever agreements they have made.

Proceeding from the assumption that no settlement can guarantee any lasting peace as long as parties that have the power to disrupt the outcome are left out of the negotiating process, or are unsatisfactorily accommodated, it is clear that third-party interveners and neutral mediators have a vital role to play. It is unlikely that the NP or the ANC will be too concerned about accommodating the smaller parties. The way in which the rapprochement between Mandela and Buthelezi has been thwarted by elements within the ANC, for example, indicates their determination that Inkatha will have no seat at the negotiation table.

Third-party interveners and neutral mediators will be able to make valuable contributions. Dennis Worrall, co-leader of the Democratic Party (DP), underscored this point. He has stated in Parliament that the National Party could not govern the country, supervise negotiations, and be a participant at the same time.

In this respect, it is also necessary to reemphasize the need for pressure from the outside on the parties concerned. The case for the complementarity of coercion and negotiation has been made elsewhere.[10] Whereas in the past it was the government that had to be coerced into a position of willingness to negotiate, coercion is now needed on all parties concerned: at the ANC in order to guard against authoritarian and one-party rule and the violation of human rights; at the PAC and the CP to persuade them to enter into negotiations. An important proviso remains that any form of coercion or sanctions should be constructive and conditional, not destructive and vindictive, and based on a rational cost-benefit analysis.[11]

There is a major need for public education to promote the knowledge that a negotiated settlement is a compromise. After generations of propaganda in an adversarial win-lose frame of mind, the public must be educated into a new process of problem solving. Without an extensive educational program, the public may not accept the agreements reached by their leaders around the negotiating table.

CONTINUING MANIFESTATIONS OF SOCIAL CONFLICT

So far we have been discussing the process of reaching a negotiated settlement between the major political parties in South Africa. Unfortunately, however, it is not possible to predict an end to all manifestations of destructive and violent conflict once agreement on a new constitution has been reached. It must be accepted that the demise of apartheid and the acceptance of the ideal of a constitution free from racism will not be the end to apartheid-induced conflict. The effects of such drastic social engineering as apartheid cannot be eradicated just by the signing of an agreement. Furthermore, it is a truism to state that, quite apart from apartheid, South Africa has in its history and demography a concentration of those same problems and tensions that beset the world at large. For the past four decades, apartheid has absorbed the major part of the human energy available, either in efforts to establish and maintain it, or in efforts to tear it down. Apartheid has at the same time suppressed the urgency of some of these diverse problems, and aggravated them as well, since the preoccupation with apartheid has tended to obscure objective analyses and understanding of the major issues underlying the conflict in South Africa.

The remaining areas of conflict in South African social life will be discussed in the following sections.

Racism and Ethnicity

It has become fashionable, under the influence of Marxist theory, to explain the existence of racism and the tenacity of ethnicity in terms of the class struggle. Racism, in this light, is a factor of exploitation. By dehumanizing those about to be exploited, the act of exploitation becomes morally easier, whereas the result of the process of exploitation—the dehumanized person—inevitably continues to reinforce the stereotype. There is doubtless an element of truth in this assessment; but the reduction to economic and political dimensions of basic contributors to human conflict worldwide, such as racism and ethnicity, cannot be accepted.

The roots of these phenomena lie not only in the political and economic behavior of people, but also in the domain of the human psyche. V. D. Volkan, for example, argues that the three psychological mechanisms of externalization, projection, and displacement are the chief defense mechanisms in the human psyche that contribute to inter alia ethnic prejudice.[12] In addition, in the formation of personal identity, ethnicity plays a vital role.[13] John Burton has identified identity among other things, as a basic human need that cannot be frustrated in its drive for fulfillment without serious consequences.[14] The frustration of such basic human needs, according to Burton, is at the heart of all deep-rooted conflict.

J. V. Montville discusses the role of victimhood in interethnic conflict.[15] The collective historical memory of victimization will continue to create aggressive behavior unless a mourning process is completed, which requires "that the victimizers accept responsibility for their acts or those of their predecessor governments and people, recognize the injustice done, and in some way ask forgiveness of the victims."[16]

Enough has been said to make the point that the forces of racism and ethnicity will continue to be sources of conflict in South Africa. It is an unfortunate but likely prospect that, under influence of the need to establish nonracialism as a nonnegotiable value (which in itself is an expression of the basic human need for recognition and participation), the underlying seriousness and intensity of these phenomena will be suppressed.

Protest Violence Because of the Absence of Shared Social Values

Plural societies are prone to instability and violence, especially when traditional patterns of life are disrupted and the masses are drawn into a modern economy and lifestyle with inflated high expectations. The frustration of these high expectations is a major cause of violence.

It is important to understand that the modernizing process in South Africa had its unique features. The traditional societies of South Africa inevitably faced the same unsettling or even traumatizing urge to modernize (i.e., urbanize, industrialize) that every other society in the world faced. This process, wherever it took place, involved the breaking down of traditional structures that had existed for centuries, as well as the traditional world view that gave coherence and meaning to those structures. However, in South Africa these processes were firmly controlled by apartheid legislation, i.e., laws like those governing influx control, job reservation, occupation rights, sexual relations, etc. The process of modernization inevitably led to feelings of alienation, but in South Africa the alienation was strengthened by factors such as the breakup of family structures by the migrant labor system and the almost total lack of control by blacks over these events. The modern world into which they moved was very firmly a "white" world, where the rules of the game were laid down by the whites.

With white control over the institutions and systems that shaped South African society slipping, it can be expected that many of these institutions and systems will experience disintegration. Not only will they be allowed to disintegrate because of their association with "The System" (i.e., apartheid), but perhaps more important because their rationale—their raison d'être—in the eyes of whites is not shared by a great number of blacks. This is the crisis of meaning. The serious alienation of large proportions of black people from that which makes the white world tick spells trouble for a smooth transition to black rule. It is unlikely that the social unrest—the result of this process of alienation and the concomitant distorted expectations—will be treated in any way other than by means of the existing legal forms of repression. There is no prospect of retiring the riot police.

Township Violence

It is a tragic fact that township violence, sometimes referred to as black-on-black violence, has left more deaths in its wake than any form of overt white-black violence. Since 1985 this particular form of violence led to a state of near anarchy, especially in Natal. It involved a wide range of antagonistic groups: clans, families, ethnic groups, gangs, criminals, and innocent victims.

Political factors, such as the difference between those willing to work within the system for gradual change and the noncollaborationists, or between the free-marketeers and socialists, contributed to the initial phases of the conflict. But it is clear that many of these communities have entered a spiral of violence, whereby revenge and retribution have become the dominant driving forces. It is obviously an enormously complex situation that has been fed by the general situation of deprivation. What is clear is that this is a particularly tragic form of violence that will not be solved by merely reaching a political settlement.

Education

A deep, simmering dissatisfaction with the heritage of apartheid education exists in the black community. Education has symbolized the possibility of entering and participating in the modern world, sharing its affluence and glitter. The anger that blacks have felt upon realizing that they have been cheated out of this dream has been uncontainable during recent years.

The cumulative result of the neglect of decades, however, cannot be wiped out within a short space of time. The rate of population growth places additional unbearable burdens on the financial and logistical ability to cope with the demand. Political liberation will raise tremendous expectations that no new black government will be able to satisfy. How will the anger be contained?

Consumer Protest

Consumer action against shops, local authorities, and public transport have become a widespread tactic, and its success has ensured that such action will be continued in the future. While black consumer action was largely aimed at white businesses in the past, it was essentially concerted action of the poor against the rich. Price increases in essential services such as transport, housing, electricity, medicine, etc., are likely to be met with consumer resistance. It should be noted that socialist and communist governments in

Eastern Europe were brought down by consumers.

Labor-Management Conflict

The trade union movement has become a very effective tool in the process of black empowerment. It has become a concentration of political power that is a potential threat to any government. It is an open question whether nationalization will dissolve the perceived conflict of interests between management and labor, since historical examples in other countries point in a different direction. The current alliance between the Congress of South African Trade Unions (COSATU) and the UDF/ANC should not detract from potential differences that could lead to major confrontations.

This brief review of the potential sources of conflict leads to two conclusions:

- While white-black conflict is continuing, and with a preponderance of whites on one side and blacks on the other side of all conflicts, there are other new sources of conflict that increasingly cut across racial divides.
- The end of apartheid does not mean the end of violent conflict.

THE CASE FOR MEDIATION SERVICES

For many years van der Merwe has advocated the establishment of a professional body of mediators.[17] Central to his argument at that time was the fact that neutrality within the polarized situation was so rare that very few, if any, people qualified. Therefore, rather than seeking neutrality and credibility in individuals, it should be sought in a professional body of people functioning as a team and earning credibility on the grounds of their expertise. Some of the stagnated political polarization of earlier times has been defused in the new situation, making the role of an impartial mediator somewhat more acceptable. The establishment of such a professional body of mediators can therefore be pursued with more confidence.

Burton has pointed to a development worldwide that has important implications for the South African conflict.[18] He discusses the growing impotence of centralized authorities to maintain control over their subordinates and the exponential growth in occurrences of violent conflict worldwide. This, he says, can be related to the fact that centralized power frustrates the development and fulfillment of basic human needs. It is in the nature of human beings to be driven by basic needs such as identity, development, recognition, and security. In the long run, human beings refuse to compromise the fulfillment of these needs, and therefore we find the "universal decay of authoritative processes unable to satisfy basic human needs."[19]

He distinguishes between disputes, which can be settled by traditional methods of negotiating and bargaining, and deep-rooted conflicts caused by the frustration of irrepressible human drives, which cannot be solved by traditional methods of negotiation: "If conflict is caused by some frustration of irrepressible human drives, the appropriate response would be to analyze the nature of the problem and *adjust the institutional and normative environment accordingly*" (emphasis added).[20]

A possible scenario for South Africa is that a new constitution will be adopted and that power will be transferred to a dominantly black government. South African society, however, will continue to be plagued by violent conflict as analyzed above. The establishment of a body of people professionally equipped to mediate in these situations can make a major contribution to promote peace.

Since 1981, the Centre for Intergroup Studies in Cape Town has been offering courses in the general field of conflict management, and in recent years more organizations have been providing such services in community and political relations. The Centre for Intergroup Studies, the Religious Society of Friends (Quakers), the Independent Mediation Service of South Africa (IMSSA), and Wilgespruit Fellowship Centre have pioneered the establishment of networks of facilitation and mediation services for community and political conflict.

The various manifestations of conflict in South Africa have deep roots, however, and have to be treated with the seriousness and respect that deep-rooted conflicts demand. This is probably the greatest challenge for those interested in fulfilling a mediating role in South Africa. We are in need of a process that will be indigenous, that will take the whole spectrum of basic human needs represented in the conflict seriously, and that will adequately appreciate the behavior of parties to the conflict as determined by their various histories and cultures. In light of the decay of centralized authority and the crisis of meaning, such a process must contribute to resolving conflict in such a way that a grassroots process of building new South African political and socioeconomic institutions and values will be the result.

Serious and urgent research is still necessary, but it is equally urgent to establish a nationwide network of people who will be available and who will have adequate understanding of this process in order to assist the nation in the hour of great need.

NOTES

1. Hylke Tromp, "Peace Research at the End of the Cold War," paper presented at the opening plenary session of the Twenty-fifth Anniversary Conference of the International Peace Research Association (IPRA), Groningen,

Netherlands, 3 July 1990.

2. Issa G. Shivji quoted by Birgit Brock-Utne, "The Changing Face of Europe," paper presented at the opening plenary session of the Twenty-fifth Anniversary Conference of the International Peace Research Association (IPRA), Groningen, Netherlands, 3 July 1990.

3. Ibid.

4. Hendrik W. van der Merwe, "Is There a Shift from Race to Class Conflict in South Africa?" *South African Sociological Association Papers* (Pretoria: South African Sociological Association, 1982), 323-338.

5. W. A. De Klerk, *The Puritans in Africa: A Story of Afrikanerdom* (London: Rex Collings, 1975), 199.

6. D. J. Bosch, "Nothing But a Heresy," in *Apartheid Is a Heresy,* ed. J. de Gruchy and C. Villa-Vicencio (Grand Rapids: Eerdmans, 1982).

7. Van der Merwe, "Is There a Shift from Race to Class Conflict in South Africa?"; Henrik W. van der Merwe, *Pursuing Justice and Peace in South Africa* (London: Routledge, 1989), 53.

8. Van der Merwe, *Pursuing Justice and Peace in South Africa.*

9. W. Thomas, "Mandela en nasionalisering: Debat oor ekonomiese stelsels kom aarde toe," *Die Suid-Afrikaan* 26 (1990): 5-7.

10. Hendrik W. van der Merwe and S. Williams, "Pressure and Cooperation as Complementary Aspects of the Process of Communication Between Conflicting Parties in South Africa," *Paradigms* 1 (1987): 8-13; H. W. van der Merwe, J. Maree, A. Zaaiman, C. Philip, and A. D. Muller, "Principles of Communication Between Adversaries in South Africa," in *Conflict: Readings in Management and Resolution,* ed. J. W. Burton and F. Dukes (New York: St. Martin's Press, 1990).

11. Van der Merwe, *Pursuing Justice and Peace in South Africa,* 84-86.

12. V. D. Volkan, "Psychoanalytic Aspects of Ethnic Conflicts," in *Conflict and Peacemaking in Multiethnic Societies,* ed. J. V. Montville (Lexington, Mass.: Lexington Books, 1989), 81.

13. Ibid., 86-88.

14. John W. Burton, "Conflict Resolution as a Political System," Working Paper 1, Center for Conflict Analysis and Resolution, George Mason University, 1988, 13.

15. J. V. Montville, "Epilogue: The Human Factor Revisited," in *Conflict and Peacemaking in Multiethnic Societies,* ed. J. V. Montville (Lexington, Mass.: Lexington Books, 1989), 537-540.

16. Ibid., 538.

17. Hendrik W. van der Merwe, "Proposal for the Establishment of a National Facilitation and Mediation Service in Community and Political Conflict," *Con-Text* 1 (1988): 69-80.

18. Burton, "Conflict Resolution as a Political System."

19. Ibid., 23.

20. Ibid., 11.

CHAPTER 12

Silently: How UN Good Offices Work

JUERGEN DEDRING

Multilateralism has experienced a great resurgence since 1988, but this comes none too soon, as new threats and new confrontations are anticipated throughout the world, including Europe. Reference may be made here to nonmilitary clashes, such as waves of ethnic tensions, numerous environmental crises, religious and language differences, and other novel instances of violent encounters. The new dimensions of international relations have appeared at the same time that the international community has witnessed breakthroughs in conflict resolution in which the United Nations has played a leading role and has designed new tools to overcome complex cases of interstate and intrastate enmity.[1]

CONFLICT RESOLUTION IN THE UNITED NATIONS

The evolution of multilateralism as practiced in the United Nations family of organizations has been fascinating; the tentative process in the early years of the organization has since developed in a fashion not envisaged by the "founding fathers" in 1944 and 1945. The Security Council's inability to fulfill its role as guardian of international peace and security under conditions of US-Soviet hostility forced the actors in the international organizations to develop alternative approaches to conflict resolution. The General Assembly, for its part, was hampered in its endeavor to pick up the tasks left undone by a frequently paralyzed Security Council. Uniting for Peace worked in a few instances but did not equip the Assembly with a lasting tool for peaceful settlement. Normative declarations also have not been sufficient to end wars and to resolve conflicts.

The organ that assumed growing significance as a result of the Security Council's weakness was the office of the Secretary-General. The main architect of the new power structure in the United Nations was Dag Hammarskjöld, the dynamic Swedish administrator and diplomat. When his tenure ended in an airplane crash over Africa, it was clear to everybody that he had moved the position of Secretary-General to a level equivalent to that of the collective bodies of the Security Council and the General Assembly.

The subsequent years of UN history, up to the end of Pérez de Cuellar's second term in 1992, constitute an unbroken chain of events that have further enhanced and strengthened the office of the Secretary-General. This should prevail also in a new era of close cooperation among the permanent members of the Security Council and at a point in time where other important states rise to similarly high status in the contemporary international system. The role of the Secretary-General is unlikely to be challenged by groups of states or individual states.

This new pattern of authority in the organized international community has had a direct impact on the way peace and security matters have been handled by the United Nations. The innovations in the Security Council revolve around the systematization and formalization of complex consultative procedures and the dominant search for consensus, avoiding voting altogether where possible. The discussions in the General Assembly and in its committees regarding international conflicts and their resolution are usually abstract and of little effect. The difference, however, has developed in the work of the Secretary-General. His functions have expanded continuously, especially his good offices function, which has grown into something sui generis, unique to the UN and its efforts at conflict resolution.

While the Secretary-General's good offices and quiet diplomacy do not constitute the whole of conflict resolution activities in and by the United Nations, a large part of the actual work of the organization either involves or touches upon this aspect. A review of recent cases in the UN shows very quickly how much has been affected by the Secretary-General. Even if a group of states is handling a particular issue, they still stay in close touch with the Secretary-General and seek his assistance in various aspects of the procedure employed to advance the search for a just peace.

The quiet application of the good offices function serves multiple purposes: it offers an invitation to make use of the services of the Secretary-General if and when parties so desire; to customize the involvement as the parties wish; to change the direction at any point; to pursue efforts confidentially without being exposed; to disavow the good offices whenever necessary or convenient; to make concessions without losing face; and to yield to discrete suggestions of one man, instead of surrendering to the political power of the adversary or a powerful third-party state. Moreover, good offices are completely malleable and can be shaped like clay in the hands of the sculptor. The mix of quiet services covering both procedure and substance in the pursuit of a peaceful solution is made available to the parties, but it is not to be imposed. No wonder states and governments seek out the help of the Secretary-General and entrust their concerns and complaints to him, expecting from him not only the services of an honest broker, but frequently calling upon him to draw up a full-fledged blueprint for peace and to take up the challenge of implementation.

The Secretary-General's exercise of the good offices role embedded in quiet diplomacy could have emerged only in the context of major UN cases involving new approaches in conflict resolution. The description of four such cases will illustrate the interplay of the principal organs for peace and security and, specifically, the activities of the Secretary-General. Once the evidence has been put forward, a second review of conflict resolution in the UN system can be carried out; its focus will be those aspects that really constitute new roles for the UN in conflict resolution.[2]

FOUR CASES

The four recent cases chosen for this review are typical of the work of the United Nations, but they vary in the way the conflict situations are configured and how the efforts at their resolution are shaped. The patterns are highly complex, but by juxtaposing these brief case histories, the common as well as the divergent elements will be understood.

Afghanistan

Soon after the ceremony in Geneva in April 1988, when the representatives of Afghanistan, Pakistan, the USSR, and the United States convened under the Secretary-General's chairmanship to sign the four Geneva accords under which the Soviet forces would be withdrawn, it became clear that the highly delicate set of agreements had been achieved at the expense of the important question of the future social and political order in the new Afghanistan. The Secretary-General and his special representative, whose discretion, determination, and persistence had led, after more than eight years, to a major success in quiet diplomacy, realized quickly that an equally difficult challenge awaited them; the search had begun for ways and means to allow the Afghans to establish a broad-based government under whose rule the wounds of the decade of fratricidal struggle would be healed.

While the initial mandate for the Secretary-General derived from a General Assembly resolution adopted shortly after the events of December 1979, the General Assembly also entrusted the Secretary-General with the task of assisting in the search for a broad-based Afghan government. Since 1988, the Assembly has each year renewed the short resolution that provides the basis for the ongoing sensitive initiatives.

Since spring 1989, after the USSR successfully concluded the total withdrawal of its troops from Afghan soil, the Secretary-General, supported by a very small team of officials, has become involved in a most difficult and time-consuming second phase of the good offices process, in which the initial aim is to negotiate a so-called international consensus involving the United States, the Soviet Union, Pakistan, Iran, Saudi Arabia, China, and India. The purpose of that consensus is to terminate all outside military assistance and to declare jointly, but not necessarily in public, that the fight over the future of the ravaged country must be ended. Second, the United Nations team must try to find a "magic" formula that would enable the Afghans to overcome their deep-seated religious and sociopolitical antagonisms and initiate a dialogue that could lead to an Afghan act of self-determination and then to the formation of an indigenous broad-based government. This twofold assignment is significant for several reasons; the role of the Secretary-General does not relate to an international conflict but to an issue, internal in nature, that has been internationalized by several state actors whose motives are not necessarily peaceable. Moreover, the good offices exercise trespasses the limits of what usually falls under state sovereignty and territorial integrity. Last, contacts with the various factions and individuals are essentially unrestricted and fully accepted, revealing the range and force of the UN engagement in that troublesome situation.

While the outcome of this second phase in the Afghan crisis is uncertain and the time frame open-ended, the case offers a striking demonstration of the novelty of the assignment entrusted to the Secretary-General and the extent to which the world organization and its executive head are drawn into intricate details of the history and politics of a closed social system such as that of the Afghans, with its special mix of tribal, religious, and linguistic differences and with the weakness of its cohesion as a nation. Time will tell if the multilateral mechanism and the good offices of the Secretary-General can conquer the Afghan challenge. However, the fact that the challenge has been put to the Secretary-General and been accepted by him is significant for a better understanding of how the United Nations has been functioning in the area of peace and security.[3]

Namibia

The admission of newly independent Namibia in April 1990 as the 160th member of the United Nations received top billing in the international media. Following the 1966 decision of the General Assembly that South African control over South West Africa was illegal and that South Africa should relinquish control and turn the country over to the United Nations, other tribunals also became active in the pursuit of Namibia's independence. In 1971, the International Court of Justice supported the General Assembly viewpoint that South Africa's presence in Namibia was illegal. The Security

Council took up the Namibian question and invited the Secretary-General to name a representative for Namibia to intensify the drive for international political action. In 1978, in close cooperation with the Secretary-General, the Security Council adopted a plan of action for the transfer of authority from South Africa to an independent Namibia.

After more than ten years, the political situation at last allowed the United Nations to set in motion the 1978 Namibia blueprint. A threefold UN operation was to be set up that would oversee (1) the preparation for elections in Namibia, (2) the deliberation and adoption of a constitution for Namibia, and (3) the formation of an independent government that would replace the South African administration. The actual political decision and the financing of the UN operation caused difficulties and delays; as a consequence, the United Nations Transition Assistance Group (UNTAG) was launched under unfavorable conditions. The preparations were not complete, and knowledge about the territory and its inhabitants was devoid of practical experience, so that the excitement of 1 April 1989 nearly ruined the operation.

With such troubled beginnings, the Secretary-General realized immediately that only the closest monitoring and steering at the highest level could ensure the successful implementation of the Namibia transition plan. From April 1989 to March 1990, the Secretary-General's task force at headquarters met every day to discuss the latest developments and to decide on the next moves.

What did the UNTAG operation entail? The first part of the task was carried out by the group of military observers who brought calm and order to the towns and villages and monitored the phased withdrawal of the South African contingents from the Namibian territory. A civilian component arrived to prepare the voting lists and to monitor the return of many Namibians who had lived in exile abroad. Various UN agencies, among them UNHCR, assisted in welcoming the returnees and getting them settled as soon as possible. When the South African government presented a biased and discriminatory electoral law for the first free Namibian elections, the UN acted swiftly, insisting on the revision of that law by a senior UN legal expert who rewrote the law to enforce a free ballot. For the Namibia elections, monitors were sent by the UN itself, many of them made available by governments of member states eager to help in this great event. Police were also brought in to ensure calm conditions during the days of balloting. The basic UNTAG civilian and military teams stayed in the territory while the elected Namibian representatives gathered in the Constituent Assembly to deliberate on and adopt the most democratic constitution on the African continent. Since the operation developed very smoothly, the Secretary-General and his representative in Namibia decided to accelerate the timetable and set the date for independence for the second part of March 1990 rather than April 1990. The rest is history.

What makes Namibia so significant is (1) the interaction between the Secretary-General, the Security Council, the General Assembly, and various member states and groups of states in the prolonged pursuit of the goal of Namibian independence; (2) the multiple functions secured by UNTAG's expanding the scope beyond the normal diplomatic and peacekeeping roles found in other cases; (3) the tight link between the Secretary-General and the operation in the field; and (4) the comprehensive authority placed into the hands of the Secretary-General by the United Nations and by the principal governments and regional groupings. The fact that Namibia was set on such a promising path of independent statehood is due largely to the circumspection that characterized the moves in the United Nations in the years before 1989, and also during the launching of UNTAG and its successful implementation.

Election monitoring, public order, legal advice, basic administration, and humanitarian assistance all added to the long-standing practice of peacekeeping by military personnel and of traditional multilateral diplomacy. The fact that the UN system has been able to handle this transition operation underlines vividly the widening range of UN activities and the growing sophistication with which approaches to conflict resolution are applied in highly complex situations.[4]

Central America

In terms of an ongoing UN operation that fits the label of conflict resolution, the evolving Central American situation must be seen as the most unusual and innovative case. In the shadow of an overpowering military and political giant, events have taken place in the last three years that have surprised the general public as much as the seasoned experts. The regional governments, under the imaginative and dynamic leadership of former President Arias of Costa Rica, activated on their own and in close cooperation with their neighbors, a process of understandings whereby the role of the Northern hegemony could be neutralized or at least mitigated and tentative steps toward an end to fighting and violence initiated. The calculation of President Arias paid off. The five regional presidents met several times and resolved, in time-consuming and difficult talks, to set certain signposts on the anticipated road to recovery. The necessary modicum of goodwill and trust was available to transform the abstract vision into practical measures and to structure the process in a way that would allow each participant to ask for review and revision down the road.

The functions assigned to the United Nations as well as to the Organization of American States (OAS) were multiple. The whole package of agreements was to be monitored by the UN and the OAS, through a commission to implement the accord (CIAV). Furthermore, when it was decided that Nicaragua would prepare and hold an open and free election, the UN and the OAS were requested to provide personnel to monitor the elections so that the international community could be sure the ballot had not been tampered with or manipulated. ONUVEN was set up for that crucial purpose and carried out its mission smoothly and effectively, despite allegations and fears voiced on all sides. In addition, it was agreed that an international observer force should monitor the borders in Central America in order to detect, report on, and, if possible, interdict illicit traffic in weapons and troops, especially between Nicaragua, Honduras, and El Salvador. ONUCA, the border observer force, was established in spring 1990 and enlarged to monitor the borders, to receive weapons from Contras willing to surrender their arms and return to civilian life in Nicaragua, and to assist in related tasks.

While the Security Council and the General Assembly had dealt with the Nicaraguan issue and with the wider problem of Central America, it should be emphasized at this juncture that the most decisive role was entrusted to the Secretary-General. His overall consulting and supervising function was specifically focused on his position of trust and discretion. This was a position that the Central American leaders held in high esteem and made use of, as they took all precautions not to arouse open antipathy from the Reagan administration. Since the UN Secretary-General had just been persuaded by the representatives of the five permanent members of the Security Council to accept a second term as head of the world organization, it was unquestionably clear to President Arias and his colleagues that it was the symbol of the office of the UN Secretary-General that could sway even the most reluctant members of the UN community. The stratagem worked, though there were critical moments when the viability of the Arias plan seemed in doubt.

Furthermore, it should be noted that the concrete tasks assigned to the United Nations, ONUVEN, and ONUCA were of a type not yet experienced in the history of the United Nations. The close supervision and certification of the election in Nicaragua constitutes a first, in that a sovereign state and its government accepted international monitoring of a supremely internal act. What moved the Sandinista government to acquiesce in this innovation is still not fully ascertained. Their act has opened new vistas for international organizations in matters of domestic jurisdiction. The next step, the establishment of ONUCA, is also quite remarkable, as the interdiction of weapons and troops presents an extraordinary challenge to the soldiers of peace serving the United Nations. The recent broadening of the ONUCA mandate to serve as the recipient of demobilizing Contra troops in Nicaragua ranks as another advance in international peacekeeping. This mandate is a triumph of internationalism over parochialism.

During April 1990, the Central American operation went through another evolution. The adversaries in the Salvadoran civil war approached the

Secretary-General, urging him to make his good offices available to help end the internal fight of many years and overcome the deep chasm that separated the conservative regime and the leftist opposition. The opening meetings in Caracas, Venezuela, give strong evidence that the trust factor has swayed even hardened adversaries to turn to the United Nations, more specifically to the Secretary-General.

This radical departure from past practices highlights the dramatic sequence of events, revolutionary in character as regards conflict resolution in and by the United Nations and exemplified most strikingly in the expanded utility and responsibility of the Secretary-General.[5]

Cambodia

The utterly complex issue of Cambodia is of significance in this examination as it relates to a conception of a UN presence in that troubled land. It represents a vision of an exercise of governmental authority by an international organization for a transition period of possibly three or four years—unique and unprecedented in a sovereign country. The international debate on this subject is still inconclusive, but the recent turn of events makes it very likely that some UN presence will be established, with the details yet to be settled. What is envisaged amounts to a central role of a UN transition mechanism involving basic administrative functions in Cambodia and, specifically, the preparation, conduct, and monitoring of free elections that would, it is hoped, enable the Cambodian people to put the grim past of the Pol Pot terror behind them and to restore the traditional civility of the Khmer society. To envision international officials as administrators acting on behalf of and for the inhabitants of an established sovereign country is unprecedented, but the participants in the search for a Cambodian solution appear to be fully determined to travel this new road, since all earlier efforts have thus far failed.

The partners in this lengthy deliberation are not only the immediate parties, i.e., the coalition around Prince Sihanouk and the present government in Pnom Penh, but also the regional powers of ASEAN, and more recently, the five permanent members of the Security Council, who have entered the discussions as a group. In addition, the UN Secretary-General has maintained a discrete presence in these efforts at solution and is drawn into most of the ongoing consultations because all states foresee a major role for the United Nations.

The decisive reason for the envisaged participation of the international machinery of the UN is the recognition by the various state actors that the symbolic power of the UN *chapeau* for the eventual transition arrangements is critically important. The chain of recent successes in peacemaking and peacekeeping has demonstrated the versatility of the multilateral instruments and the capacity of the UN to grapple with immense and delicate problems. The key spot occupied by the Secretary-General, who enjoys wide support and great trust among political leaders and the general public, helps us understand the dynamic factors in the pursuit of the formula to obtain the elusive peace for the Cambodians, victims of terrible events not easily forgotten. Although it may still take years before Cambodia is ready for the transition process, the position of the UN as central to the administrative process seems assured. It will constitute a new threshold in international conflict resolution and peacekeeping.[6]

INNOVATIONS IN CONFLICT RESOLUTION

The above case histories present in brief the emergence of decisive innovations in peacemaking and the good offices of the UN and the Secretary-General. The breakthroughs are manifold; yet, while the evidence so far is compelling, further developments should be awaited before we regard the new features in conflict resolution as more or less permanent.

A word first of all with regard to the procedure used in these delicate efforts at conflict resolution. The focus has been primarily on the Secretary-General, whose quiet diplomacy and good offices constitute the principal venue in affecting international events, but his functioning must also be seen as intertwined with a complex web of other international movements and interaction patterns. As was pointed out, the other organs of the UN system, especially the Security Council and the General Assembly, have contributed to the advancing process of conflict resolution, but state actors and regional groupings have also had a share in the evolution of policies that have eventually produced the anticipated results. This very special mix that defines the context and essence of UN policymaking cannot be overemphasized. The widespread lack of awareness of United Nations decisionmaking demands further study of the existing patterns and a refinement of our understanding, in particular, of informal, confidential approaches that make up most of the communication flows in peacemaking and conflict resolution.[7]

The reluctance to seek public declarations and firm policy positions was not that uncommon in earlier times. But while secret diplomacy was often employed to protect the *arcana imperii*, the discrete uses of quiet diplomacy and the support structures provided by an intricate pattern of multilateral consultations have little in common with traditional practices. The need for confidentiality has become undeniable, and the fact that the United Nations community has accepted that ingredient of successful peacemaking underlines the significance of the principle. Only a case-by-case examination of pertinent instances of conflict resolution could bring out the full evidence, assuming the researcher-analyst has full access to the processes as well as the files. In the meantime, we must be satisfied with partial findings as actors and observers give testimony about how issues were handled in the search for the formula or framework to resolve a concrete issue.

The multilateral political process as found in the UN system, especially as regards conflict resolution and the services of the Secretary-General, is in need of further conceptual clarifications and analytical studies. However, the insight that it differs substantially from classical interstate diplomacy does not require principal confirmation, since a good number of practitioners and scholars have examined various facets of multilateralism of this sort. It should nevertheless be stressed that the work of the Secretary-General and his immediate aides calls for a deeper and more thorough assessment distinct from an organization study, because it takes place in an intricate network of linkages. Each network of linkages has an impact on the moves of the Secretary-General and belongs in the set of factors with which the "good officer" must reckon in his initiatives to open doors, to prepare the path toward dialogue and conciliation, and to prevent the immediate parties from abandoning an emerging understanding. The ability to play this complicated instrument is the basic prerequisite for a successful stewardship in the post of Secretary-General. It has been said repeatedly that Secretary-General Pérez de Cuellar displays knowledge and intuition in utilizing the given elements to advance the issues entrusted to him. To what extent the personality variable will shape the outcome, i.e., a successful package deal or blueprint for a peaceful accommodation, remains an open question. It should be noted that the predecessor in the office of Secretary-General did not display those necessary skills too visibly.[8]

The skill of the individual has been emphasized here because the other aspects of the multilateral decisionmaking process are less pertinent and also less unusual. The systemwide choice of consultative formats for meetings and negotiations—also found in the European Community, in ASEAN, in the OAU, and in ad hoc international gatherings—is noted here, but it simply strengthens the view that the personal skills of individual actors, in particular the Secretary-General, are of paramount significance.

The cases discussed above also help to shed light on the terminological as well as substantive debate about the concept of conflict resolution. If the meaning of the term is taken literally, we see either that no resolution has yet occurred in the Afghan, Central American, or Cambodian situations or that no clear-cut conflict situation was given, e.g., in the Namibian situation or in Central America. Quoting the UN Charter language as to disputes and situations and the pacific settlement of disputes, it is undeniable that the reference is to interstate conflicts, not to internal issues or tensions. Moreover, the terminological differentiation between the prevention, management, containment, resolution, and transformation of conflicts should also be taken into consideration in order to give full justice to the specific quality of each of these complex questions.

In the case of Afghanistan, the Secretary-General currently seeks the termination of what is essentially a civil war in which several outside powers are still openly interfering. This would be accomplished by initiating a dialogue among Afghans with the aim of forming a broad-based Afghan government. These objectives are as treacherous as the mined fields and mountains of Afghanistan. Standard techniques of conflict resolution are inadequate; new ideas in management, containment, and transformation are in demand to custom-tailor a set of proposals that would please the Afghan factions and their disunited leaders and would be acceptable to the USSR, the United States, Pakistan, Iran, Saudi Arabia, India, and even China. The far-reaching search for formulae, venues, and incentives exceeds the boundaries of what the founding fathers of the UN had in mind when they adopted the Charter.

A similar imprecision applies in the case of Namibia. The lengthy pursuit of a peaceful transformation of political, social, economic, and ethnic conditions in Southern Africa cannot be pressed into the narrow confines of a Charter article or of a concept of social scientists. The diplomatic accord was as significant as the multidimensional campaign to prepare the Namibians for their eventual freedom and independence and to rally the international community to their just cause. The tremendous range of functions assigned to the UN became especially clear during the nearly twelve months in which UNTAG delivered Namibia out of South African bondage into its sovereign statehood. The diversity and strength of the assistance provided by the organized international community can be grasped in their full extent only in a detailed account of the manifold events that defined the path toward Namibia's independence. All the skills of administration, planning, and accommodation were brought to bear on the time-consuming activities undertaken in the name of the United Nations and under the Secretary-General's responsibility.

When we turn to the Central American process, it becomes difficult even to label the various engagements of the UN system and Secretary-General. The interplay between the Security Council, the General Assembly, and the Secretary-General on the one hand and the growing role of the OAS and its secretary-general on the other are important contributory factors that led the Central American leaders to crucial decisions. Finally, the point of no return was reached, short of a willingness on the part of any one of them to ruin the whole "peace process" in their region. The two secretaries-general acted as symbolic guarantors of the Central American plan. They were called in to monitor the preparations and conduct the outcome of free elections in Nicaragua; they were further requested to monitor the regional borders and to fulfill critical tasks in the return of the Nicaraguan Contras to their country and to civilian life. Oddly enough, the role of the UN Secretary-General as mediator in the strictly internal confrontation between the Salvadoran right and left is the only function that comes close to the concept of conflict resolution or peaceful dispute settlement. However, it takes place in a context clearly defined as a matter of domestic jurisdiction—in which the UN as a rule is not permitted to interfere.

Cambodia, also, is not easily classified as an instance of conflict resolution. Again, the internal and international threads of this knot are so intertwined that to disentangle them is nearly impossible. The UN is little involved in the current search for a way in which conflicting aspirations could be reconciled so that the Cambodian people would find peace and rebuild their war-torn land. The principal actors at this juncture are the five permanent members of the UN Security Council, who act outside the framework of the Council, and the regional states, ASEAN members, and a few others, who attempt to persuade the Cambodian rivals to remove the last remaining barriers that block the passage to a just and stable peace. It is also symptomatic that the specific role the UN is expected to play is that of administrator and organizer/manager of the eventual elections. It would be hard to find an activity more oriented to domestic jurisdiction than the challenging assignment to serve as transition authority in Cambodia.

From this reassessment of the four cases in which specific functions have been performed by the United Nations, the most striking feature of these new developments that emerges is a considerable shift in the understanding and application of the provisions of Article 2(7).[9] All four situations depict United Nations involvement in strictly domestic matters. That seemingly amounts to a breach of the noninterference clause of the UN Charter. Under what circumstances do these conditions arise? In the case of Afghanistan, the title of the government and other claimants is contested; the task of the Secretary-General, as mandated by the General Assembly, is to help the various factions come to a binding and viable arrangement of how to establish a government that would be acceptable, at least to the wide majority of the Afghan people. While the Kabul government accepted the UN role, the representatives of the Mujahedeen were not directly asked, nor is it clear to what extent their *pourparlers*, the Pakistani authorities, were consulted. Nevertheless, it is correct to stipulate that the barrier of Article 2(7) was removed by specifically issuing an invitation to the Secretary-General to take up that challenging assignment.

Similarly, the role in Namibia was a function that did not fall outside the terms of the noninterference clause. However, here the situation is more easily resolved in that the authority of South Africa was not accepted by the international community. Instead, since 1966, the United Nations had assumed the administrative authority over that territory, although its claim could not be realized until 1989-1990; even then the authority was shared by South Africa and the UN, with the UN definitely playing the lesser part.

Nevertheless, Article 2(7) was clearly bypassed in shaping the wide-ranging mandate as administrator, supervisor, and election monitor that was practiced in the UNTAG deployment.

The actual UN role in Central America, especially in Nicaragua and El Salvador, and the envisaged deployment in Cambodia emphasize the point stressed thus far: the domestic jurisdiction clause in these operations is largely suspended, since otherwise the UN could not credibly carry out its many varied tasks. The governments affected and the international community document, through their willing agreement and cooperation, that the danger of external interference from the UN system is remote. The UN is perceived as facilitator, not as meddler. As long as the governments that benefit from the UN involvement approve the operation or acquiesce in its presence, there is no reason for concern with regard to the nonobservance of the Charter prohibition.

Still, the breakthrough in this area should be studied, as it expands remarkably the space of operations for the UN as a whole and the Secretary-General in particular. Governments adhere to their definition of state sovereignty in its legal and political meaning, but admit that in certain situations the response to a given critical problem requires the lowering of the wall between internal prerogatives and international emergency operations. Aid, especially humanitarian aid, knows no boundaries, because human suffering also transcends the artificial divisions of the political map.

The pertinence of this particular development for other aspects of UN involvement is to be stressed. The expansion in the applications of peacekeeping operations in the four cases as well as in other recent endeavors is due in part to the widening political space for UN service. The singular achievement in election monitoring is tied to the same phenomenon. The experiment in civilian administration cannot be understood unless it is seen as part and parcel of the enlargement of the UN's utility as perceived by a growing number of member states. The last dimension to be added here is the field of humanitarian assistance that has opened up as a result of the activation of the UN capacity for peaceful settlement, conflict resolution, and peacekeeping.

If we see the current changes as indicators for a major reshuffling of the international system, the impact of the recent developments fore-shadows a further enlargement of the peacemaking and problem-resolving capacity of the UN system. The imaginative exercise of his good offices has put the Secretary-General into the forefront of multilateralism in the service of the international community and its constituent parts. As long as discretion and quiet diplomacy prevail, the number of tasks entrusted to the United Nations will expand, solidifying the achievements of the last few years.

CONCLUSION

As international challenges increase in number and complexity, the pressure increases on the UN system and on the Secretary-General, its helmsman, to further diversify the instruments of peacemaking and peacekeeping to fine-tune the approaches to particular situations and to shape appropriate responses to the challenges as they arise. Great flexibility is called for so that the methods of multilateralism can be kept totally malleable for the emerging crises and dangers. In this regard, the United Nations will continue to offer a rich field for observation and research.

NOTES

1. This chapter is primarily a report on evolving UN practices in the resolution of international conflicts and does not constitute a full-fledged research paper.

2. From a growing body of literature on the United Nations and multilateralism, a few titles of special relevance should be listed here: Jacob Bercovitch, "International Mediation: A Study of the Incidence Strategies and Conditions of Successful Outcomes," *Cooperation and Conflict* 21 (3) (1986): 155-168; Harold K. Jacobson, *Networks of Interdependence: International Organizations and the Global Political System,* 2d ed. (New York: Knopf, 1984); James O.C. Jonah, "The Military Talks at Kilometer 101: The UN's Effectiveness as a Third Party," *Negotiation Journal* 6 (1) (January 1990): 53-70; Arthur Lall, ed., *Multilateral Negotiation and Mediation: Instruments and Methods* (New York: Pergamon Press for the International Peace Academy, 1985); Paul E. Mason and Thomas F. Marsteller, Jr., "UN Mediation: More Effective Options," *SAIS Review* 5 (2) (Summer/Fall 1985): 217-284; Christopher Roger Mitchell and Keith Webb, eds., *New Approaches to International Mediation* (New York: Greenwood Press, 1988); Donald Puchala and Roger Coate, "The Challenge and Relevance: The United Nations in a Changing World Environment," *ACUNS: Reports and Papers* (1985): 5; Hasan-Askari Rizvi, "Geneva Parleys on Afghanistan," *Pakistan Horizon* 39 (1) (1986): 74-91; Saadia Touval and I. William Zartman, eds., *International Mediation in Theory and Practice* (Boulder, Colo.: Westview Press, with the Foreign Policy Institute, Johns Hopkins University, 1985); Saadia Touval, "Multilateral Negotiation: An Analytic Approach," *Negotiation Journal* 5 (2) (April 1989): 159-173; "United Nations Mediation of Regional Crisis," *Proceedings* (American Society of International Law 80th Meeting, 1986): 135-151; William L. Ury, "Strengthening International Mediation," *Negotiation Journal* 3 (3) (July 1987): 225-229.

3. For the Afghanistan issue see especially the following UN documents: S/19835; A/43/720, S/20230; S/RES/622 (1988); A/44/203, S/20549; A/44/661, S/20911.

4. Regarding Namibia, see especially the following UN documents: S/20412 and Adds. 1 and 2; S/20457; S/20579; S/20967 and Adds. 1 and 2; S/20974; S/221215; and the *UN Chronicle* 6 (4) (December 1989).

5. With regard to the complex situation in Central America, see especially the following UN documents: A/43/729, 2/20234; A/44/288, S/20463; A/44/304; A/44/344 and Add. 1; S/20640; A/44/451, S/20778; A/44/270,

S/20802; S/20857; S/20895; S/RES/644 (1989); S/20952; S/21011; A/44/872, S/21019; A/44/856, S/21029; S/21194; A/44/921; S/RES/654 (1990); S/21274.

6. For the still unresolved Cambodian question see the following UN documents: A/44/168, S/20511; A/44/414, S/20748; A/44/439, S/20770; S/20768; S/20880; A/44/670; A/44/699, S/20932; A/44/720, S/20959; A/44/733; A/44/1; S/21087; S/21115; A/45/56, S/21021; A/45/127, S/21149; A/45/89, S/21095; A/45/81, S/21082; A/45/91; A/45/95; S/21119; A/45/209, S/21240; A/45/167, S/21196.

7. See my essay entitled "Multilateral Aspects of Conflict Resolution," to be published (fall 1991 or spring 1992) by Sage Publications in a volume of essays on conflict resolution edited by Raimo Vayrynen.

8. On the Secretary-General's good offices see Bertrand G. Ramcharan, *Humanitarian Good Offices in International Law: The Good Offices of the United Nations Secretary-General in the Field of Human Rights* (The Hague: Nijhoff, 1983). The recent evolution in the good offices practice deserves serious attention by academic researchers who specialize in conflict resolution.

9. The panel discussion on the relevance of Article 2 (7) at the 1990 International Studies Association Annual Meeting in Washington, D.C., should be mentioned here, especially the stimulating discussion paper by Benjamin Rivlin. The debate on the nonintervention clause in the UN Charter has just begun.

CHAPTER 13

The Challenge of Peace Education: Replacing Cultures of Militarism

—————————————— RIITTA WAHLSTRÖM

The deadly culture that surrounds us—the culture of militarism—has held societies captive with tenets so pervasive that it is difficult to realize in our confinement the darkness in which we live. Henry K. Skolimowski says that nearly all current cultures are sick;[1] this sickness is the atrophy of values. Consumerism and militarism are the sick values of most societies. Peace education is one of the lines of thought that try to break the value and power structures of militaristic culture in society.

In militaristic cultures, military institutions dominate civil institutions, resulting in the decline of individual liberties and the erosion of democratic principles. The *Encyclopedia Americana* defines militarism as follows:

> Militarism is applied to the policy of giving exceptional emphasis to military preparedness, exalting military virtues and relying on force in international relations. Preparation for war encourages the growth of the militaristic spirit to strengthen the combatants for battle.[2]

Militarism is characterized by nationalism, political conservatism, authoritarianism, a pessimistic conception of human nature, and alarmism in estimating the probability of war.

Malvern Lumsden states that the primary role of the military is to maintain the present world economic order, an order that is characterized, on one hand, by global competition between competing industrial systems and, on the other hand, by vast discrepancies in the utilization of resources. He defines militarism as follows: "Militarism is the military exploitation of 'mythology' in order to 'legitimize' the expropriation of surplus produce for illegitimate macroparasitic purpose."[3]

Militarism today, global in scope, has become part of (and affects) economic, political, technological, and ecological systems. An international weapons market supports all the mechanisms that lead to war. C. Clausewitz defines war as a rational instrument of national policy: "War is an act of violence intended to compel our opponent to fulfill our will."[4]

The policy of oppressive ruling groups is being influenced by complex cultural-historical factors and by the infiltration of armament industries and arms trade into political decisionmaking systems. Structural violence is an essential underlying factor of war. Jan Oberg writes that disarmament cannot be addressed without giving analytic attention to the symbiotic relationship between armament and structural violence.[5] Peace education is one line of thought trying to break the value and power structures of militaristic culture in society.

THE CULTURES OF MILITARISM:
MYTHS, SYMBOLS, AND IMAGES OF HUMAN BEINGS

The cultures of militarism promote war and armament. As Y. P. Häyrynen states, the cultural armament that utilizes art, education, and mass communication creates the basis for war, which is violence organized by society.[6] The reality of war, which is unnatural to human nature, cannot be created without cultural and educational manipulation. Robin Luckham even uses a term, *armament culture*.[7] Arms modify human consciousness through a phenomenon that we can call "armament culture." According to Luckham, armament has a deep effect on all forms of culture. Science, technology, and even everyday language are militarized.[8] Weapons are mythologized to represent force, scientific progress, and the exercise of power. Luckham writes that weapons have become myths of power. Weapons are named making use of traditional images of power and strength. Such weapons carry names like Eagle, Tornado, Tor, and Atlas, symbolizing traditional and mythological images of power and strength.[9] In cultural production, war toys, video games, and movies based on violence use this same mythology. Throughout the world there are military parades, rituals, marches, and heroes with guns to reinforce military solidarity at the expense of solidarity with the civilian population.[10]

Human beings act not only on the basis of what they believe is probable (cognitive aspect), but also on the basis of what is believed to be desirable (affective aspect). In social interactions, therefore, the main function of militaristic mythology is not so much to explain why things exist but rather to reinforce in-group identification and to create the image of the possible threat. The manipulation of uncertainty and associated anxiety and the reinforcement of group solidarity are the two social functions of mythology that are important in the study of militarism. Human beings are willing to pay those who can reduce uncertainty for them.

The typical features of militaristic culture are ethnocentrism, belief in authority, nationalism, and a pessimistic conception of human nature.[11] Betty Reardon states: "Militarism is a belief system founded on the basic assumption that human beings are by nature violent, aggressive and competitive and on the corollary assumption that social order must be maintained by force and power."[12] The image—of the human being as evil, violent, and competitive by nature—leads logically to the perception that security and social order can be maintained only by power and coercive means. Häyrynen states that most of the arguments that war is a necessity contain mystification of human nature[13] (e.g., "War cannot be avoided because human beings are what they are," "War is a part of human nature," etc.). Thus, the concept of the human being maintained by militarism is based on the idea that war is accepted as a necessity, as an eternal plague. According to Kirsti Lagerspetz, this view has been presented in many popular writings.[14] Richard Leakey's statement in *Making of Mankind* that violence is innate in human beings[15] is one of the most dangerous and destructive ideas that mankind has ever had. Our beliefs influence our actions. As Anthony Wilden states: "Unlike animals, what we do or do not is never independent of what we have learned to believe is possible or impossible, right or wrong."[16] Warfare is not genetically programed; it is learned behavior.[17] The purpose of peace education is to "free" people of such beliefs that support militarism.

MILITARISM AND SEXISM

Reardon points out that because there is a symbiotic relationship between armaments and structural violence, it is impossible to politically separate the problems of militarization from those of poverty and oppression; and this provides a precedent and a paradigm for consideration of the kind of relationship that exists between sexism and the war system.[18] Militarism is based on patriarchy and sexism. Patriarchy is a set of beliefs and values supported by institutions and backed by the threat of violence, postulating the supposedly "proper" relations between men and women, between women and women, and between men and men. Men in most societies are taught very early to be "masculine," to respect only other men who are "masculine," to compete with each other, to use women as modes of exchange with each other, to hide their fears and compassion from one another, and to treat their sons differently than they treat their daughters.[19] The military is the distilled embodiment of patriarchy.[20]

Sexism humiliates women. Military training underlines openly that women are inferior to men. This kind of belief system makes it easier for men to abandon women and wives and rape and humiliate women during war. Equality between men and women is a threat to militarism; as long as women are seen as inferior it is easier to assault them. In military training young men learn to underestimate women and to oppress and violate their needs.

Education for equality between women and men is a threat to militarism. This education teaches men to respect women and to adopt their set of values. The women's set of values is opposed to the militaristic way of thinking—to the emphasizing of power, competition, and violence. The typical male image in the Euro-American culture underlines toughness and macho-masculinity. The education for equality alters this image of "maleness." When fathers care for their children more often and function as affectionate objects of identification, the macho male image breaks down. The sexist culture and the closely associated militarism weakens when fatherhood becomes culturally and psychologically equal with motherhood. It can be assumed that the equality of parental roles in the family will decrease sexism in cultures as well.

Feminine values that nurture life and acknowledge the need for transcending competition and violence are needed to guide policy formation to avoid and abolish war.[21] The same values—nurturing, caring, and sharing—exist in the same way in masculine culture, while competition and desire for power exist in feminine culture as well. It is simply more openly and culturally taught that males are allowed to be competitive, powerseeking, and violent. It is the responsibility of the whole society, both male and female, to rid itself of militarism and to seek out true cultural values of life.

MILITARISM CREATES AN ENEMY IMAGE

To legitimize the maintenance of a vast military establishment during peacetime, great efforts are made to exploit new items that create public anxiety about the intentions of a possible enemy. The militaristic conception of the human being, emphasizing violence and competitiveness, legitimizes the idea that, in principle, there always exists an enemy that might attack. According to Lynne Iglitzin, supranational militarism always portrays the enemy as an anonymous object that is continuously present.[22] The enemy can be another nation; an ethnic, ideological, or religious group within one's own community; or people of a different race or language group. The existence of an enemy justifies the use of violence. During war, the fighting troops become enemies to each other, and so to protect one's own life one "has to kill." In peacetime, the maintenance of the enemy image is a dangerous preparation for war.

The concept of an enemy image is very familiar to war propaganda. Harold Lasswell writes that if you want to arouse a nation against an enemy, describe the enemy as a threatening and murderous attacker;[23] portray the enemy as an obstacle to the ideals and dreams cherished by the nation and each of its central groups.[24]

Both the attitude and the behavior toward "enemies" are violent. The enemy is believed to threaten everything regarded as good and valuable in national identity. The formation of enemy images is characterized by dualistic thinking. This kind of thinking induces people to view different sets of morals, values, ideologies, and religions as either "right" or "wrong," and people as either "good" or "bad." I have described the enemy image as a psychological phenomenon:

> The enemy image is the commonly-held, stereotyped, dehumanized image of the outgroup. The enemy image provides a focus for externalization of fears and threats. In addition, a lot of undesirable cognitions and emotions are projected onto the enemy. This definition contains three important points: the enemy image is connected with an outgroup; dehumanization of the enemy legitimizes violence and the enemy image provides a focus for projections.[25]

The enemy image has a scapegoat function. Weaknesses and failures are transferred to an external target so that one's own identity or that of the nation is protected.[26] The enemy is blamed for the failures of internal politics. The enemy always becomes the embodiment of what we fear or reject in ourselves. The enemy is always "other" and feared. Society reinforces and exacerbates this perception of otherness. "Othering" is a psychological mechanism delineating people as better or worse, good or bad, etc. Sexist societies and war systems are kept in order by the capacity to use or threaten the use of violence against those "others."[27]

The central element in the formation of the enemy image is the dehumanization of the enemy. This dehumanization process involves the removal of all human facets; it can be observed in various forms in military training and in the arousal of nations against their enemies. The dehumanization of the enemy is clearly seen in the cruelties that occur in many internal conflicts. Savage murders and the torturing and killing of unarmed children and women are directly related to seeing victims as dehumanized enemies. For example, many internal conflicts are characterized by the killing of not only "real" enemies, but of completely defenseless people as well. The mental image of seeing somebody as an enemy makes this sort of cruelty possible. "Otherness," in its negative form, connotes hierarchies in human worth based on fundamental assumptions that make possible the dehumanization of members of another sex, race, or class; citizens of another state; or adherents to another religion or ideology.

Images that are connected to our emotions and values are much more powerful than reality. Emotional reasoning is part of the image world of the human mind. Fear, hate, and feelings of being threatened, humiliated, worthless, or powerless are ingredients in the emotional reasoning related to the development of enemy images.

The mass media and propaganda have a very important role in creating the enemy image. The propagandist brainwash is an essential part of militaristic culture. Militarism supports the creation of the enemy image in all possible ways, e.g., by utilizing rumors, mass media, and propaganda.

THE POWER STRUCTURE AND
EDUCATION FOR MILITARISTIC CULTURE

Militarism is promoted by organizational forms in which orders are obeyed without question and actions are executed without knowledge of their purpose. Militarism is connected to patriarchal society. Patriarchy is, according to Marilyn French, a doctrine that rests on the assumption that the human being is superior to the animal. This superiority is based on the human being's relation to the higher power/knowledge called God, reason, or the ability to govern. Human beings have created a substitute environment where they no longer seem to be dependent on nature.[28]

The education of militaristic culture reflects a patriarchal power structure and set of values. Educational methods and institutions are characterized by authoritarianism, hierarchies, discipline, and submission to the power of the "one," who is stronger and higher in the hierarchical structure. Both men and women teach children to worship, serve, and fear the powerful. Women's part in this teaching process is important. Mothers are said to instill in their offspring the idea that fame, power, and prestige lead to happiness.[29]

Militaristic education tolerates neither creative curiosity nor speculative attitudes. Critical attitudes are forbidden; rules and regulations are to be followed without criticism or questioning. Equality is impossible in militaristic culture. Hierarchy creates a pecking order where it is impossible to express real and sincere feelings. The respect for authority and the virtue of obedience are legitimized through education, culture, and religion.

Power is either covertly or openly controlled by the economic-military alliance. Many politicians function merely as marionettes of the militaristic power system. The studies of Scilla McClean[30] on decisionmaking processes concerning nuclear weapons show that the war industry obliges politicians to follow its orders. In reality, the opinions of voters come second. Power defines what is important in society, what is less important, and what issues are regarded as problems. The influence of power ranges from the definition of problems to the measures taken to solve them. Only when the power system is revealed is criticism possible. The armament manufacturers, the military, and the economically powerful are behind the culture of militarism.

Environmental problems are also defined through the prism of social power. For example, it is a scientific fact that private cars are the worst pollutants of cities. But which solution should be chosen—the development of mass transportation or the installation of catalyzers—is defined by those in power, and if the latter alternative is chosen, the solution to the problem is only postponed.

Power also defines social development. The maintenance of economic growth is regarded as development, even though this ideology should be weighed critically. If the military-political power system expresses a concern that the state lacks weaponry, this concern then becomes a social problem. Supported by the mass media, the military-political power system guides the population to the need to acquire such weaponry.

Under militarism, power is hierarchical and leads to competition, struggle, and oppression, the core of the patriarchal exercise. Violence is its ideology; it is the extreme form of the power struggle and contributes to the legitimization of violence as a solution to struggle. Competition, also regarded as an essential component of the militaristic culture, is expressed as inherent in human nature and thus legitimized in all sectors of the society— from the arts to sports, from education to the economy.

In militaristic culture, festivals and national holidays underline the themes of struggle and battle. The values of the culture require that people participate in the power struggle, but there might simultaneously prevail a religious or ethical opinion that emphasizes self-sacrifice and altruism. Individuals with such religious and ethical values are deeply concerned about the destruction of others, and this complicates their reaction to the value/system and to the power struggle imposed by the culture.

Those who possess nondemocratic power are fearful of the heightened consciousness of the people, of the moment they become fully aware of the injustice of the system under which they live. The militaristic power system tries to make everyone conform to the dominant culture. Such domination will, in time, through peace education, be understood as injustice of the imposed system and be the catalyst for change.

Peace education shifts the focus of education from the male child to human beings of both sexes, destroys the basis for paranoia between men and women, and liberates both from slavery to socioeconomic power.[31] The pressures to conform to the dominant culture are removed.[32]

CRITICAL THINKING—A TOOL AGAINST MILITARISM

Peace education aims to develop reflective, critical, and individual thinking. Reflective and critical thinking is important in various fields: in direct personal relationships, in vocational and professional relations, as part of the political involvement of the adult, and with regard to the influence of the mass media in shaping the perceptions of citizens today. Critical thinking can aid in opting for a process whereby war can be eliminated as a means to solve international conflicts. Reflective and critical thinking becomes a productive and positive activity. People are actively engaged in life as they see themselves in a creative and recreative political life.[33]

The pessimistic image of the human being in militaristic culture is being questioned in peace education. A positive and humane image of the human being is replacing this negative image. In peace education the human being is regarded as an intrinsically good and loving creature. Evil and violence are seen as the products of false beliefs, wrong attitudes, and education.[34]

Peace education replaces *vis pacem para bellem* with a vision of the world without war. The belief that arms increase security is seen as false. Peace education guides people to contemplate a better world. As Yrjö Engeström states: "People face situations where they must engage in formulating what shall be a desirable culture."[35] Fred Polak says that societies move toward what they image;[36] and Elise Boulding asserts,

> We need to begin picturing the new order in our minds, fantasying it, playing with possibilities. An exercise in first stepping into a desired future in imagination, then consciously elaborating the structures needed to maintain it, and finally imagining the future history that would get us there is a very liberating experience for people who feel trapped in an unyielding present.[37]

Peace education creates a new kind of paradigm for perceiving the world. In this new perception, humankind is experienced as a unity, people are seen as children of the same Mother Nature, and one and the same universal life manifests itself in each individual human life. Human meaning has a cosmic meaning.[38] While perceiving the world in a new way, the human being understands how important and enriching is the diversity of cultures, and how all the world's creatures have a value *an sich*.

There is no place in this new image of the world for patriarchal hierarchy and power structures, or for conforming to a set of "norms." The aim of militaristic rule is to merge minority cultures with the dominant culture. In the culture of peace the preservation of each minority culture is important. Peace education provides an optimistic and realistic vision of the future where solidarity prevails among people and toward nature.

The task of humans is to understand that they are only one of the organisms in the complex and vulnerable ecosystem. They have to be aware of this basic bond between self and nature, and in this process peace education has an important role. Peace education enables people to act for their peace convictions.

EDUCATION FOR NONVIOLENCE

Peace education aims to create a new male culture in which fatherhood is equal with motherhood. Being permitted to take paternity leave after the birth of one's child exemplifies the importance of fatherhood. Paternity leave is possible in Sweden and Finland. We can talk about a new male culture where such qualities as fatherliness, care, affection, and sensitivity are included in the definitions of normal and healthy masculinity. The violent, dominating, and possessive macho image propagated by the militaristic culture appears ridiculous and dangerous in this new male culture. In this new culture, courage is the ability to find peaceful means to resolve conflicts, and it is possible to take off the straitjacket of competition without threatening this healthy and self-confident masculinity.

Peace education includes the development of cooperative play and games in early childhood education and school education.[39] Peace games (new games) should be created to counterbalance violent and competitive games. Modern culture is overloaded with games and play that have "losers and winners"—a tradition that identifies enemies and ourselves as losers or winners. Competition within school is emphasized by a battery of professional educators, counselors, and testing officials who determine normal distributions and establish grading curves that condemn many students to mediocrity. Birgit Brock-Utne points to this as structural violence built into the school system.[40] Children learn frustration and violence at school through such authoritarian structures.

Nonviolence includes, as an essential task of peace education, an ability to listen and to understand the view of the other(s). We can find peaceful means to solve the problems caused by war and structural violence by trying to understand and take into consideration the views of minorities and the oppressed.

It is essential to develop the ability of role taking. Flavell has introduced a four-phased model that illustrates the role-taking ability. The four phases are:

- *Existence:* to observe that other people have different opinions
- *Need:* an attempt to define another person's different way of thinking
- *Drawing a conclusion:* an ability to define another person's perspective
- *Applying:* an ability to utilize the other person's point of view to change one's own attitude[41]

Thus, the role-taking ability also requires the ability to apply the other person's view to one's own thinking and activity, which presupposes respecting the other as an equal. However, the different ways (which can be learned) to perceive and define existence and need are not sufficient for reaching the level of application. To reach that level one must not only acquire information, but must also have experiences that awake emotions and empathy. These feelings awaken in activity. Peace education attempts to create situations where people can practice various roles. The contemplation of true moral problems and the practicing of conflict resolution in real situations develop the role-taking ability.

Peace education undertakes an enormous task when it challenges the authoritarian educational tradition of militaristic culture to the transformation process in which the educator and the one who is educated meet each other as equals, respecting and listening to each other's views. Through these experiences human beings learn to understand that there exist different views and that one's own way of perceiving the world is only one among others. These experiences are needed to reach the highest level of moral development. Peace education develops the ability to contemplate and evaluate one's own convictions and ethical principles and to maintain continuous spiritual development.

FROM MILITARISTIC STRUCTURES TO PEACE

Peace-blocking factors and militaristic structures can be changed into peace-promoting factors. This process can be described schematically (the scheme is in part based on Jensen[42]) in Table 13.1.

When the cultural values that idealize competition and violence are replaced by more peaceful and humane values, new attitudes elicit new behaviors. If peace education were regarded as a socially important and necessary activity, it would bring about a transformation of militaristic power structures. It is probably for this reason that peace education has been seen as dangerous.

Peace education creates a basis for the education of civil society, for whose members it is not important to possess, win, and rule, but rather to encourage sympathy to defend the weaker by nonviolent means. As Johan Galtung has said, an integral part of peace education is to listen carefully to the voice of even the most distant nations and people.[43]

The support of nonviolence takes courage at a time when it is a widespread practice for people to promote their own interests by means of violence or power politics. Everyone who chooses nonviolence and solidarity shows great civil courage. Peace education reminds us that courage is needed every day to protect life and nature and to oppose militarism. As Betty Reardon has written:

> The whole of human society is faced with the challenge of making global policy choices that will determine whether or not our species will survive. Education must therefore face up to the need to prepare the young for global responsibility, to understand the nature and implications of global interdependence, and to accept the responsibility to work for a just, peaceful, and viable global community on planet Earth.[44]

Table 13.1 Peace Education Aims at Conversion

From	To
cultures of militarism	peace culture
authoritarian education	democratic education
military training	disarmament education
propagation of prejudiced enemy image	counteracting of prejudice
violent actions	nonviolent actions
militaristic concepts, myths, and images	alternative concepts, myths, and images
neglect of fatherhood	promotion of fatherhood
support of sexism	promotion of equality between men and women
obedience, uniformity	self-reliance, independence, and critical thinking
neglect of equality, justice, and human rights	respect for equality, justice, and human rights
racism and nationalism	tolerance and global responsibility

NOTES

1. Henryk Skolimowski, "The Role of Philosophy and Values in the Right Model of Peace," *International Journal of World Peace* 5 (1987): 3-39.

2. *The Encyclopedia Americana, International Edition*, Vol. 19 (New York: American Corporation, 1975), 59.

3. Malvern Lumsden, "Militarism: Cultural Dimensions of Militarization," in *Peace, Development and New International Economic Order*, ed. L. Herrera and R. Väyrynen (Tampere: Vaasa OY, 1977), 54-60.

4. Anatol Rapoport, "Introduction," in *On War*, ed. C. Clausewitz (New York: Penguin Classics, 1982), 11-80.

5. Jan Oberg, *Myter om vor sikkerhed.* (Myths about our security) (Copenhagen: Mellemfolkelighet Samvirke), 1981.

6. Yrjö-Paavo Häyrynen, "Peace Research in the Field of Psychology and Pedagogy and Their Share in Anti-War Efforts," *Peace Newsletter* 1 (1985): 1-4.

7. Robin Luckham, "Of Arms and Culture," *Current Research on Peace and Violence* (Tampere Peace Research Institute) 7 (1) (1984): 1-64.

8. Paul Chilton, "Nukespeak, Language, Culture and Propaganda," in *Nukespeak: The Media and the Bomb*, ed. Crispin Aubrey (London: Comedia

Publishing Group, 1982), 94-112.

9. Luckham, "Of Arms and Culture," 2-3.

10. See Brian Easlea, *Fathering the Unthinkable: Masculinity, Scientists and the Nuclear Arms Race* (London: Pluto Press, 1983); Birgit Brock-Utne, "Listen to Women for a Change," paper presented at A Meeting of the Worlds, Joensuu, Finland, 19-23 June 1990.

11. Luckham, "Of Arms and Culture"; Riitta Wahlström, "Educating Preschool Children for Shared Responsibility and Peace," *Reprints and Miniprints*, No. 590 (Malmö: School of Education, 1988).

12. Betty Reardon, *Sexism and the War System* (New York: Teachers College Press, 1985), 14.

13. Häyrynen, "Peace Research in the Field of Psychology and Pedagogy."

14. Kirsti Lagerspetz, *Are Wars Caused by Aggression?* paper presented at the International Congress of Psychology, Acapulco, Mexico, 1984.

15. Richard Leakey, *The Making of Mankind* (London: Shema, 1981), 219.

16. Anthony Wilden, *Man and Woman, War and Peace: The Strategist's Companion* (London, New York: Routledge & Kegan Paul, 1987), 226.

17. Leakey,*The Making of Mankind.*

18. Reardon, *Sexism and the War System,* 4.

19. Birgit Brock-Utne, "Kvinner i fredsarbeid" (Women in peace work), in H. Sivertson, F. Stockholm, and L. Vislie (eds.) *Kvinne Viser Vei* (A woman leads the way). Festschrift to Eva Nordland. Oslo: Aschehong, 1981.

20. Reardon, *Sexism and the War System,* 15.

21. Brock-Utne, *Educating for Peace: A Feminist Perspective* (New York: Pergamon Press, 1985); Reardon, *Sexism and the War System;* and H. Kekkonen, "Peace Education for Adults," in *Adult Education, Development, and Peace* (Sri Lanka: National Association for Total Education [NATE], 1986).

22. Lynne Iglitzin, "War, Sex, Sports and Masculinity," in *War: A Historical and Social Study,* ed. L. L. Farran, Jr. (New York: Liveright, 1978), 4.

23. Harold D. Laswell, *Propaganda Technique in the World War* (New York: Knopf, 1927).

24. Heikki Luostarinen, *Perivihollinen* (The traditional enemy) (Tampere: Vastapaino, 1986), 32.

25. Riitta Wahlström, "On the Psychological Basis of Peace Education: Enemy Image and Development of Moral Judgement," paper presented at the Eleventh Conference of the International Peace Research Association (IPRA), Brighton, England, 13-18 April 1986; Riitta Wahlström, "Enemy Image as a Psychological Antecedent of Warfare," in *Essays on Violence*, ed. J. Ramírez et al. (Sevilla: Publicaciones de la Universidad de Sevilla, 1987), 21-45; Riitta Wahlström, "Enemy Images and Peace Education," *Reprints and Miniprints, No. 660* (Malmö: School of Education, 1989).

26. Vamik Volkan, "The Need to Have Enemies and Allies: A Developmental Approach," *Political Psychology,* 6 (2) (1985): 219-247.

27. Betty Reardon, *Educating for Global Responsibility* (New York: Teachers College Press, 1988), 7; Pierre Bourdieu, *Sosiologian kysymyksiä* (Tampere: Vastapaino, 1985).

28. Marilyn French, *Beyond Power: On Women, Men and Morals* (London: Abacus, 1985), 429-430.

29. Claudia B. Pacheco, *Women on the Couch: An Analysis of the Female Psychopathology* (São Paulo: Proton Publishing House, 1987), 112.

30. Scilla McClean, *How Nuclear Weapons Decisions Are Made* (London: Macmillan Press, 1986).

31. Pacheco, *Women on the Couch,* 64.

32. Michel Foucault, *Naissance de la prison* (Paris: Editions Gallimard, 1985).

33. Paul Dikstra, "Adult Education for Peace," *Convergence* 22 (1) (1989):5-9.

34. Norberto R. Keppe et al. *Liberation of the People—The Pathology of Power* (São Paulo: Proton Publishing House, 1988).

35. Yrjö Engeström, "Activity Theory and Individual and Societal Transformation," in *International Congress for Research on Activity Theory* (ISCRAT), Lahti, Finland, 1990.

36. Fred Polak, *De Toekomst is Verleden Tyd* (Image of the future) (Utrecht: W. de Haan 1953), 2 vols. Translated by Elise Boulding from the Dutch; English version published by Oceana Press, 1961. Also, one-volume abridgment by Elise Boulding (San Francisco: Jossey-Bass/Elsevier, 1972).

37. Elise Boulding, *Building a Global Civic Culture: Education for an Interdependent World* (New York: Teachers College Press, 1988; and Syracuse University Press [paperback], 1990), 242.

38. Skolimowski, "The Role of Philosophy and Values in the Right Model of Peace."

39. Wahlström, "Educating Preschool Children for Shared Responsibility and Peace"; Riita Wahlström, "Emagen de Enemigo: Educación de Paz" (Enemy image and peace education), *Gernika-Gogoratuz,* (2), 1990.

40. Birgit Brock-Utne, "Disarmament Education: The European Evolution," in *Peace Education,* ed. D. Ray (London: Third Eye, 1988), 96.

41. John H. Flavell, *The Development of Role-Taking and Communications Skills in Children* (New York: Wiley, 1968).

42. Paul Jensen, "Human Rights and Education for Peace," presentation at the conference Human Rights and Education for Peace, Ministerio de Educación y Ciencia, Madrid, 5-7 March 1990.

43. Johan Galtung as referred to in Kekkonen, "Peace Education for Adults," 49.

44. Reardon, *Educating for Global Responsibility,* xv.

Epilogue: Challenges for the Peace Research Community in an Era of Transition

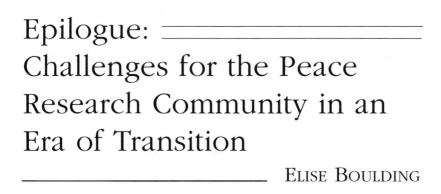

ELISE BOULDING

The invasion of Kuwait by Iraq and the subsequent military buildup in the Middle East by allied forces with the consent of the United Nations Security Council followed within weeks of the International Peace Research Association Conference in peaceful Groningen. The Gulf War can be considered a case history in the interconnectedness of internal and external conflicts. As those of us who live far away see and smell in our imaginations the burning oil wells of Kuwait and the ravaged deserts and cities of Iraq, and as we ponder the social and economic disasters that have struck many thousands of refugees from neighboring continents, we can see how little protection from harm armed forces can provide.

The big question now is, What new security technologies of a peace-building nature can emerge from within Arab society itself, not dependent on the vagaries of current foreign policy of the United States and its allies? How can the creativity of the UN beyond the use of its peacekeeping forces be made available? We may also ask, What can peace researchers and peace educators offer? IPRA formed the Commission on Peace Building and War Termination in the Middle East at the start of the Gulf War. It is the commission's goal to bring together new visions of social and structural arrangements originating in the Middle East itself, with visions from other regional perspectives. The larger context is a world order based on the rule of law and on principles of equity, justice, and human rights applied to the relations among peoples and states. Democratization; the participation of women; demilitarization initiatives; regional collective security arrangements; how Islam and other communities of faith can contribute to peace building; solutions for ethnic communities; environmental problems of air, water, soil, sand and oil; economic futures; education futures; and models of dispute settlement for different problems at different levels, as well as related

185

problems as they appear, are being explored with our Arab colleagues. The underlying issue is the rebuilding of the Arab civil society, which has many historical strengths as well as current weaknesses, and the nurturance of its vision of itself and its place in the world. For the West, a difficult lesson of giving up old habits of intervention has to be learned.

For the International Peace Research Association this is an important moment, as we move from theory, research, and education to more emphasis on the exploration of peace-building practice. The academic discipline of peace research has now reached a point of maturity, where responsibility for the application of knowledge in crisis situations becomes clearer. This will be increasingly done through IPRA's fifteen study groups and commissions, each formed to deal with one particular aspect of conflict and peace building. The list of study groups and commissions, together with the names and addresses of their conveners, will be found in the Appendix, with information about the current secretariat of IPRA. Inquiries are welcomed.

About the Authors ⎯⎯⎯⎯⎯

ELISE BOULDING, past secretary-general of IPRA, is professor emerita of sociology, Dartmouth College. A futurist, she writes on local and global peace building, development, family life, and women. A founding member of IPRA, she served on the commission to recommend the establishment of the US Institute of Peace, was a member of the UN University Council, and served on the UNESCO Peace Prize jury.

LOTHAR BROCK, professor of international relations at the Johann Wolfgang Goethe University in Frankfurt, is project director of the Frankfurt Peace Research Institute. A former member of the IPRA Council, he writes on security, development, and ecology.

BIRGIT BROCK-UTNE, professor on leave from the University of Oslo, is now working at the University of Dar es Salaam, Tanzania. She is best known for her analysis of peace studies from a feminist perspective.

WINIFRED K. BYANYIMA is ambassador from Uganda to UNESCO, a member of the UNESCO Executive Council, and a consultant on science and technology policy to the government of Uganda.

JUERGEN DEDRING studied in Germany and the United States and received degrees from the Free University in Berlin and from Harvard. Currently in the Secretary-General's Office of Research Collection and Information (ORCI), he has worked for the United Nations in New York since 1972. His fields of interest include peace research, conflict resolution, multilateralism, and international relations.

RANDALL FORSBERG is the founder and director of the Institute for Defense and Disarmament Studies in Cambridge, Massachusetts. She also directs the East-West Conventional Force Study. Her areas of interest include the study of policies that would limit the use of armed force to narrowly defensive roles.

HENDRIK W. VAN DER MERWE is director of the Centre for Intergroup Studies in Cape Town, South Africa, which conducts research into conflict and peace and facilitates communication among groups in conflict.

PATRICIA M. MISCHE, cofounder of Global Education Associates and coeditor of its journal, *Breakthrough*, has worked with teachers and community development activists in all parts of the world. An initiator and coordinator of the transnational Earth Covenant Project, she writes on peace education, nonviolent approaches to international security, and the care of the earth.

SOLOMON NKIWANE is professor and deputy dean of the Faculty of Social Studies at the University of Zimbabwe; he has also been a visiting professor at several universities throughout the United States and Canada. He is president of the African Peace Research Association and a member of the Executive Committee of the IPRA Council.

ANDRIES ODENDAAL is senior lecturer and head of the Department in Missiology at the University of the North, Qwa-Qwa Branch; he was visiting fellow at the Centre for Intergroup Studies in Cape Town in 1990.

URSULA OSWALD is a professor at the Centro Regional de Investigaciones Multidisciplinarias of the Universidad Nacional Autónoma de México. She is currently the national coordinator of the Food, Social Debt, and Survival research project, the coordinator of the IPRA Food Policy Study Group, and chair of the IPRA Council. She is an adviser to urban and rural grassroots development organizations and writes on food, the debt crisis, water resources, ecology, and survival strategies in Third World countries.

KUMAR RUPESINGHE is a senior researcher at the International Peace Research Institute, Oslo (PRIO). He is the convenor of the IPRA Commission on Internal Conflicts and Conflict Resolution (ICON) and consultant to the United Nations University on Identity Conflicts and Governance. He is the editor of a forthcoming three-volume series for Macmillan on internal conflicts and their resolution.

EVA SENGHAAS-KNOBLOCH is an assistant professor of peace and conflict research at the University of Bremen. Her research and writing focuses on issues related to intrasocietal and intersocietal conflicts and democratic integration.

HYLKE TROMP is professor of peace research at the University of Groningen and director of its Polemological Institute. He was visiting professor of international relations and peace research at the Free University in Berlin and the J. W. Goethe University in Frankfurt. He has recently written *On War, Peace and Peace Research* (Aldershot: Dartmouth Publishers, 1992).

RIITTA WAHLSTRÖM is director of the Peace and International Education Project and researcher at the Institute for Educational Research at the University of Jyväskylä, Finland. She has published widely in the peace research field and is a member of IPRA and vice-president of Finnish Psychologists for Peace.

Appendix

- **Communications Study Group**, Omar Souki Oliveira, University Federal De Minas Gerais, Rua Curitaba 8327 Sala 1101, 30170 Belo Horizonte MG, Brazil.
- **Defense and Disarmament Study Group**, Hans Gunter Brauch, Alte-Bergsteige 47, 6950 Mosbach, Germany. Tel: [49] (6261) 12912. Fax: [49] (6261) 15695.
- **Ecological Security Study Group**, Clovis Brigagão and Muricio Andres, Fundacão Cidade de Paz, Cx Postal 020021, CEP 70001 Brasilia DE, Brazil. Tel: [55] (61) 553 1202 or [55] (61) 553 1885.
- **Food Policy Study Group**, Ursula Oswald, La Habana No. 7, Barrio Ixtlahuatlan, Yautepec, Morelos, Mexico. Tel: [52] (73) 130555/130316. Fax: [52] (73) 175981.
- **Human Rights and Development Study Group**, Michael Stohl, Director, Programs for Study Abroad, Purdue University, 1104 Schleman Hall, Room 223, West Lafayette, IN 47907-1104, USA. Tel: [1] (317) 494 2383. Tlx: 276147 AGAD-PU LAF. Fax: [1] (317) 494 9613. BITNET MSTOHL@PURCCVM.
- **Internal Conflicts and Their Resolution Study Group**, Kumar Rupesinghe, International Peace Research Institute Oslo, Fuglehauggate 11, N-0260, Oslo, Norway. Tel: [47] 2 557150. Fax: [47] 2 558422. Tlx: 72400 FOTEX N ATT: Peace Research.
- **International Conflict Resolution Study Group**, Louis Kriesberg, Program in the Analysis and Resolution of Conflict, 712 Ostrom Avenue, Syracuse University, Syracuse, NY 13244, USA. Tel: [1] (315) 443 2367. Fax: [1] (315) 443 1954.

- **IPRA Commission on Peace Building in the Middle East**, Elise Boulding, Campus Box 327, University of Colorado, Boulder, CO 80309-0327, USA. Tel: [1] (303) 492 2550 Fax: [1] (303) 492 6388.
- **Nonviolence Study Group**, Chaiwat Satha-Anand, Department of Political Science, Thammasat University, Prachan Road, Bangkok 10200, Thailand. Tel: [66] (2) 391 3259. Fax: [66] (2) 224 8099.
- **Peace Education Commission**, Ake Bjerstedt, School of Education, Box 23501, S-200, 45 Malmo, Sweden. Tel: [46] 4032 0000. Fax: [46] 40 32 02 10.
- **Peace Movements Study Group**, Katsuya Kodama, Department of Humanities, Mie University, 1515 Kamihama, Tsu 514, Japan. Tel: [81] (592) 32 1211, ext. 2679. Fax: [81] (592) 31 2966.
- **PEC University Peace Studies Network**, Thomas Daffern, Initiative for Peace Studies, Institute of Education, London University, 28 Woburn Square, London WC1H OAA, UK. Tel: [44] (71) 636 8000, ext. 4310. Fax: [44] (71) 436 2186. E-Mail: T.DAFFERN@UK.AC.LON.EDUC.isis.
- **Refugee Study Group**, Ayok Chol, PO Box 35100, Dar es Salaam, Tanzania. Tlx: 41000 TPTC TZ. Fax: (255) 51 34794. Tel: 49192, ext. 2650. Syed Sikander Mehdi, A-413 Block L., North Nazimabad, Karachi 33, Pakistan.
- **Religion and Conflict Study Group**, Roger Williamson, 136 Grosvenor Road, Forest Gate, London E7 8JA, UK. Tel: [44] (81) 552 6423.
- **Research Team on Changes in Eastern Europe**, Wojciech Kostecki, Polish Institute of International Affairs, 1a Warecka Street, 00-950 Warsaw, PO Box 1000, Poland. Tel: [48] (22) 26 30 21. Fax: [48] (22) 27 47 38.
- **Secretary-General of IPRA**, Paul Smoker, IPRA, Antioch College, Yellow Springs, OH 45387, USA. Tel: [1] (513) 767 6444. Fax: [1] (513) 767 1891. E-Mail: PEACENET: antiochcol. BITNET: PSmoker@WSU.
- **Women and Peace Study Group**, María Elene Valenzuela, Chilean Peace Research Association, Casilla 19078, Santiago, Chile. Tel: [56] 2 273 244 9. Fax: [56] 2 46 04 33 or [56] 2 22 57 35.

Index

Afghanistan, 5, 164; conflict resolution in, 165, 166; drug trade in, 49, 50; Soviet withdrawal from, 69, 73, 157–158

Africa, 1, 2–3, 23, 26, 30, 43, 48, 56, 59, 88, 124; conflicts in, 145–146; democracy in, 34–35; political systems in, 24–25, 33–34; sovereign states in, 28–29; in World War II, 27–28. *See also various countries*

African National Congress (ANC), 146, 147, 148

Agriculture, 37, 122

Alcoholism: in Soviet Union, 9–10

Algeria, 34, 56

Alienation, 150

Amathila, Ben, 34

Amathila, Libertine, 34

Amazon, 85

Amin, Idi, 133–134, 135, 142, 143–144

ANC. *See* African National Congress

ANC/UDF, 147, 152

Andizhan-Ost, 55

Anglican Church, 131

Angola, 26, 31(n9)

Anthrax, 87

Apartheid, 145, 151

Arbatov, George, 13–14

Argentina, 11

Arias, Oscar, 160, 161

Armament culture, 172

Arms control, 112. *See also* Disarmament

Arms industry, 68, 75, 76, 77

Arms race, 11–12, 51, 68, 71

Arms sales, 51, 144; and drug trade, 49–50; and internal conflicts, 52–53

ASEAN. *See* Association of Southeast Asian Nations

Asia, 1, 43, 51, 59. *See also various countries*

Assimilation, 26

Association of Southeast Asian Nations (ASEAN), 162, 164, 166

Austro-Hungarian Empire, 11

Authority, 53, 55–56

Autonomy, 17, 53, 55–56

Azanian People's Organization (AZAPO), 147

AZAPO. *See* Azanian People's Organization

Azerbaijan, 55

Babiito dynasty, 130

Bakiga, 130

Baltic Sea, 87

Bangladesh, 99

Barsh, Lawrence, 59

Belgium, 26

Benin, 33, 56

Berlin Conference, 25, 26

Biological weapons, 87

Bloom, William, 57–58

Bolivia, 49

Boycotts, 39

Brazil, 70, 85

Brezhnev Doctrine, 14

Brock-Utne, Birgit, 179

Bronze Age: warfare during, 106–107

Buganda, 130, 131

Bukiiko. *See* Resistance Committees

Bunyoro, 130

Burkina Faso, 56

Bush administration, 69

Buthelezi, Mangosuthu, 148

Calha Norte project, 85

Cambodia, 5, 73, 162–163, 164, 166

Canada, 39

Capital, 121

Capitalism, 35, 46

Catholic Church, 131

Central America, 5, 43, 164; United Nations role in, 160–162. *See also various countries*

Central Europe, 15

Centre for Intergroup Studies, 153

CFE, 76

CFE 1 Treaty, 69, 77

Chad, 69

Chalice and the Blade, The (Eisler), 39

Chemical weapons, 52–53, 63(n31), 87

Children, 122

Chile, 55, 82

China, 51, 56, 70, 87, 124, 158, 165

Christianity, 131, 146

Churches, 92, 146

Clauseqitz, C., 172

Club of Rome, 83

Cold War, 2, 10, 47

Collective consciousness, 125

Colombia, 49, 50, 55, 85

Colonialism: in Africa, 24, 26, 27, 30–31(n2); in Uganda, 130–132, 142–143

193

Nuclear-free zones, 15
Nunn, Sam, 96, 104
Nyere, Julius, 35–36

OAS. *See* Organization of American States
OAU. *See* Organization of African Unity
Obote, Milton, 133, 134, 135, 142, 144
Oil, 82–83
Okello, Tito, 141
ONUKA, 161
ONUVEN, 161
Oppression, 173
Organization of African Unity (OAU), 29,
  135, 164
Organization of American States (OAS),
  160–161, 165
Ottoman Empire, 11
Ozone depletion, 99

PAC. *See* Pan-African Congress
Pakistan, 49, 50, 51; and Afghanistan, 157,
  158, 165, 166
Palestinians, 50
Pan-African Congress (PAC), 146
Panama, 69
Paraguay, 55
Parks: peace, 4, 88, 99–100
Patriarchy, 176
Peace: through cooperation, 88–89;
  defining, 45–46; and ecological
  security, 109–110; and environment,
  80–81; with nature, 92–93
Peace Treaty of Wesphalia, 23
Peacekeeping forces, 5–6, 60–61, 67, 74
Perestroika, 30
Pérez de Cuellar, Javier, 156, 164
Peru, 49, 54, 55, 82, 85
Pol Pot, 162
Poland, 14, 16, 37
Political systems, 47; modern
  international, 23–24, 27, 28; one-party,
  33–34; in Uganda, 138, 139–140
Politics: African, 24–25; broad-based,
  138–139; post-Cold War, 10–11; South
  African, 146–147, 152; Ugandan, 132–
  133
Pollution, 9, 18, 83–84, 90
Population growth, 47–48, 110
Portugal, 26, 28
Poverty, 9, 36, 48, 122, 173
Power, 54, 82; economic, 11, 70, 124;
  political, 132–133, 146–147; social, 53,
  176–177
PPW. *See* Protracted People's War
Pragmatopia, 39–40
Prebish, Raul, 122
Private sector, 113
Privatization, 147
Project Global 2000, 116–118
Propaganda: war, 174
Protracted People's War (PPW), 136, 137–
  138

Quebec, 44

Race, 2, 56–57
Racism, 149–150
RCs. *See* Resistance Committees
Reagan, Ronald, 10, 47, 161
Reardon, Betty, 173, 180
Rebellions: drug-financed, 43
Reciprocity, 94
Recolonization, 48
Recycling, 125
Refugees, 51, 56
Religion, 2, 131, 132–133
Religious Society of Friends, 153
Resistance Committees (RCs), 139, 140,
  141
Resources, 38
Revenge, 4, 142
Revolution, 54
Role-taking, 179–180
Russian Empire, 11

Sahel, 48
Salinization, 122
Saudi Arabia, 124
Schmidt, Helmut, 112
Schools, 143
Secession, 55
Second Indochina War. *See* Vietnam War
Second Sino-Japanese War, 87
Sectarianism, 143
Security, 18, 19, 76, 85, 125, 185; defense-
  oriented, 67–68; ecological, 3–4, 80,
  93–98, 103–105, 107–108, 109–110,
  113–114; redefining, 116–117; systems
  of, 105–106; in Uganda, 140–142
Seko, Mobutu Sese, 34
Self-determination, 16, 27, 129
Self-sufficiency, 125
Sendero Luminoso, 54
Senegal, 50
Sexism, 173–174
Shevardnadze, Eduard, 88, 93–94, 112
Shivji, Issa G., 34–35
Sihanouk, Prince, 162
Skolimowski, Henry K., 171
Slavery, 23, 24, 25, 30(n1)
Socialism, 35, 47, 55
Society, 2, 5, 16, 19, 53, 98, 125, 130;
  security of, 105–106
Songhai, 25
South Africa, 5, 28, 34, 56, 153; economy
  in, 147–148; and Namibia, 158–159,
  165; politics in, 146–147; violence in,
  150–152
South America, 43. *See also various
  countries*
Southeast Asia, 43, 49. *See also various
  countries*
Sovereignty, 17, 108, 116–117
Soviet Germans, 56
Soviet Union, 14, 15, 17, 20(n5), 36, 47,

About the Book

Confronting a changing post–Cold War Environment—in which North-South conflicts have superseded those between East and West, and the boundaries between internal and interstate conflicts have all but disappeared—peace researchers reexamine in this book the concepts of conflict and security.

In Part I, the authors explore the old and new conflicts from European, Third World, and feminist perspectives. Part II examines reconceptualizations of security, critically analyzing the appropriateness of using environmental and development concepts to expand earlier formulations of strategic security. Part III offers dramatic insights into creative new approaches to conflict and violence, concluding with a look at the process of replacing cultures of militarism with peace cultures. An epilogue highlights the challenges facing peace research now—in its twenty-fifth year of development as a discipline—and in the decades to come.